Praise for *Make Sure It's Deductible*

Evelyn Jacks is well-deserving of her reputation as Canada's most trusted tax advisor. This book could save thousands of tax dollars for anyone who is self-employed, runs a small business, or is thinking of starting one.

Gordon Pape

The day you opened your small business is the day you stepped up to the plate to play ball with Canada Customs and Revenue Agency. In characteristic friendly style, Canada's foremost tax author lays out the rules of the game so that you and your family can minimize stress and maximize deductions. Prepare to be surprised and rewarded.

Michael Kane — *The Vancouver Sun*

Ms Jacks draws on her expertise in a way that makes the argument for self-employment in this tax-oppressed country almost compelling.

Jonathan Chevreau — *The National Post*

Evelyn Jacks knows tax and writes about it in a way the average person can understand. That's a very unusual combination. Reading her advice will make you richer, especially if you deduct business expenses the way she tells you to in this book.

Ellen Roseman — *The Toronto Star*

For guidelines on the home office and all self-employment issues, I would recommend you read Evelyn Jacks' book *Make Sure It's Deductible* as a really good general and specific guide.

David Christianson — *Winnipeg Free Press*

Praise for Other Books by Evelyn Jacks

Jacks' style is direct and concise. For the answer to "What does this line on the tax return mean?" it is where I would turn first.

George Hartman — *Investment Executive*

The most obvious choice for income tax do-it-yourselfers, Ms Jacks' book is a line-by-line guide ...

Catherine Mulroney — *The Globe and Mail*

... long on plain English and an easy guide for the average person.

Alan Caplan — *The Edmonton Sun*

Tax expert Evelyn Jacks shares her tips on how to take advantage of key incentives in preparing your tax return.

Kristin Goff — *The Ottawa Citizen*

When it comes to being up to date, *Jacks on Tax Savings* is definitely the winner. The author has taken time to analyse the changes arising from the federal mini-budget.

Ellen Roseman — *The Toronto Star*

... And that, says tax specialist Evelyn Jacks, makes tax planning just as important as tax preparation for submitting your return by the April 30 deadline.

Brian Lewis — *The Province*

Fortunately, there are more concise books that try to translate tax matters into everyday English. In recent years, the two main popularizers have been tax educator Evelyn Jacks ...

Jonathan Chevreau — *The National Post*

Tax *Secrets* for Tough Times

Evelyn Jacks

McGraw-Hill Ryerson

Toronto • Montréal • Boston • Burr Ridge, IL • Dubuque, IA • Madison, WI • New York
San Francisco • St. Louis • Bangkok • Bogotá • Caracas • Kuala Lumpur • Lisbon • London
Madrid • Mexico City • Milan • New Delhi • Santiago • Seoul • Singapore • Sydney • Taipei

McGraw-Hill
Ryerson Limited
A Subsidiary of The McGraw-Hill Companies

This edition has been carefully researched and verified for accuracy; however, due to the complexity of the subject matter and the continual changes occurring in the subject matter, neither the author nor the publisher can be held responsible for errors or omissions, or consequences of any actions resulting from information in this book. Examples discussed are intended as general guidelines only, contain fictional names and characters and any resemblance to real persons or events is purely coincidental. Tax law and policies referred to in this book include proposals of the Year 2000 federal and provincial budgets, December 2001 federal budget, and draft regulations and announcements by governments throughout 2001. The reader is urged to seek the services of a competent and experienced professional should further guidance in income tax preparation, tax planning, or financial planning be required.

ISBN: 0-07-090962-8

1234567890 JFM 098765432
Printed and bound in Canada.

National Library of Canada Cataloguing in Publication Data

Jacks, Evelyn, 1955-

Tax secrets for tough times

Includes index.

ISBN 0-07-090962-8

1. Income tax—Law and legislation—Canada—Popular works.
2. Tax planning—Canada—Popular works. I. Title.

HJ4661.J32 2002 343.7105'2 C2001-904232-9

Publisher: **Joan Homewood**
Editorial Co-ordinator: **Catherine Leek**
Research Assistance: **Walter Harder and Associates, Profort Financial Services**
Production Co-ordinator: **Sandra Deak**
Electronic Page Design and Composition: **Heidy Lawrance Associates**
Cover Design: **Inklings Design Studio/Anne Dunnett**
Cover Image: **Peter Dazeley/Getty Images/Stone**

Credit for Page 83: Statistics Canada Catalogue No. 13–595, The assets and debts of Canadians: An Overview of the Results of the Survey of Financial Security, page 16

Statistics Canada information is used with the permission of the Minister of Industry, as Minister responsible for Statistics Canada. Information on the availability of the wide range of data from Statistics Canada can be obtained from Statistics Canada's Regional offices, its World Wide Web site at http://www.statcan.ca, and its toll-free number 1-800-263-1136.

Secrets for Those Going Through Tough Times

1. Tough Times are usually Temporary.
2. If Action is required, act with Knowledge.
3. If you don't know, seek help from Knowledgeable Sources.
4. Sometimes, Tough Times are disguised as Opportunities.
5. Be Ready.

EJ

Table of Contents

"There is a tide in the affairs of men, which, taken at the flood, leads on to fortune. . ."

William Shakespeare

Acknowledgements

I wish to thank and acknowledge the hard work and dedication to the publication of this book by all those involved, but in particular to Joan Homewood, for believing in the project, Cathy Leek, for her cheerful determination and dedication to excellence in seeing it to editorial completion, to Walter Harder, who knew no time boundaries in preparing the calculations for the various scenarios and charts in this book, and to Al Jacks for staying up those extra nights to help make this happen.

When skill, hard work, dedication to excellence and kindred spirits collaborate to produce a new work, the process and the result fill one with the warmth of pride.

Introduction

KEY PERSONAL TAX CONCEPTS:

- In tough times, many Canadians find themselves with unexpected financial assets to manage
- When income and asset bases fluctuate, the personal income tax system can often provide cash flow relief
- Recent tax changes will result in reduced marginal tax rates for most Canadians ... and that means there are savings and investment opportunities
- When taxes are scheduled to reduce over time, it's usually best to defer income into the future; maximize RRSP deductions
- All Canadians can benefit from higher tax free zones due to indexing
- Special provisions have been introduced for the sick and disabled
- New support has been given to those improving their skills with education
- Investors have received significant tax breaks on capital gains
- Low interest rates have made borrowing for investment purposes more attractive
- The Child Tax Benefit has been increased for low and middle income families, which can create monthly cash flow once parents' tax returns are filed

TOUGH TIMES AND NEW TRENDS

For the first time in decades, the tax burden of average Canadians has been dropping ... welcome news in a new millennium that has presented itself in an otherwise spectacular fashion.

As we look forward to an improved global economy, and from the devastating terrorism that rocked our world in the fall of 2001, individuals may be surprised to find that they can look to the tax system to find a number of certainties. In fact, it is often when things change that the biggest opportunities for long term tax planning and tax savings arise.

When you think about it, taxpayers are most likely to make important long term decisions about significant sums of money during times of crisis and change. It is not unusual, for example, for people to receive very large lump sums of money in these times as outlined in Figure 1.

Because some of these personal and financial events can bring with them an elevation of stress, the worst thing an individual can do is to make an uninformed decision with the potential for long term consequences; consequences that can be compounded, if tax liabilities arise after the money has been spent.

LAW, ORDER AND BURIED TREASURE

The tax system is the first place to turn for significant relief when incomes fluctuate or personal circumstances change. It is possible, for example, to enhance the monthly income of families with children through the Canada Child Tax Benefits (CCTB), to transfer portions of severance packages on a tax free basis to RRSPs, to apply capital or non-capital losses to prior years' taxable income to recover previous taxes paid, to defer taxes when a replacement business is acquired after the sale of another, or to minimize taxes upon the death of a loved one.

But beware, nobody likes to wait for their money and the good folks at the Canada Customs and Revenue Agency (CCRA) are no exception. Also, there can be significant penalty and interest charges for those who choose to test the agency's patience. This often happens in tough times when people are short of cash. For this reason, it is important to mention that when financial hardship strikes, CCRA has the power of leniency. It can accept tax remittances over a period of time, instead of in a lump sum, and voluntary compliance by the taxpayer negates penalties.

There's more good news: CCRA's "Fairness Provisions" can be tapped to recover prior-filed errors back to 1985 for most federal provisions, to waive late filing penalties during times of severe personal stress (like death or disability) and to waive both penalties and interest where factors beyond the taxpayer's control result in late filing.

Figure 1
Changes in Circumstances

Life Circumstance	Potential New Assets to be Managed
1. Disability	Lump sums from wage loss replacement plans, Canada Pension Plan Disability Benefits, equity from sale of residences and vacation properties, vehicles, personal properties
2. Divorce	Equity from liquidation of family residences, splitting of registered and non-registered investments, children's education funds
3. Death	Life insurance benefits, death benefits, tax free rollover of assets to spouse, taxable transfer of other property to trusts, children, grandchildren
4. Early Retirement or Job Termination	Severance package, access to public and private pension plans, non-registered accounts
5. Emigration	Liquidation of Canadian holdings
6. Gifts	Cash or property gifted during one's lifetime by parents, other relatives who are liquidating assets
7. Inheritances	Lumps sums from insurance policies, sale of deceased's asset accumulations
8. Landing a Job	Signing bonus, new cash flow available for investment
9. Lawsuits, Judgements, Settlements	Net proceeds after legal fees
10. Marriage	Saved assets of two parties; residence purchases, retirement planning, education fund planning, insurance
11. Retirement	Pensions, non-registered savings, insurance
12. Sale of Business	After-tax sales proceeds; signing bonuses at new employment or consulting positions, taxation windfalls, acquisition of replacement business.
13. Sale of Residences	Equity from homes, cottages, offshore properties
14. Tax Savings	Recovery of missed tax provisions of prior years; tax refunds from RRSP deposits, significant moving expense claims, refundable and non-refundable credit claims
15. Windfalls	Lottery and gambling proceeds, unexpected market gains

In fact, there may be significant "gold" in those dreaded tax filings, either as a result of requesting adjustments to prior-filed returns or some tax planning for the future. For several common examples of errors and omissions, and their recovery values, we present "Digging for Gold" at the end of this book. These adjustments are presented in the order that the tax provisions appear on a general tax return, a sample of which is presented in the Appendix.

If you find as you read through this book that you have forgotten to mention something in meetings with your professional advisors, discuss requesting an adjustment to your prior-filed returns. While Statutes of Limitation provide some deadlines for tax recovery, it's never too late to review your affairs with a view to maximizing your benefits under the tax system. If you can do this before a significant life event occurs, you'll keep more money and control.

THE ROLE OF PROFESSIONAL ADVISORS

While change challenges us in the best of circumstances, knowledge and a well-executed action plan can help us win back control. When coupled with the use of legitimate and available tax provisions, new capital formation and long term wealth creation can be accomplished, even in the worst of times. Common circumstances experienced in difficult periods are profiled throughout this book from a tax viewpoint. It is our hope that the reader will come across a tax nugget or two regarding his or her own personal affairs and then discuss these with a qualified financial advisor(s).

The relationship with your financial advisor can be the most profitable one in your lifetime. Good advice from your financial planner, tax accountant and lawyer can help you leverage the assets you and your family have now and in the future.

While tax planning is an integral part of any financial plan, tax sheltering should not unduly influence any investment decision. Before acquiring any investment, or acting on any of the ideas in this book, work the numbers with your financial advisors, understand the short and long term ramifications of your investment decisions, including yield, liquidity and opportunities for income splitting and diversification. Most important, question whether the investment fits into your long term objectives for risk and reward.

KEEPING UP WITH CHANGES

The "Tax Secrets" discussed in this book are based on many taxation changes that have been announced over the last several years. Understanding and applying these provisions to a taxpayer's own changing circumstances and a myriad of investment options can be a bit like trying to hit three moving targets—a task generally not recommended for amateurs. It is therefore very important to take the time to become an informed taxpayer and investor to maximize your relationship with your financial advisors.

How have life circumstances in the new millennium been impacted by tax changes? The following overview will help you understand some of the significant provisions that could affect you and your loved ones.

December 10, 2001 Federal Budget Changes

The following new provisions were announced in this short budget, which endorsed previously announced personal taxation provisions, giving Canadians comfort that tax reductions would continue at least on a short term basis.

- **Tax Burdens will Fall Until 2004.** The taxation revenue projections, highlighted on the Finance Canada Web site and in the Budget Documents released on December 10, 2001, show expected decreases in tax revenues, some resulting from a slowing of the economy, others from personal tax changes announced in 2000 and 2001, at least until 2004.
- **Deduction for New Tool Costs of Apprentice Vehicle Mechanics.** Those who are enrolled in an educational program leading to a designation as a licensed motor vehicle mechanic may deduct, starting in 2002, the cost of tools acquired against the income made in their employment as an apprentice. If those costs exceed income, the amounts can be carried forward to a subsequent tax year. The deduction will be limited to the total cost of the tools and ancillary equipment required for the apprenticeship and the greater of $1,000 and 5% of the individual's income for the year from the apprenticeship.

  The cost of the tools will be reduced by the deduction received in the year and this will be used as the cost base of the tool. Later, that adjusted cost base will be used to compute further tax consequences on disposition.
- **Exemption for Adult Basic Education.** Retroactive to the 1997 and subsequent taxation years, a tax deduction will be allowed to individuals who received and included in income a taxable amount to take an educational program in adult basic education approved by Human Resources Development Canada or under the Employment Insurance Act or a provincial Labour Market Development Agreement, provided that the assistance did not qualify for the tuition fee credit. Adjustments to prior-filed returns should be requested all the way back to 1997.
- **Expansion of the Education Tax Credit.** This amount—$400 a month for full-time students and $120 a month for part-time students—will be available to those who received taxable assistance for post-secondary education under programs approved by Human Resources Development

Canada or under the Employment Insurance Act or a provincial Labour Market Development Agreement, effective the 2002 taxation year.

- **Extension of Credit on Donations of Certain Publicly Traded Shares.** The amount included in the income of a donor of eligible securities to public charities will be one-half the normal income inclusion amounts. This provision was scheduled to expire on December 31, 2001, but has now been extended permanently for donations made after 2001. In addition, employees who donate eligible securities through stock option plans will receive parallel tax treatment on securities acquired after 2001.
- **Speedier Payment of Goods and Services Tax Credits (GSTCs).** The GST Credit is paid quarterly to low income Canadians to offset the GST paid on non-discretionary spending. It is based on net family income reported upon filing a return and the credit begins each year in July following the tax assessment. To ensure that the money is available to needy families on a more timely basis, the entitlement for the credit will be based on family circumstances in the previous quarter. What this means is that if your circumstances change, such as due to the birth of a child, separation, death, divorce, the reaching of age 19 (this is when a young adult qualifies to file for his/her own GSTC), etc., notify CCRA and they will recalculate your eligibility based on the new family net income figure.
- **Tax Breaks for Construction Work Camp Businesses.** The deduction of business means and entertainment is generally limited to 50% of the expenditure to reflect personal consumption. Starting in 2002 full deductibility of such expenses will be allowed in cases where temporary work camps are set up close to urban areas that cannot support a large temporary construction workforce.
- **Cash Flow Assistance for Corporations.** Tax instalments owed by qualifying small corporations for the first three months of 2002 can be deferred for at least six months without interest or penalties as a temporary measure that responds to economic times.

NOTE: RRSP Deductions. It is worth noting that maximum RRSP contribution limits have not changed over the last several years. Canadians are allowed to contribute 18% of their "earned income" up to a maximum of $13,500 annually. This maximum is achieved when earned income is $75,000. These levels will stay in effect until 2004, when the maximum dollar amount will increase to $14,500 (earned income of $80,556 required). It is scheduled to increase again in 2005 to $15,500 (earned income of

$86,111 required). After this the maximum dollar amount will be indexed to the growth in the average industrial wage in Canada.

A Short Synopsis of New Trends

The following tax provisions have altered the Canadian tax system significantly over the past couple of years. If you haven't paid attention, you might be missing out on taking home more dollars on an after-tax basis and those windfalls could be invested to leverage your tax savings. In other cases, altered provisions have hurt Canadians, particularly unincorporated small business owners who have faced cash flow problems due to increases in Canada Pension Plan premiums.

1. Indexation

Canadians stand to gain tax savings each and every year as their tax brackets, personal amounts, refundable tax credits and clawback zones are indexed for inflation. The indexing factor is 3% for 2002, which, simplistically speaking, is based on increases in the Consumer Price Index.

Specifically, the Department of Finance uses the following two pieces of information in setting the indexing factor that is effective every January 1:

- the percentage increase in the average consumer price index (CPI) for Canada, as determined by Statistics Canada for the 12-month period ending on September 30 of the previous year
- the average CPI for the 12-month period ending on September 30 of the year earlier.

So, to arrive at the 3% indexing factor that was effective for January 2002, the government calculated the percentage increase in the average level of the CPI from October 2000 to September 2001, relative to the average level of the CPI from October 1999 to September 2000.

As a result, personal income tax brackets, non-refundable tax credits and their clawbacks, refundable tax credits and their clawbacks and certain social benefit repayments will all be adjusted for inflation. In general, this is good news for taxpayers, as they should experience increasing tax savings every year as a result of this provision.

This presents the opposite phenomenon of "Bracket Creep," the hidden taxes that had characterized our tax system through much of the 90's. Rather than being bumped into a higher tax bracket by inflation, Canadians now may find themselves in a lower tax bracket due to inflation adjustments, as time goes on.

2. New Tax Brackets and Rates

The 2000 Federal Budget of February 28, reduced all tax rates applied to taxable incomes and created a new tax bracket for incomes between $60,000 and $100,000. Together with the restoration of full indexing, this was most welcome news for managers and other professionals. In addition, the removal of the high income surtax for those with incomes over $85,000 came into full effect for tax years 2000 and beyond. The results of these changes are illustrated in Figures 2 and 3 using approximate average combined federal and provincial tax rates in the right hand column.

Figure 2
Federal and Provincial Tax Brackets and Rates 2001

Taxable Income	Federal Tax Rates	Average Combined Fed/Prov. Tax Rates
$0-$7,412	0%	0%
$7,413 to $30,754	16%	25%
$30,755 to $61,509	22%	31%
$61,510 to $100,000	26%	41%
Over $100,000	29%	45%

Figure 3
Federal and Provincial Tax Brackets and Rates 2002

Taxable Income	Federal Tax Rates	Average Combined Fed/Prov. Tax Rates
$0-$7,634	0%	0%
$7,635 to $31,677	16%	25%
$31,678 to $63,354	22%	31%
$63,355 to $103,000	26%	41%
Over $103,000	29%	45%

The effect of indexing is evident in Figures 2 and 3. Not all income sources are taxed alike, however, as illustrated in Figure 4, and this is important information for those looking to average their tax burdens downward with income diversification.

3. New Personal Amounts

The federal tax free zone (or Basic Personal Amount) rose to $7,412 in 2001 (indexing pushes it up to $7,634 in 2002), making it possible for every Canadian to earn approximately $600 a month on a completely tax free basis.

Figure 4
Average Federal and Provincial Marginal Tax Rates on Different Income Sources for 2001

Taxable Income	Federal Tax Rates	Income Type: Interest	Dividends	Capital Gains
$0-$7,412	0%	0%	0%	0%
$7,413 to $30,754	16%	25%	5%	12%
$30,755 to $61,509	22%	31%	16%	16%
$61,510 to $100,000	26%	41%	23%	20%
Over $100,000	**29%**	**45%**	**29%**	**22%**

Each province determines its own tax brackets and rates to these average figures may not be accurate in your province of residence. The provincial rates for 2001 are shown in Figure 7 below.

4. New Spousal Definitions and Amounts

Spouses, in the meantime, could earn up to $6,923 (or about $577 a month) in 2001 or $7,130 in 2002 (or about $594 a month), before the Amount for Spouse or Common-Law Partner was eliminated. The full amount was $6,294 for 2001 and $6,482 in 2002. Also, same sex partners are now recognized for tax purposes. The term "spouse" now applies only to heterosexual couples who are legally married. All others in conjugal relationships will be considered to be "common-law partners" if certain criteria are met:

- The couple lives together at the end of the year and has lived in a conjugal relationship for a continuous period of 12 months during the year or a prior year, or
- The partners live together as at the end of the year and are the natural or adoptive parents of child they have together.

5. Other Changes to Personal Amounts

Personal amounts increase the "tax free zone" available to families in different circumstances. Indexing and budget enhancements have recently increased these amounts significantly, as outlined in Figure 5.

Figure 5
Changes to Additional Personal Amounts

Taxpayer Profile	2002 Amounts	2001 Amounts
Seniors:		
Age Amount	$3,728	$3,619
Clawback begins at Individual Net Income of	$27,749	$26,941
The Sick and Disabled and Their Caregivers		
Amount for Infirm Dependant Adult	$3,605	$3,500
Clawback begins at Individual Net income of	$5,115	$4,966
Caregiver Amount for in-home care of adult	$3,605	$3,500
Clawback begins at Individual Net Income of	$12,312	$11,953
Disability Amounts for Adults	$6,180	$6,000
Supplemental Amount for Minors	$3,605	$3,500
Allowable child care and attendant care before clawback	$2,112	$2,050
Medical Expense Net Income Ceiling (expenses must exceed 3% of net income to a maximum of this figure)	$1,728	$1,678
Refundable Medical Expense Supplement (25% of medical expenses claimed to a maximum of this)	$535	$520
Minimum earnings from employment, self-employment	$2,676	$2,598
Family net income at which clawback begins	$20,296	$19,705

6. New Eligibility for Refundable Federal Tax Credits

More families also qualified for the federal refundable tax credits: The Canada Child Tax Benefits (CCTB) and The Goods and Services Tax Credit (GSTC).

In the case of the CCTB, it is now possible to receive the full benefits for minor children (without taking into account the National Child Benefit Supplement—NCB—for lower earners) if combined family net income is just under $33,000. Partial benefits are available when income exceeds this level, depending on the number of children in the family and the NCB Supplement begins to phase out when family net income levels reach $22,000.

Income thresholds and credit amounts for the GST have been similarly increased, as shown in Figure 6.

7. New Increased Employment Insurance Clawback Ceilings

Also known as the "Social Benefits Repayment" on the tax return, it is important to note that this clawback will no longer apply to those on "special benefits"—maternity, parental or sick benefits—and for those on regular benefits, the clawback ceiling has risen from $39,000 to $48,750.

Figure 6
Federal Refundable Tax Credits in 2002 vs. 2001

	2002	2001
Canada Child Tax Benefit (CCTB) *		
Basic benefit	$1,151	$1,117
Additional benefit for third child	$80	$78
Additional benefit for children under 7 years	$228	$221
National Child Benefit (NCB) Supplement		
First child	$1,293	$1,255
Second child	$1,087	$1,055
Third child	$1,009	$980
Family net income at which CCTB begins to phase out	$32,960	$32,000
Family net income at which NCB begins to phase out	$22,397	$21,744
Goods and Services Tax/Harmonized Sales Tax credit*		
Adult maximum	$213	$207
Child maximum	$112	$109
Single supplement	$112	$109
Phase-in threshold for the single supplement	$6,911	$6,710
Family net income at which credit begins to phase out	$27,749	$26,941

*The GST/HST credit and the CCTB are paid on a "benefit-year cycle" that begins every July based on net family income reported on the prior year's return.

8. Increased Old Age Security Benefit Clawbacks

The individual net income level at which the Old Age Security benefit is clawed back has also been increased to $56,968 from the 2001 threshold of $55,309.

9. Capital Gains Inclusion Rates

Starting with transactions after October 17, 2000, the capital gains inclusion rate for tax purposes was reduced to 50%, which is good to know by those who must consider "cashing in" their non-registered investments earlier than anticipated to meet cash flow requirements.

10. Other Significant Personal Tax Changes Announced in 2000

The following measures all effect tax filing in the Year 2001 and beyond:

- **Tuition and Education Credits.** The amounts on which the education tax credit is based have doubled to $400 a month for full-time students and $120 a month for part-time students.

- **Capital Gains Tax Rollovers.** A tax free rollover allows individual small business owners who sell their companies to defer the tax on capital gains from eligible small business investments, if the individual reinvests in another eligible small business.
- **CPP/QPP Deduction for Proprietors.** Starting in January 2001, self-employed individuals may claim a deduction for the employer's portion of the Canada Pension Plan and Quebec Pension Plan contributions, rather than claiming those amounts as a non-refundable credit.
- **CPP Premiums Payable.** These premiums have increased significantly recently. In 2001 the premiums were 4.3% of earnings up to $38,300. In 2002 they will again increase to 4.7% on earnings up to $39,100. In 2001, proprietors who are required to pay both the employer and employee's portion of the premiums which were subject to a maximum of $2,992.80 (the employee maximum was $1,496.40); that number will rise to $3,346.40 (or $1,673.20 for employees).
- **EI Premiums Payable.** These premiums were $2.25 for each $100 in insurable earnings in 2001, $2.20 for 2002, $2.10 for 2003 and are projected to be $2.00 thereafter.

11. Provincial Budget Changes

With the introduction of Tax on Net Income in all provinces, the calculation of provincial taxes has been "de-linked" from the federal tax system. The provinces are now allowed to develop their own tax brackets and rates as well as to increase or supplement non-refundable tax credits, providing only that they extend at least the same tax credits as the federal government. In addition both levels of government must use the same definition of taxable income.

As a result, there are some significant tax variations between the provinces, and in particular in Ontario and Alberta, who have been competing strongly for taxpayers via their tax systems. But it is important to note that these differences can rise and fall with different income levels. That is, taxpayers at the lowest tax bracket currently fair better in Ontario than they do in Alberta; whereas the highest income earners fare best in Alberta.

Because Canadians are taxed for the whole year in their province of residence as at December 31, it is important to become informed on the latest provincial tax outcomes before making a move.

Federal/provincial tax rates quoted for illustrative purposes in this book are approximations only; readers should visit with their tax advisors for preliminary actual tax calculations before making any tax planning decisions. See Figure 8 for details of provincial tax brackets and rates for 2001. At the time of writing, British Columbia and Ontario have announced their rates for 2002 and each province shows a decrease in rates. Brackets are expected to be indexed annually.

GOING FORWARD IN TOUGH TIMES

Decisions made during times of crisis can make or break the family legacy. When times are tough, remember these three basic tax concepts:

1. It is your legal right and duty to arrange your affairs within the framework of the law so as to pay the least amount of taxes possible.
2. Pay only the correct amount of tax—not one cent more. It's important to stop overpaying your taxes through your periodic pay cheque or through quarterly instalment payments.
3. Your biggest lifetime expense will not be your investment in your home mortgage or your RRSP. It will be the taxes you pay day in and day out in a productive lifetime of approximately 40 years ... for most this is a large six figure sum. If you can shave just 10% off this large number, you could significantly change one or two aspects of your current and/or future lifestyle.

So, the secret's out. You too could make and save money by learning more about tax planning ... *pass it on.*

Figure 7
Provincial Tax Brackets and Rates for 2001

Province	Tax Brackets	Rate	Surtax
Alberta		Flat Tax of 10%	
British Columbia	$0 to $30,484	7.3%	
	$30,485 to $60,969	10.5%	
	$60,970 to $70,000	13.7%	
	$70,001 to $85,000	15.7%	
	Over $85,000	16.7%	
Manitoba	$0 to $30,544	10.9%	
	$30,545 to $61,089	16.2%	
	Over $61,089	17.4%	
New Brunswick	$0 to $30,754	9.68%	
	$30,755 to $61,509	14.82%	
	$61,510 to $100,000	16.52%	
	Over $100,000	17.84%	
Newfoundland and Labrador	$0 to 29,590	10.57%	9% > $7,032
	$29,591 to $59,180	16.16	
	Over $59,180	18.02%	
Northwest Territories	$0 to $30,754	7.2%	
	$30,755 to $61,509	9.9%	
	$61,510 to $100,000	11.7%	
	Over $100,000	13.05%	
Nova Scotia	$0 to $25,590	9.77%	10% > $10,000
	$25,591 to 59,180	14.95%	
	Over $59,180	16.67%	
Nunavut	$0 to $30,754	7.2%	
	$30,755 to $61,509	9.9%	
	$61,510 to $100,000	11.7%	
	Over $100,000	13.05%	
Ontario	$0 to 30,814	6.16%	20% > $3,560
	$30,815 to $61,629	9.22%	+
	Over $61,629	11.16%	36% > $4,491
Prince Edward Island	$0 to 30,754	9.8%	10% > $5,200
	$30,755 to $61,509	13.8%	
	Over $61,509	16.7%	
Quebec	$0 to $26,000	17%	
	$26,001 to $52,000	21.25%	
	Over $52,000	24.5%	
Saskatchewan	Up to $30,000	11.5%	
	$30,000 to $60,000	13.5%	
	Over $60,000	16%	
Yukon	$0 to $30,754	10.12%	5% > $6,000
	$30,755 to $61,509	11.96%	
	$61,510 to $100,000	13.34%	
	Over $100,000	7.36%	

CHAPTER 1

Creating Legacies in Tough Times: Family Focus

KEY PERSONAL TAX CONCEPTS:

- When family income fluctuates, provisions within our tax system can help families cope
- Canadians overpay their taxes throughout the year and receive tax refunds—over $16 billion is refunded annually—an unnecessary drain on monthly income that can affect Canadian lifestyles in times of change and in retirement
- Taxpayers, who consider tax savings as "windfalls" to be invested, can significantly improve their wealth, even in turbulent times
- Employed taxpayers are often unaware that they qualify to claim out-of-pocket expenses on their tax returns
- 90% of Canadians do not use all their RRSP contribution room, which means they miss out on tax savings of 22% to over 50% of every dollar so invested, as well as tax-sheltered investment earnings over time
- RRSP contributions can create cash flow in tough times by reducing net income, thereby increasing non-refundable and refundable tax credits
- By crystallizing annual tax savings, other family priorities can be managed, including education savings, home ownership and retirement income accumulation and estate planning
- Annual tax savings can be further enhanced with investments in tax-efficient mutual funds and Labour-Sponsored Investment Funds

REAL LIFE

Donald Grant, an Ontario-based retail store manager who earns a gross base salary of $65,000 annually, was exasperated. He was just able to make ends meet in the past two years with his commission-based bonuses ($10,000 in each year) but world political and economic events have affected his young family dramatically in 2001.

Sales within his company had dropped off; there would be no commission sales bonuses in 2001 at all and the money left for the family's discretionary needs was tight. Fortunately, Donald had managed his credit card debt well, but he knew that his young family was quickly outgrowing their rented home. This year two of the couple's children needed glasses and Donald's spouse, Meredith, was scheduled for expensive root canal surgery. The family had no private health care coverage. In addition, changes to his spouse's career priorities would soon put more pressure on the family.

Meredith, mother of their four pre-school children, had been helping out financially with her home-based babysitting enterprise, netting $1,000 each month. It seemed to cost more and more to feed and care for her wards, however, and Meredith had been questioning whether the effort was really worthwhile over the longer term. She decided to go back to university full-time in the fall to take her Bachelor of Nursing degree. This move was financially challenging in the short term. Fortunately, Donald's mother was available to provide child care for the little ones. Meredith and Donald agreed that now was the right time for this decision, so that the family could benefit from the potential for higher earnings by Meredith in the future.

As a result, Meredith and Donald had no plans to make RRSP contributions this year, despite the fact that each had over $15,000 in RRSP room. The couple had previously accumulated $10,000 each in their RRSPs, primarily before their children were born.

Donald had been making contributions to a Canada Savings Bond investment through a payroll deduction plan at work and had accumulated $5,000 there. The family's immediate priorities included the incorporation of regular contributions to their retirement savings plans, initiating life insurance coverage, saving for a home and for their children's future post-secondary education.

THE CHALLENGE

How was it possible for this family to make plans for wealth creation at a time when their current income level was threatened? It seemed impossible.

In fact, Donald and Meredith were already reaping rewards from recent changes to the personal taxation system. Thanks to federal income tax reductions announced for the period 2000-2005, the family would benefit from increased monthly cash flow in the short term. They needed the ability to identify those savings and the resolve to invest these tax windfalls, in order to save for their long term priorities more effectively.

Wisely, the couple sought the advice of a financial advisor with tax knowledge who was able to create an action plan. Specifically, this family qualified for:

- Reduced federal tax rates
- Increased federal tax brackets and clawback threshholds
- Increased non-refundable tax credits
- Increased refundable tax credits
- Significant tax savings opportunities through the use of RRSPs and possibly Labour-Sponsored Fund Investments
- Cash recovery as a result of errors and omissions made on prior-filed returns.

The advisor went on to demonstrate to the couple that a tax focus could in fact help them meet their goals to create a comfortable retirement income, fund their children's education and their life insurance policies over the long term and even a down payment on a new home in the short term.

Despite tough times, Donald and Meredith discovered much more could be done to create new capital for investment purposes in the future:

- Donald's income tax withholding could be reduced at source to account for tax deductions and credits his employer did not know he qualified for during the tax year.
- Donald's employer could be asked to annualize the withholding of taxes on any future bonuses.
- Donald could also be writing off his home office and car expenses, as he has no office at his place of employment. Donald's employer should provide him with a signed *Form T2200 Declaration of Conditions of Employment* to validate this claim. (See Figure 1-2.)
- A strategy for a systematic investment into Donald's RRSP could be adopted, not only to help Donald and Meredith benefit from tax-deferred retirement savings, but also to assist them in using this principal to fund home ownership and education priorities.
- An education savings plan could be created for the children.
- Finally, both Donald and Meredith's prior-filed tax returns could be reviewed for errors and omissions. He was sure to qualify for missed employment expenses in the previous two years. She was not sure she had claimed all she was entitled to as a self-employed babysitter

and wondered about missing medical expenses and charitable donations. As well, three years ago the family had moved from Quebec to Ontario, but had not made a claim for moving expenses.

Through their advisor the couple discovered they could request adjustments for errors and omissions on most federal provisions all the way back to 1985 (provinces allow adjustments for the current year and two prior years only).

FACTORS TO CONSIDER

There are at least a dozen alternatives available to Donald and Meredith to increase tax savings and create wealth to reach their short and long term goals.

1. Identify Savings from Reduced Tax Burdens, Then Invest

Recent federal tax changes have predicted a reduction in taxes for Canadian families by up to 27% by 2005, as outlined in the Introduction of this book. Donald's income of $65,000, for example, is no longer taxed at the highest marginal rates as in previous years. In 2001 he qualifies for a 26% federal rate and a 9.22% provincial rate for a total of 35.22%. Further, there are no longer any federal surtaxes applied to these taxes.

Meredith's income of $12,000, on the other hand, falls into a 16% federal tax bracket. Combined with the provincial rate of 6.16%, her combined marginal tax rate is 22.16%. If we assume for illustrative purposes that the *same income* was received in each of 1999, 2000, and 2001, tax savings from these changes are significant over the taxes the family had been paying in the prior two years. Figure 1-1 illustrates this point.

Figure 1-1
Tax Savings Due to Tax Reductions Available Since 2000

Taxpayer	Income	Taxes in 1999	Taxes in 2000	Difference 1999 to 2000	Taxes in 2001	Difference 2000 to 2001	Savings since 1999
Donald	$65,000	$18,604	$17,524	($1,080)	$15,738	($1,786)	$2,866
				(6%)		(10%)	15%
Meredith	$12,000	$1,631	$1,572	($59)	$1,510	($62)	$121
				(4%)		(4%) *	7% *
Total	$77,000	$20,235	$19,096	($1,139)	$17,249	($1,847)	$2,986

*Being self-employed, Meredith's savings gains have been reduced by increases in Canada Pension Plan rates. For more information, see Chapter 5.

The key to new prosperity in tough times, from a tax point of view, is to identify and then invest these tax savings windfalls ... a 15% reduction in personal tax liabilities since 1999 can go a long way in offsetting losses due to economic circumstances. In other words, the new tax measures introduced by governments since 2000 have brought new capital of close to $3,000 to the family in our example over two years; this is money that could be used for a variety of purposes, including investments, if financial discipline can be exercised.

2. Reduce Tax on Employment Income

It is always important to be on the look-out for new tax savings opportunities, particularly in years in which personal, financial or career opportunities change. Donald started his current employment in 1999 and earns his compensation in part from salary ($65,000 per year) and in part through commissioned sales bonuses. In the dark, from a tax point of view, Donald was unaware that he qualified to write off some of the expenses he incurs to earn employment income. Because the majority of taxpayers are employees, Donald's omission is worth reviewing in detail. See the discussion under the categories following.

Allowable Employment Expenses: Salary Only

Those who earn salary only may deduct the following out-of-pocket expenses:

- Accounting and legal fees, not including income tax preparation
- Motor vehicle expenses including Capital Cost Allowance (CCA), interest or leasing costs, as well as operating costs
- Travelling expenses, including rail, air, bus or other travel costs
- Meals, tips and hotel costs providing each excursion is for at least 12 hours away from the taxpayer's metropolitan area (meals and tips are subject to a 50% restriction)
- Costs of parking (but generally not at the place of employment)
- Supplies used up directly in the work (stationery, maps, etc.)
- Salaries paid to an assistant (including spouse or children, if fair market value is paid for work actually performed)
- Office rent or certain home office expenses, described below.

Allowable Employment Expenses: Salary and Commission

Employees who earn their living negotiating contracts for their employers or selling on commission may claim expenses for travel and sales costs if they are required to pay their own expenses and regularly perform their duties away from their employer's place of business. In addition, expenses are claimable only if the employee is not in receipt of a tax-free travel allowance.

Deductible travel expenses include:

- Automobile-related operating expenses like gas, oil, repairs
- Automobile-related fixed costs like licenses, insurance, interest, leasing and capital cost allowance. The latter three expenses are limited to annual maximums. At the time of writing, those maximums were:
  - For CCA: – $30,000 plus GST and PST is maximum capital cost
  - For Interest: – $300 a month
  - For Leasing Costs: – $800 a month plus GST and PST
- The cost of air, bus, rail, taxi or other transportation which takes the employee outside the employer's metropolitan area
- When travel expenses only are claimed, the amounts may exceed commissions earned. Excess expenses may be used to offset other income for the year.

Deductible Sales Expenses include:

- Promotional expenses, like brochures, trade show costs, gifts, etc.
- Meals and entertainment (subject to the 50% restriction)
- Travel and auto expenses
- Home workspace expenses.

Note: Those who claim "sales expenses" may not claim expenses that exceed commissions earned in the calendar year, except home workspace may be carried forward.

Common Errors on Asset Purchases

Deductible equipment costs are subject to special rules of which most taxpayers are unaware. Employees are not allowed to make a claim for capital expenditures with the exception of the purchase of vehicles, musical instruments or aircraft. Therefore it is wise tax planning to lease computers, cell phones or other equipment.

Deductible Home Workspace Costs

Employed taxpayers may claim home workspace costs but are limited to the following if they earn salary only:

- Rent
- Utility costs
- Cleaning materials and minor repairs for the office

Employed commission salespeople may add the costs of property taxes and insurance.

Employees may never claim costs relating to mortgage interest or capital cost allowance. In addition, a loss may not be created by claiming home

Figure 1-2
T2200 Declaration of Conditions of Employment – Sample

Canada Customs and Revenue Agency — Agence des douanes et du revenu du Canada

DECLARATION OF CONDITIONS OF EMPLOYMENT

- You have to complete this form to deduct employment expenses from your income. You complete **Part A**, and your employer completes **Part B**.
- You do not have to file this form with your return. However, you have to keep it in case we ask to see it.
- For more information, see the guide called *Employment Expenses*, or Interpretation Bulletins IT-352, *Employee's Expenses, Including Work Space in Home Expenses*, and IT-522, *Vehicle, Travel and Sales Expenses of Employees.*

Part A – Employee information (to be completed by the employee)

Last name	First name	Social insurance number
Home address	Business address	

Part B – Conditions of employment (to be completed by the employer)

1. Did this employee's contract require the employee to pay his or her own expenses? ☐ Yes ☐ No

2. a) Did you normally require this employee to work away from your place of business, or in different places? ☐ Yes ☐ No
   b) If *yes*, what was the employee's area of travel? ____________

3. Indicate the period of employment during the year. **From**: ______ (Year) ______ (Month) **To**: ______ (Year) ______ (Month)

4. a) Did this employee receive an allowance? ☐ Yes ☐ No
   b) If *yes*, indicate:
   i) the amount received as a fixed allowance, such as a flat monthly allowance. $ ______
   ii) the per km rate used ______ ($/km), and the amount received. $ ______
   iii) the amount of the allowance that was included on the employee's T4 slip. $ ______

5. a) Did this employee receive a repayment of the expenses he or she paid to earn employment income? ☐ Yes ☐ No
   b) If *yes*, indicate the amount that was:
   i) received upon proof of payment. $ ______
   ii) charged to the employer, such as credit-card charges. $ ______
   iii) included on the employee's T4 slip. $ ______

6. a) Did you require this employee to pay other expenses for which the employee did not receive any allowance or repayment? ☐ Yes ☐ No
   b) If *yes*, indicate the type(s) of expenses. ______

7. a) Did you pay this employee wholly or partly by commissions or similar amounts according to the volume of sales made or contracts negotiated? ☐ Yes ☐ No
   b) If *yes*, indicate the amount paid, $ ______ and the type of goods sold or contracts negotiated. ______

8. Did you require this employee to be away for at least 12 hours from the municipality and metropolitan area (if there is one) of your business where the employee normally reported for work? ☐ Yes ☐ No

9. a) Did you require this employee under a contract of employment to:
   - rent an office away from your place of business, or use a portion of his or her home? ☐ Yes ☐ No
   - pay for a substitute or assistant? ☐ Yes ☐ No
   - pay for supplies that the employee used directly in his or her work? ☐ Yes ☐ No

   b) Did you or will you repay this employee for any of the expenses in 9a)? ☐ Yes ☐ No

   c) If *yes* to 9b), indicate the amount you did or will repay. $ ______

Employer declaration

I certify that the information provided in Part B is, to the best of my knowledge, true, correct, and complete.

______ Name of employer (print) ______ Name and title of authorized person (print)

______ Date ( ) ______ Telephone ______ Signature of employer or authorized person

T2200 (01) (Français au verso) Canadä

workspace expenses. Therefore if commissions or employment income are insufficient to cover these costs (perhaps because the employee started working late in the year), the unclaimed portion of costs can be carried forward and used to offset future income.

Employee and Partner GST/HST Rebates

Employees who claim employment expenses on Line 229 of the tax return may receive a cash rebate of any GST/HST, paid on these expenses on Line 457. *Form GST 370* must be completed. Many employees have missed this provision in the past. The amounts can be recovered by filing an adjustment back to the inception of the GST: 1991 (HST 1997).

Tax Overpayment Recovery

As Donald was unaware of his rights to offset employment income with the provisions above, he can adjust prior-filed returns all the way back to 1985 to recover taxes overpaid due to this oversight. See the Digging for Gold section at the end of this book for detailed examples of common tax error adjustments.

Documentation

All employees who claim employment expenses must complete *Form T2200 Declaration of Conditions of Employment* for each year in which tax deductible expenses are claimed, and have this signed by their employers. A sample of this form is shown in Figure 1-2.

Donald, who benefited from a stronger economy in each of 1999 and 2000, earned commission sales income in the amount of $10,000 in each of those years, over and above his base salary. He is now aware that he could have claimed approximately $1,200 in home workspace expenses, $500 in net entertainment expenses, $850 in promotional expenses and $6,000 on auto expenses (total $8,550) and a GST rebate of $250 in each year. As a result, he had missed out on significant savings as detailed in Figure 1-3.

Figure 1-3
Tax Savings Available After Deduction of Employment Expenses

Year	Gross Income	Deductions	Net Income	Tax Savings	CGST Rebate	CCTB Increase	Total Savings
1999	$75,000	$8,550	$66,450	$4,169	$250	$428	$4,847
2000	$75,250 *	$8,550	$66,700	$3,968	$250	$428	$4,646

*Income increases by inclusion of GST rebate received.

3. Increase Monthly Income with Reduced Tax Withholding

Any Canadian who receives a tax refund after filing a tax return is overpaying taxes all year long and giving the federal and provincial governments an interest-free loan. It is important to arrange your affairs so that you pay yourself first, particularly if you have trouble making RRSP contributions or paying monthly debt of any type.

Taxpayers can request that taxes withheld by their employers at source be reduced. This is possible when tax deductions and credits the employee is entitled to do not show up on the *TD1 Personal Tax Credits Return,* upon which income tax withholding deductions are normally based. Following is a list of the many provisions that can reduce the income tax you pay and, in turn, permit you to request that the income tax withheld by your employer be reduced. See which circumstances apply to you.

- Registered Retirement Savings Plan (RRSP) contributions
- Union and professional dues not paid on a payroll deduction plan
- Child care expenses
- Moving expenses
- Allowable Business Investment Losses
- Employment Expenses on Line 229
- Carrying charges including interest costs for investment loans
- Repayments of social benefits like Employment Insurance
- Deductible alimony or maintenance payments
- Net business or rental losses
- Loss carryovers (capital or non-capital)
- Northern Residents' Deductions
- Significant medical expenses or charitable donations
- Overseas Employment Tax Credits
- Labour-Sponsored Funds Tax Credits
- Any other provisions that will reduce the taxpayer's taxable income.

To reduce tax withholding, *Form T1213 Request to Reduce Tax Deductions at Source* (see Figure 1-4) is forwarded to CCRA by the taxpayer, outlining the type of deduction that will reduce net income during the year. From this information, CCRA will forward a *letter of authority* to the employer, allowing the employer to reduce tax withholding for the employee.

As a result, any employee who begins making RRSP contributions during the year may have tax withheld at source reduced to take into account this legitimate deduction. This means more dollars go into your retirement savings plan faster or monthly bills can be paid without incurring interest costs.

Figure 1-4
T1213 Request to Reduce Tax Deductions at Source - Sample

Canada Customs and Revenue Agency | Agence des douanes et du revenu du Canada

REQUEST TO REDUCE TAX DEDUCTIONS AT SOURCE FOR YEAR(S) ________

- Use this form to ask for less tax deductions at source for any deductions or non-refundable tax credits that are not part of the TD1 *Personal Tax Credits Return.*
- All your income tax returns that are due have to be filed and amounts paid in full before you send us this form.
- If you have deductible support payments that are the same or greater for more than one year, you can make this request for two years.
- Send the completed form with all the supporting documents to the Client Services Division of your tax services office. You can find the addresses on our Web site at: **www.ccra-adrc.gc.ca/contact/tso-e.html**, or by calling us at **1-800-959-8281**.
- We will notify you in writing within four to eight weeks, whether or not we approve your request.

Identification

First name	Last name		Social Insurance Number
Address			
City/Town	Province	Postal code	Telephone: Residence / Business
Employer Name	Contact person		Telephone and fax numbers
Address			

Request to reduce tax on

Salary ☐ Lump sum ☐ If lump sum, give amount and details (for example, a bonus or paid vacation).

$ ________ ________________

Deductions or non-refundable tax credits

Registered retirement savings plan contributions $ ________
- Give details or a copy of the payment arrangement contract.
- Do not include contributions deducted from your pay by your employer.

Child care expenses $ ________
- Give details on a separate sheet.

Alimony or maintenance, or support payments $ ________
- Attach a complete copy of your signed judgment or written separation agreement, if not previously filed.

  Recipient's name and social insurance number

  ________________ | | | | | | | | | |

Employment expenses $ ________
- Attach a completed T2200 form signed by your employer and a statement of expenses.

Interest expense and carrying charges on investment loans $ ________
- Attach a copy of statements from the lender confirming the purpose and amount of loan(s) and the interest payments to be made in the year.

Other—specify (for example, charitable donations or rental losses)
- Attach all supporting documents. Use a separate sheet to give details, if necessary.

________________ $ ________

Total amounts to be deducted from income $ ________

Subtract income not subject to tax deductions at source (interest, net rental or self-employed income) - ________

Net amount eligible for **tax waiver** $ ________

Certification

I request authorization for my employer to take less tax deductions at source based on the information given. I certify that the information given in this statement is, to the best of my knowledge, correct and complete.

________________ Signature ________________ Date

T1213 (Français au verso) Canada

4. Understand the Value of RRSP Contributions

The RRSP is such a versatile, multi-faceted tax provision because its power to influence wealth stretches beyond the present, well into the future. It provides a guaranteed return on the investment of 22% to almost 50% (depending on the tax bracket and province of residence) in tax savings to all who are taxable, it influences monthly income from social benefits like Child Tax Benefits and it influences the size of transferable, inter-family credits like tuition and education and disability amounts. Its primary features are overviewed in the RRSP Tip Sheet in Figure 1-5.

Ideas for the use of tax savings created by the RRSP investment will support the real life scenarios presented throughout this book.

5. Should Scarce Resources be Invested in Registered or Non-Registered Accounts? It's Your Decision

With recent federal tax changes, the generally-accepted wisdom of making RRSP contributions has been under attack. The primary controversy surrounds its tax efficiency upon withdrawal in retirement. At that time, both principal and accumulated earnings within the RRSP are subject to 100% income inclusion.

Gains on capital property, on the other hand, are included at 50% under current rules. (Details surrounding the taxation of non-registered accounts is covered in more detail in Chapter 4.)

The speculation is that upon withdrawal, when 100% of principal and earnings within an RRSP must be included in income, a tax-deferred capital gain included at 50% or less may be more tax efficient, particularly if clawbacks of Old Age Security (OAS) and other credits which are based on net income are involved at that time.

However, broad-based generalizations on this theory may be imprudent, at best, and dangerous, at worst, depending on the age of the taxpayer and the number of years to retirement. The further out retirement is, the less able we are to compare future apples to current apples. That is, we cannot predict whether future tax provisions, such as capital gains income inclusion rates, federal and provincial tax brackets and their respective rates, clawback zones, and the taxpayer's income, marital status and health will remain the same in the foreseeable future. All of these factors can have a major impact on today's RRSP contribution decision and tomorrow's wealth accumulation.

When faced with such a dilemma, it is generally wise to turn to what we know:

- **Tax savings earned today are worth more in your pocket than the government's.** RRSP contributions made by those who are taxable today will return approximately 22% to close to 50% in tax savings, depending

Figure 1-5

Tip Sheet—RRSP

Eligibility

Allowable contributions to an RRSP are based on available RRSP contribution room. This space is based on a taxpayer's "earned income" from active sources, like employment income, net rental or self-employment income, and taxable alimony or maintenance payments. Passive investment income or social benefits like Employment Insurance do not qualify. There is no lower age barrier in making contributions; however there is an upper age limit of 69. A taxpayer may contribute in the 69th year and, even if over 69, may contribute to spousal RRSP if spouse is under 69.

Upper Age Limit

RRSPs must be collapsed by the end of the year in which the taxpayer turns 69. The accumulations can be taken out in a lump sum (not usually a good idea as the amounts are often taxed at the highest marginal rate at that time), but most commonly will be transferred to an investment that will enable a periodic taxable income from this source: either an annuity (which provides for equal monthly payments over a period of time) or a Registered Retirement Income Fund (RRIF—which provides for gradually increasing payments over time).

Net Income Reductions

Contributions to an RRSP based on RRSP contribution room will reduce net income. Generally, the higher the tax bracket in which the income falls, the greater the benefit will be received from the RRSP contribution. However, because net income is reduced, reduction in clawback of other benefits may be significant in any tax bracket.

Maximum Contributions

A taxpayer may contribute 18% of earned income to a maximum of $13,500 annually (this dollar maximum is scheduled to rise in 2004).

Contribution Deadlines

Contributions can be made throughout the year or within 60 days of the year end to qualify for deduction.

Tax Sheltering and Withdrawal Implications

While in the plan, the earnings on the RRSP principal is completely sheltered from tax. However, upon withdrawal, 100% principal and earnings are included in income.

RRSP Contribution Room

The ability to contribute to an RRSP—together with an ability to carry forward unused RRSP contribution room—has been accumulating based on the earned income of those who filed tax returns since 1991. Taxpayers who missed filing returns in this time period will have understated RRSP contribution room if they had "earned income." So it is important to file those returns to open the proper RRSP contribution room, bring tax liabilities up to date or reap tax refunds on overpaid taxes in those years.

Overcontributions

Taxpayers who are over the age of 18 may contribute the full amount of their contribution room plus a $2,000 overpayment.

Cumulative Excesses

RRSP contributions in excess of $2,000 (or those in excess of contribution room for taxpayers under 19) are subject to a penalty of 1% per month on the excess. A complicated form called a *T1-OVP Individual Income Tax Return for RRSP Excess Contributions* must be completed in that case and the penalty must be paid by March 31 of the year following the cumulative excesses. Excess contributions may be withdrawn from RRSP with no further tax consequences. If not withdrawn, the penalty continues.

Planning with Undeducted Contributions

Taxpayers who make contributions have the option of taking a tax deduction for these amounts or they may carry forward undeducted contributions for deduction in a future year, when income is higher and therefore marginal tax benefits better.

Spousal RRSPs

Taxpayers may contribute to their own RRSPs based on available RRSP contribution room, but may also contribute some or all of the amounts to a spousal RRSP. This allows a couple to accumulate and then split tax deferred pension income in retirement. However, there are special restrictions on withdrawal from these plans: the money must be left in the spouse's RRSP for at least three years from the last RRSP contribution to the plan; otherwise withdrawals will be taxed in the contributor's hands.

Home Buyer's Plan

First time homebuyers (or those who have not owned a home in the current year or preceding four years) may withdraw up to $20,000 of funds saved within their RRSPs for the purpose of buying a home, on a completely tax free basis. However, the funds must be repaid back into the RRSP over a 15 year period beginning in the second calendar year after the withdrawal. Missed repayments are added to income and do not qualify for an RRSP deduction.

NOTE: Tax free withdrawals from an RRSP may also be made for the purpose of making home renovations or purchasing a compatible home to meet the needs of a disabled person.

Lifelong Learning Plan

RRSP savings help taxpayers go back to post-secondary school—a common occurrence in times of layoffs or job termination. In this instance, the taxpayer is allowed to withdraw up to $10,000 per year from the RRSP over a maximum of four years. Withdrawals may not exceed $20,000 in total. Repayments back into the RRSP must be made at least over a ten year period, and must begin within 60 days after the end of the fifth year following the first withdrawal or, where students fail to qualify as "full-time," the year following the last year in which the taxpayer was enrolled as a full-time student. Again, missed repayments are added to income.

on province of residence and the taxpayer's tax bracket. Generally those guaranteed double-digit tax savings are available within a period of two weeks to two months, depending on CCRA's return processing time. This immediate return of capital is lost if RRSP contributions are not made.

- **Earnings within the RRSP remain tax deferred until withdrawal.** Such withdrawal is mandatory by the end of the year the taxpayer turns 69. However, taxes can be further deferred on balances remaining by transferring RRSP accumulations to a Registered Retirement Income Fund (RRIF) or an annuity, or both. In general this tax deferred growth, accumulating in the RRSP throughout the accumulation period, results in significantly increased before-tax wealth accumulations by comparison to investments in non-registered accounts, particularly if annual tax savings are continually reinvested in the RRSP.
- **Spousal RRSP contributions provide for a retirement income-splitting opportunity,** while reaping the normal tax savings return; something that is not possible with a non-registered equities investment.
- **RRSP deductions reduce net income on the tax return,** which can result in new capital in tax savings from a variety of other provisions like:
  - The Age Amount
  - The Spousal Amount
  - The Amount for Infirm Dependent Adults
  - The Caregiver Amount
  - Amounts transferred from spouse
  - Medical expenses
  - Charitable donations
  - Child Tax Benefits
  - Goods and Services Tax Credits
  - Provincial Refundable Tax Credits
  - Old Age Security Clawbacks
  - Employment Insurance Benefits Clawbacks.

  The cost of foregoing savings on these and other benefits (like the transfer of tuition and education credits from a dependent spouse or child) must be factored into the equation before an informed decision can be made on the registered/non-registered investment question. In short, investment decisions should not be made in absence of tax and investment planning for the whole family.
- **Based on the 2000 and 2001 Federal Budgets,** we know that, through existing tax provisions expected to take effect between 2000 and 2005, taxes are expected to be reduced for the majority of Canadians. Reductions range between 20 and 27% when one takes into account indexing

of tax brackets and clawback zones, the new five-level taxation rate structure, the capital gains income inclusion changes and generous enhancements to the Child Tax Benefit. This means that an RRSP contribution —at least in the short term—is worth more in tax savings this year than it will likely be in the foreseeable future.

One could say that given these changes, the worst mistake a taxpayer could have made in 1999 and 2000 was to miss his or her RRSP contribution, as each dollar was worth more in tax savings than it is today. It is possible the same could be said of the opportunity in 2001 vs. 2002, 2003, 2004 or 2005.

- **Those very close to retirement may make different choices.** It is possible that in certain instances those close to retirement or those who are close to age 69 may benefit from choosing not to make registered investments. This may be the case if they know taxes in retirement will be significantly higher than before retirement. Such decisions, however, should take into account the ability (or inability) to carry forward undeducted RRSP contributions, the ability to make spousal RRSP contributions for a younger spouse and clawbacks to the age credit and Old Age Security. It is important to prepare preliminary tax calculations before making this decision.

6. Families Should Consider the RRSP Investment Opportunity First

Unless there is an obvious contrary scenario, taxpayers and their advisors should consider all of the following in determining their RRSP contribution strategies this year:

- **Longer Time Horizons; Taxable Income.** Make RRSP contributions, reap the tax rewards, then reinvest the savings within next year's RRSP immediately, unless there are priorities to reduce non-deductible debt. If cash is tight before March 1, contribute from non-registered investments to RRSPs if necessary—keeping the superficial loss rules in mind, however. That is, capital losses created by a flip of equities or bonds into an RRSP will not be allowed.
- **Arrange for Periodic Pre-tax RRSP Contributions.** RRSP contributions should be made through payroll deduction plans on a pre-tax basis. Not only is this a good way to average back into the marketplace, but the benefit of the tax refund is received immediately, allowing you to invest more, sooner.
- **Income Splitting Opportunities.** Use the spousal RRSP option to split future income and thereby reduce exposure to clawbacks on social benefits.

- **Maximize Use of Transferable and Refundable Tax Credits.** Invest in RRSPs for all lower income earners in the family who have RRSP contribution room, to maximize tax savings from transferable non-refundable credits and benefits available under refundable credits like the CTB.
- **Diversify Use of RRSP Savings.** The versatility of the RRSP allows for tax-free withdrawals for those who need funds to go back to school (under the Lifelong Learning Plan) and those who need to finance a house purchase (under the Home Buyer's Plan), options unavailable under other non-registered investment alternatives. Those with only non-registered equity savings, for example, would need to generate sufficient pre-tax gains or losses to finance either additional learning or home purchases, and borrowing for these purposes, unfortunately, is not deductible.
- **Fund Education Savings Plans.** Tax savings from RRSP contributions can be used to fund education savings for children, while RRSP accumulations can fund education for adults, as explained above. When it comes to the children, a parent may decide to invest the tax savings into a Registered Education Savings Plan (RESP). Contributors may make contributions of up to $4,000 each year, and earnings within the plan are tax sheltered until withdrawal by a student using the funds to go to post-secondary education. A portion of this RESP deposit will be matched by the federal government by way of the Canada Education Savings Grant. The matchable amount is 20% of the deposit to a maximum of $400 annually, which is reached when $2,000 is deposited.
- **Revisit the Mortgage or RRSP Question.** Young families often wonder whether it is better to contribute to an RRSP or pay down the mortgage. Much of this depends upon the family's financial focus and discipline but it is important to consider the following example: assume a 42% marginal tax bracket and a maximum RRSP contribution of $12,000, according to the taxpayer's available room. Tax savings from the contribution are approximately $5,040 in this case. This equates to $420 a month of "new capital" that can be applied to the mortgage.

  Now imagine the $125,000 mortgage amortized over 25 years at an average interest rate in that period of 6%. Monthly payments are $799.76. If this is bumped up by the $420 a month in tax savings from the RRSP, the taxpayer cuts the amortization period by 13 years. The results are as follows:

  - Accumulated tax-sheltered earnings on principal of $12,000 contributed each year for 12 years, compounding at a before-tax rate of return of 6% amounts to about $70,600.

- Interest savings on the reduced amortization period of 12 years rather than 25 years equals approximately $65,300.
- Total accumulated principal and earnings in the period will result in $214,600 in the RRSP, $125,000 in home equity and a further $65,300 in interest savings for a total of $404,900 .... all from an investment of just $144,000 over 12 years.
- While the deferred tax bite must be factored into this (at marginal rates of 22% to close to 50% this could range from $47,000 to $107,000), the challenge for equal performance from equities in a non-registered account involves the size of pre-tax returns that have to be generated consistently on a monthly basis to reap the same mortgage principal reduction.

- **Plan Early and Long Withdrawals.** In the case of taxpayers who find themselves closer to retirement, it may be valid to plan to withdraw RRSP funds over a longer period of time, starting before age 69, and with the lower income earner, if by doing so tax can be generated at a rate lower than that expected in future years or at death. The after-tax dollars can then be reinvested within non-registered accounts, for both an effective tax deferral and low-rate income inclusion upon withdrawal.

  Couple this strategy with a view to maximizing the taxpayer's deductible expenditures for medical expenses and charitable donations. Retired taxpayers who are not receiving other periodic pension income should also consider converting some of their RRSP to a RRIF to begin receiving at least $1,000 per year from the RRIF. This income is eligible for the pension income amount and, if the taxpayer is in the lowest tax bracket may be received tax free.
- **Borrow for Non-Registered Investments.** When RRSP contributions are maximized, the family can consider making tax-efficient investments within family members' non-registered accounts, borrowing to do so if necessary (interest paid should be tax deductible if there is a potential of income from dividends or other sources). This also generates the opportunity to offset taxable capital gains with capital losses, should they occur sometime in the future.
- **Draw Up Bona Fide Loans with Spouse.** Higher income earners can lend funds to lower income earning spouses for the purposes of investing within non-registered accounts and, in doing so, avoid CCRA's Attribution Rules. These rules, which will be discussed in more detail in Chapter 4, generally require earnings on money given to the lower earning spouse by the higher earner to be taxed in the hands of the higher earner. However, so long as a formal loan is drawn up and interest is paid

at fair market rates, the income becomes taxable to the lower earner. Writing inter-spousal investment loans may be an attractive option this year, given low market and prescribed interest rates. Remember, however, interest must be paid within 30 days of the end of the calendar year in which principal on the loan was outstanding.

7. Families Can Play the Labour-Sponsored Investment Fund Card

All of the RRSP contribution strategies outlined above can be further enhanced throughout the year or within the first 60 days of the next year by making contributions to a Labour-Sponsored Investment Fund (LSIF), which reaps a 15% federal tax credit on contributions up to a maximum of $5,000 ($750). Many provinces also offer matching credits against provincial taxes. The Labour-Sponsored Funds Tax Credit (LSFTC) reduces actual taxes payable. There are reasons why some taxpayers' scenarios are not suitable for this type of investment—risk tolerance, the eight-year hold period, alternate investments with guaranteed returns, etc.—however, the annual tax savings opportunity should be explored in light of the family's other financial planning priorities. LSFTCs are claimable in addition to RRSP tax deductions, so a taxpayer who uses an RRSP contribution to purchase a LSIF share can achieve tax savings in the 52% to 80% range.

In fact, the tax savings can be created without the need for additional cash—simply use assets within an RRSP to acquire Labour-Sponsored Investment Fund Shares to create the tax credit, and do so within 60 days of the end of the year.

This investment should not be made without discussion with your financial advisor. See Tip Sheet in Figure 1-6.

8. Project Investment Growth Opportunities Forward

Every tax saving analysis is enhanced when a future projection of today's savings is completed.

In Donald's case, making RRSP and LSIF contributions since he started his job in 1999 would have saved him bundles of dollars over time, as illustrated in Figure 1-7. With the potential to accumulate over $670,000 in the next 20 years, Donald was convinced that he should begin contributing to tax-preferred investments immediately.

Figure 1-6

Tip Sheet—Labour-Sponsored Investment Fund (LSIF)

Reaping the Tax Advantage

Investments in LSIFs create a tax credit that is non-refundable. That means tax savings result only if you are taxable.

Federal Labour-Sponsored Funds Tax Credits (LSFTC)

There are two levels of LSFTC available to most Canadians: federal and provincial. Federally-registered LSIFs are governed by the Income Tax Act and qualify for federal tax credits of 15% of your investment to a maximum of $5,000 per year or a credit of $750. These are the maximum investments for tax purposes; however, some taxpayers may wish to contribute more to the fund if they think it's a good investment, and this is allowed.

Provincial Tax Credit Opportunities

Many provinces also offer matching LSFTC to offset taxes payable in that province; however, their tax credit amounts may vary, as well, details of redemption and other features may vary. Provincial tax credit availability is summarized below:

Provincial LSFTC Features

Province	Rate
Alberta	No LSIF
British Columbia	15% (max. $750)
Manitoba	15% (max. $750)
New Brunswick	15% (max. $750)
Newfoundland and Labrador	No LSIF
Northwest Territories	15% of first $5,000 plus 30% of the next $95,000
Nova Scotia	15% (max. $525)
Nunavut	15% of first $5,000 plus 30% of the next $95,000
Ontario	15% (max. $750)
Prince Edward Island	No LSIF
Quebec	15% (max. $750)
Saskatchewan	20% (max. $1,000 if plan registered in Saskatchewan) 15% (max. $525 if plan not registered in Saskatchewan)
Yukon	25% (max. $1,250)

. . . *continued on next page*

Figure 1-6 . . . *continued from previous page*

Tip Sheet—Labour-Sponsored Investment Fund

Eligibility

To make a non-registered investment in a LSIF, there is no requirement for earned income, upper or lower age limits; however the taxpayer should have taxes payable against which to use the tax credit. When an investment is made within an RRSP, all the usual rules relating to earned income and age limitations must be followed. Interest on a loan taken to purchase a LSIF in a non-registered account is tax deductible.

Contribution Timing

The investment can be made throughout the tax year or if the contribution is made within the first 60 days of next year, the credit can apply to either last year's taxes payable or that of the current year, whether it is made inside or outside a registered account.

Spousal LSIFs

When a LSIF investment is made outside of an RRSP, only the contributor may claim the LSFTC. When the investment is made within a spousal RRSP, either spouse may claim the tax credit. However, only the contributor can claim the deduction.

Over Age 69

LSIF investments held outside an RRSP can be made at any age. In fact, for those at high income levels who are age-prohibited from making deductible RRSP contributions, the LSFTC provides one of the last tax tools available to shelter pension and investment income.

Holding Period

Investments in LSIFs must be held for eight years (except in Quebec).

Dispositions

When a taxpayer redeems shares of the fund within the hold period, the fund managers must remit to CCRA any tax credits earned upon investment from the proceeds. If the disposition occurs within an RRSP, the resulting gain or loss is not taxable at the time it is realized. In the case of redemption of investments held in non-registered accounts, the adjusted cost base must be increased by tax credits previously received if losses result. Excess losses are then applied to capital gains within the year or in carryover periods as per normal rules. However, the adjusted cost base for LSIF capital gains are not similarly reduced by the tax credit.

When dispositions are made after the holding period is up, there are different tax consequences. If the investment is within an RRSP, withdrawals are taxable under normal RRSP rules. At age 69 when the RRSP must be collapsed, LSIFs can be transferred to a RRIF; it is not possible to transfer these investments to annuities.

When LSIF investments are held in non-registered funds and redeemed after the holding period, a capital gain or loss is reported in the normal manner, except that capital losses again must be reduced by LSFTCs previously received.

Reinvestment Opportunities

After the hold period expires, the investment becomes fully liquid and may be redeemed at any time. Note the following important points:

- After the hold period is over, taxpayers may reinvest the funds and reap new tax credits.
- At age 69, when taxpayers must make decisions about converting their RRSP accumulations to a RRIF, LRIF or LIF or annuity, existing LSIF shares may be transferred to the RRIF. However, a RRIF, LRIF or LIF cannot buy new LSIF shares.

Investment Growth Opportunities.

Shares that are left in the LSIF continue to grow after the holding period is up. Taxpayers may not necessarily wish to cash in their fund at that time if there is an opportunity to benefit from capital appreciation. Investors will want to crystallize capital gains when performance in the fund is at its peak, so it may be wise to keep some of the funds invested should there be increased market activity in the near future. This should be discussed with your financial advisor.

Early Redemption

Early redemption is possible in case of death, terminal illness, disability (together with the permanent inability to work), or in some cases, severe financial hardship, however, tax credits may be clawed back in those cases. It is important to note, for example, that death does not trigger early redemption through a deemed disposition, which is important because early redemption generally will trigger a clawback of tax credits previously earned. As different rules exist for early redemption in various provinces, be sure to discuss this feature with your financial advisor.

Income Reporting

LSIFs may declare dividends, dividends in kind and capital gains dividends. In the case of non-registered investments, stock dividends declared will increase unit values; dividends paid in cash can be reinvested elsewhere. In either case, a taxable income inclusion results. Within registered funds, income declared stays in the plan on a tax-deferred basis.

Figure 1-7
Savings from RRSP and LSIF Contributions

Savings resulting from a $13,500 annual RRSP contribution and a $5,000 LSIF contribution. The RRSP deposits earn 5%. The tax savings generated by the RRSP and the LSIF are invested in a non-registered (NR) account returning 5% before tax.

	Registered Accumulations			Non-Registered Accumulations				
Year	A RRSP Contr.	B RRSP Yield	C RRSP Balance	D Tax Savings	E LSFTC	F Yield (D + E)	G Taxes on F	H Balance (D + E + F) – G
1	$13,500	$675	$14,175	$6,000	$1,500	$375	$167	$7,709
2	$13,500	$1,384	$29,059	$6,000	$1,500	$760	$338	$15,631
3	$13,500	$2,128	$44,687	$6,000	$1,500	$1,157	$514	$23,774
4	$13,500	$2,909	$61,096	$6,000	$1,500	$1,564	$694	$32,144
5	$13,500	$3,730	$78,326	$6,000	$1,500	$1,982	$880	$40,746
6	$13,500	$4,591	$96,417	$6,000	$1,500	$2,412	$1,071	$49,587
7	$13,500	$5,496	$115,413	$6,000	$1,500	$2,854	$1,267	$58,674
8	$13,500	$6,446	$135,359	$6,000	$1,500	$3,309	$1,469	$68,014
9	$13,500	$7,443	$156,302	$6,000	$1,500	$3,776	$1,676	$77,613
10	$13,500	$8,490	$178,292	$6,000	$1,500	$4,256	$1,890	$87,479
11	$13,500	$9,590	$201,381	$6,000	$1,500	$4,749	$2,109	$97,620
12	$13,500	$10,744	$225,625	$6,000	$1,500	$5,256	$2,334	$108,042
13	$13,500	$11,956	$251,082	$6,000	$1,500	$5,777	$2,565	$118,754
14	$13,500	$13,229	$277,811	$6,000	$1,500	$6,313	$2,803	$129,764
15	$13,500	$14,566	$305,876	$6,000	$1,500	$6,863	$3,047	$141,080
16	$13,500	$15,969	$335,345	$6,000	$1,500	$7,429	$3,298	$152,710
17	$13,500	$17,442	$366,287	$6,000	$1,500	$8,011	$3,557	$164,664
18	$13,500	$18,989	$398,777	$6,000	$1,500	$8,608	$3,822	$176,950
19	$13,500	$20,614	$432,890	$6,000	$1,500	$9,223	$4,095	$189,578
20	$13,500	$22,320	**$468,710**	$6,000	$1,500	$9,854	$4,375	**$202,557**

9. Enhance Child Tax Benefits

Families with children should be aware of the significantly enhanced Canada Child Tax Benefits they may qualify for under recent federal budget changes, as shown in Figure 1-8.

Figure 1-8
Enhancements Under the Canada Child Tax Benefits

Year	2002	2001
Canada Child Tax Benefit*		
Basic benefit	$1,151	$1,117
Additional benefit for third child	$80	$78
Additional benefit for children under 7 years	$228	$221
National Child Benefit (NCB) Supplement		
First child	$1,293	$1,255
Second child	$1,087	$1,055
Third child	$1,009	$980
Family net income at which CCTB begins to phase out	$32,960	$32,000
Family net income at which NCB begins to phase out	$22,397	$21,744

* The GST/HST credit and the CCTB are paid on a benefit-year cycle beginning in July. Benefits will vary slightly in Alberta.

Based on the figures for 2002, there are opportunities to increase the Child Tax Benefits received by reducing family net income using deductions like RRSP contributions. Figure 1-9 shows the income ranges and potential savings available to families, which should be reviewed each year and which depends on the number of children eligible for the Child Tax Benefit. For example, a family with five children and an income level of $36,000 would be able to increase their Child Tax Benefit by $37 for each $100 reduction in net income.

Figure 1-9
CCTB Clawback Rates at Various Income Levels

	NCB Supplement Phase-out		CCTB & NCB Phase-out		CCTB Phase-out	
No. of Children	Income range	Clawback Rate	Income range	Clawback Rate	Income range	Clawback Rate
1	$22,397 – $28,144	12%	$28,144 – $77,640	3%		
2	$22,397 – $32,960	23%	$32,960 – $77,640	5%		
3	$22,397 – $32,960	32%	$32,960 – $101,580	5%		
4	$22,397 – $32,960	32%	$32,960 – $36,098	37%	$36,098 – $123,320	5%
5	$22,397 – $32,960	32%	$32,960 – $39,240	37%	$39,240 – $149,460	5%
6	$22,397 – $32,960	32%	$32,960 – $42,380	37%	$42,380 – $173,400	5%

In the past, Donald and Meredith would have qualified for even more money under the CCTB if they could have reduced their family net income on Line 236. One way they could have accomplished this was to increase RRSP contributions.

For example, assume Meredith's net income stayed constant at $12,000 each year. Donald, on the other hand, earned $75,000 in each of 1999 and 2000 due to his commissions, against which he claimed $8,500 in expenses. In 2001, Donald's income was $65,000, commissions were zero and his expense claim was limited to his travel costs: auto expenses for CCA (which he opted to use next year instead), interest and insurance for a total of $1,000.

As a result, Meredith's RRSP room was approximately $2,000 each year and Donald's was around $12,000 annually. Figure 1-10 shows the family's increased tax savings resulting from this planning.

Figure 1-10
Increased Savings from RRSP Contributions

Taxpayer	RRSP Contr.	1999 Taxes	2000 Taxes	2001 Taxes	Savings over 1999	Savings over 2000
Donald	$12,000	$14,016	$13,275	$11,589	$2,427	$1,686
Meredith	$ 2,000	–$2,644 *	–$2,364 *	–$3,164 *	$520	$800

*Net of CCTB Benefits

Donald and Meredith should now consider investing any Child Tax Benefits received for their children to take advantage of a special tax loophole. Under normal rules, interest and dividends earned on funds given to children by their parents or other adults are subject to "attribution"—that is, the income is taxed to the gift-giver. However, an exception exists for Child Tax Benefit accounts. If untainted by other money, any earnings on these accounts are taxed to the child. More on attribution in subsequent chapters.

10. Maximize Individual and Transferable Deductions and Credits

Tough financial times are the best times to take a fresh look at whether the family is maximizing all tax deductions and credits they are eligible for. If you find you have missed out in the past, you can recover overpaid taxes by requesting an adjustment to prior-filed returns. See our bonus section, Digging for Gold, for instructions and sample adjustments.

11. Conquer the Documentation Challenge

Donald and Meredith found that disorganization was their primary "tax filing problem" each year. Figure 1-11 provides a documentation checklist to follow in completing this initial, time-consuming task.

Figure 1-11
Documentation Gathering Checklist

A. Income Sources

☐ **Employment:**	T4 • Tips • Research Grants • Director's Fees
☐ **Public Pension:**	OAS • CPP Retirement • CPP Disability CPP Death Benefits • CPP Survivor Benefits
☐ **Private Pensions:**	Superannuation • RRSP • RRIF • Annuities
☐ **Foreign Pensions:**	USA • Germany • Other
☐ **Taxable Dividends:**	T3 and T5 Slips • Self-reported
☐ **Interest Income:**	T3 and T5 Slips • Any self-reported amounts
☐ **Partnership Income or Losses:**	Statements/T Slips
☐ **Rental Income:**	Gross Income • Operating Expenses • Net Capital Assets
☐ **Support Payments:**	Gross • Taxable • Agreement
☐ **Capital Gains:**	Proceeds of Disposition • ACB Details • Expense Detail Capital Gains Elections • RESP Withdrawals
☐ **Other Income:**	Scholarships • RESP • Death Benefits • EI
☐ **Self-Employment:**	Gross Income • Operating Expenses • Capital Assets
☐ **Tax Exempt Benefits:**	Worker's Compensation • Social Assistance Supplements

B. Transferable Provisions

From Spouse	*From Child*
☐ Moving Expenses (if spouse has income at new location)	
☐ Dividend Tax Credit	☐ Disability Amount
☐ Age Amount	☐ Tuition/Education Amounts
☐ Pension Income Amount	☐ Medical Expenses
☐ Disability Amount	
☐ Tuition/Education Amount	
☐ Medical Expenses	
☐ Charitable Donations	
☐ Political Contributions	
☐ LSFTC on Spousal Contributions	

. . . continued on next page

Figure 1-11 . . . *continued from previous page*
Documentation Gathering Checklist

C. Provisions Available for Multi-year Carryovers

☐ **Self-employed: some commission sales agents**	Undeducted home office expenses	carry forward until net income is reported
	Undeducted CCA balances	until asset is disposed of
☐ **All taxpayers:**	Undeducted RRSP contributions	indefinitely to offset future income, assuming RRSP room
	Undeducted moving expenses	year following the move
	Undeducted medical expenses	best-12-month period ending in the tax year
	Undeducted donations	5 year carry-over
	Minimum taxes paid	7 years forward for application against regular taxes
	Capital losses	3 years back, carry forward indefinitely
	Non-capital losses	3 years back, carry forward 7 years

D. Deductions

Gather receipts for:

- ☐ RRSP Contributions
- ☐ Child Care
- ☐ Moving Expenses
- ☐ Business Investment Losses
- ☐ Support Payments
- ☐ Carrying Charges and Interest Costs
- ☐ Employment Expenses

E. Tax Credits & Other Provisions

- ☐ LSIF purchase
- ☐ Instalments paid

12. Be Tax Wise in Tax Season

The following are the biggest mistakes to be avoided in family tax preparation—tips you can take advantage of, if you are organized.

- **Never file a late return.** Penalties are stiff and unnecessary: 5% of taxes unpaid as of midnight April 30 plus 1% per month up to 12 months. It's worse if you receive a "Demand to File" from CCRA: 10% of unpaid tax plus 2% per month for up to 20 months. Interest is also charged (at 4% above treasury bill rates), compounding daily. The taxes, at this point, are the least of your problems.
- **Never forget carrying charges** like interest costs and safety deposit box charges and, in the case of interest, make sure the claim is made correctly, as these deductions are often audited. The potential to earn income from property—dividends, rents, royalties or other passive income other than capital gains—must exist. Prorate lines of credit and other arrangements to make sure only the tax-deductible portion of loans are reported. In addition, low interest or no-interest loans from employers (recorded as a taxable benefit on the T4 slip) qualify for deduction if used for investment purposes. Both the interest actually paid and the benefit are deductible.
- **Never forget moving expenses and child care costs,** which are among the most lucrative deductions available, but are usually audited. You must have receipts! See Figures 1-12 and 1-13 for Tips on claiming these expenses.
- **Never forget lucrative provisions for the sick and disabled**—medical expenses, disability amounts and caregiver amounts. These are most often missed or underclaimed. They can reap five-figure returns in some cases—especially if adjustments are requested to prior filed returns—all the way back to 1985 in the case of federal provisions. See Figure 1-14 for Tips on claiming medical expenses.
- **Always look for inter-family transferable provisions**—age amounts, spousal amounts, tuition and education credits, pension income amounts, disability amounts, charitable donations and political contributions. These, too, are often missed or claimed incorrectly. That's why it's important for families to file returns together—starting with the lowest earner and working up to the highest. This strategy will maximize RRSP contribution planning and multiply the deposits most families make this year, simply because it makes tax- and dollar-sense.

Figure 1-12
Tip Sheet—Moving Expenses

Eligible Taxpayers

To qualify, you must earn income at the new location. This income may be from employment or self-employment income. In the case of students moving to attend full-time courses at a university or other post-secondary school, that income may be the taxable portion of scholarships, bursaries, fellowships, research grants or other awards. In addition, you must cease working or operating a business at the old location.

Eligible Moves

To be eligible, the new home must be at least 40 km closer to the new work location than the old home. The distance is measured by the shortest normal route open to the travelling public. Generally, the move must be within Canada although students may claim moving expenses to attend a school outside Canada, if they are otherwise eligible.

Eligible Expenses

Eligible expenses include most expenses for moving to the new location and include the following:

- Cost of selling your former residence, including:
  - real estate commissions
  - legal fees
  - penalties for paying off a mortgage
  - advertising costs
- Costs of keeping a vacant old residence up for sale (to a maximum of $5,000) while you attempt to sell it, including:
  - Mortgage interest
  - Property taxes
  - Insurance premiums
  - Heat and power
- Expenses of purchasing the new home, including:
  - Transfer taxes
  - Legal fees (as long as the old home was owned)
- Temporary living expenses (meals and lodging) for up to 15 days
- Removal and storage costs
- Transportation costs
- Costs of meals on route
- Cost of cancelling an unexpired lease
- Cost of revising legal documents to show the new address, replacing drivers' licenses and auto permits, cost of utility connections and disconnections

Ineligible Expenses

You may not deduct any of the following expenses:

- Expenses to make the former property more saleable
- Losses on the sale of the former property
- Expenses incurred before the move (such as house hunting)
- Value of items that could not be moved (plants, frozen foods, etc.)
- Expenses to clean a rented residence
- Replacement costs for items not moved such as tool sheds, firewood, drapes, etc.
- Mail forwarding costs
- GST on new residence
- Expenses that are reimbursed

Carryover Periods

If your income at the new location is not sufficient to claim your moving expenses in the year of the move, you may carry forward your expenses until you have income at the new location.

Figure 1-13

Tip Sheet—Child Care Expense Deduction

Eligible Taxpayers

Child care expenses may be claimed by parents who must pay another individual to care for their children so that they may earn income from employment or self-employment or so that they may attend school either full- or part-time.

Eligible Dependants

Expenses are deductible for the care of dependent children who were under the age of 16 (at any time during the year) or who are physically or mentally infirm. An eligible child must be your child, your spouse or common-law partner's child or a child who was dependent on you or your spouse (or partner). If the child is not your child or your spouse's or partner's child, the child's net income must be less than the basic personal amount ($7,412 in 2001).

Eligible Babysitters

Expenses actually paid to a Canadian resident or paid to a non-resident for services outside Canada to a resident or deemed resident of Canada qualify. Babysitters may be related to you, but if they are, the sitter must be over age 17. Payments made to a parent of the child or to a supporting person are not deductible.

Earned Income Definition

The child care deduction is limited to two-thirds of "earned income." Earned income includes:

- Salaries and wages
- Net profits from self-employment
- Training allowances, the taxable portion of scholarships, bursaries, fellowships and research grants
- Disability pensions under CPP or QPP

Special Rule for Students

In addition to the limitations for all taxpayers, students have the following limitations on their claims. Full-time students' claims for child care expenses are limited to:

- $100 for each child age 7 to 16 for which the disability amount cannot be claimed, plus
- $175 per child under age 7 for which the disability amount cannot be claimed, plus
- $250 per disabled child

  times the number or weeks of full-time attendance.

Part-time students are limited to

- $100 for each child age 7 to 16 for which the disability amount cannot be claimed, plus
- $175 per child under age 7 for which the disability amount cannot be claimed, plus
- $250 per disabled child

  times the number of months of part-time attendance.

. . . continued on next page

Figure 1-13 . . . *continued from previous page*

Tip Sheet—Child Care Expense Deduction

Special Rule for High Income Earners

Generally, child care expenses claims may only be claimed by the lower income spouse (or partner). The lower income spouse is the one whose net income, before claiming child care expenses, is the lowest. The higher income spouse may only claim child care expenses during periods in which:

- The other supporting person was a full- or part-time student
- The other supporting person was incapable of caring for the child because of mental or physical infirmity
- The other supporting person was confined to a prison or similar institution for at least two weeks
- You have separated from the other supporting person due to a breakdown in your relationship for a period of at least 90 days but have reconciled within the first 60 days after the taxation year

Maximum Claim

The maximum claim for child care expenses is the least of the following:

- Eligible child care expenses paid to eligible child care providers
- Two-thirds of earned income
- The following limits
  - $4,000 for each child aged 7 to 16 for which the disability amount cannot be claimed plus
  - $7,000 for each child under age 7 for which the disability amount cannot be claimed plus
  - $10,000 for each disabled child

Marginal Benefits

Child care expenses are a deduction which reduces net income and therefore, like RRSP contributions, will affect the following refundable and non-refundable credits:

- The Age Amount
- The Spousal Amount
- The Amount for Infirm Dependent Adults
- The Caregiver Amount
- Amounts transferred from spouse
- Medical expenses
- Charitable donations
- Child Tax Benefits
- Goods and Services Tax Credits
- Provincial refundable tax credits
- Old Age Security Clawbacks
- Employment Insurance Benefits Clawbacks

Restrictions to Child Tax Benefit, Disability Amounts

In addition to having a positive affect on tax credits, amounts claimed for child care expenses have the following negative effects:

- The Child Tax Benefit includes a supplement of $228 for each child under age 7. This supplement is reduced by 25% of the child care expenses claimed by you, your spouse, or your common-law partner
- If you are claiming the disability amount for a dependant who is under age 18, your claim includes a supplement of $3,500. This supplement must be reduced by any child care expenses in excess of $2,050 claimed for the child by anyone.

Eligible Expenditures

The following expenses may be claimed:

- Babysitting costs
- Day care costs
- Costs of a live-in nanny
- Lodging paid at boarding schools, day camps, day sports camps and overnight camps to a maximum of
  - $100 per week for each child age 7 to 16 for which the disability amount cannot be claimed, plus
  - $175 per week per child under 7 for which the disability amount cannot be claimed, plus
  - $250 per week for each disabled child

Ineligible Expenditures

The following expenses may not be claimed:

- Medical or hospital care
- Clothing
- Transportation
- Tuition
- Expenses for which you did not actually pay or for which you will receive reimbursement

Figure 1-14
Common Medical Expenses

Medical Practitioners

- Dentist
- Medical Doctor
- Medical Practitioner
- Optometrist
- Pharmacist
- Psychologist
- Speech-language Pathologist
- Osteopath
- Chiropractor
- Naturopath
- Therapeutist (or Therapist)
- Physiotherapist
- Chiropodist (or Podiatrist)
- Christian Science Practitioner
- Psychoanalyst who is a member of the Canadian Institute of Psychoanalysis or a member of the Quebec Association of Jungian Psychoanalysts
- Psychologist
- Speech-language Pathologist or Audiologist
- Occupational Therapist who is a member of the Canadian Association of Occupational Therapists
- Acupuncturist
- Dietician
- Dental Hygienist
- Nurse including a Practical Nurse whose full-time occupation is nursing as well as a Christian Science Nurse
- Audiologist (after Feb 18, 1997)

Treatments

- medical and dental services
- attendant care
- nursing home care
- ambulance fees
- transportation
- travel expenses
- eyeglasses
- guide dogs
- transplant costs
- alterations to the home for disabled persons
- lip reading or sign language training
- sign language services
- moving expenses for a disabled person to a more suitable dwelling
- caregiver training
- therapy for a disabled patient
- tutoring services for a patient with a learning disability or mental impairment
- lab tests
- private health plan premiums
- prescribed drugs

Devices

- artificial limb
- iron lung
- rocking bed for poliomyelitis victims
- wheelchair
- crutches
- spinal brace
- brace for a limb
- ileostomy or a colostomy pad
- truss for a hernia
- laryngeal speaking aid
- aid to hearing
- artificial kidney machine
- van for wheelchair

Source: CCRA's Interpretation Bulletin 519R and the Income Tax Act.

THE PLAN

Donald and Meredith revamped their financial affairs to meet their personal goals using new tax savings as a driver. In particular they would do the following:

1. **Invest Proceeds from the Good News Budget Provisions.** The family would identify and invest within their RRSPs, the savings they automatically will reap from their new lower tax brackets.
2. **Reduce Employment Income.** Donald will claim the employment expenses he was entitled to for his home office and car and adjust his prior-filed returns to recover overpaid taxes on these amounts for the past, including a GST rebate on his employment expenses. This windfall would be used to fund RESPs for their children.
3. **Recover Previously Overpaid Taxes.** Meredith will adjust her tax returns to recover tax overpayments by missing her medical expense claims, safety deposit box costs and moving expenses. The family will also consolidate their donations and claim them all on Meredith's return for a better tax result. Meredith will then fund her tuition fees this year with those savings.
4. **Reduce Tax Withholding.** The family will reduce tax withholding at source to account for Donald's allowable employment expenses, child care expenses incurred when Meredith goes back to university and his RRSP contributions, which were to be made directly from the payroll to their RRSPs. Donald filed *Form T1213* with CCRA, following which a letter of authority was forwarded to his employer.
5. **Invest in Spousal RRSPs.** Donald will invest half of all RRSP savings into a spousal RRSP plan for Meredith to set up income splitting in retirement. The tax savings from the RRSP would be reinvested in future RRSPs to save for their new home. They wanted to make a down payment of $25,000 on the $150,000 home and hoped to use the Home Buyer's Plan as a way to accomplish this in 2003.
6. **Flip Investments.** The family will flip some of their capital accumulations into a Labour-Sponsored Fund, using the tax savings to fund their life insurance needs.
7. **Invest Child Tax Benefits.** As a result of their reduced family net income the family would receive enhanced Child Tax Benefits which would be invested in non-registered accounts for their children, making earnings taxable in the children's hands.

THE RESULTS

Let's look at how each of these steps will affect the family's goals.

1. **Almost $600 a Month is Recovered through Reduced Tax With-holding.** By filing *Form T1213* to reduce withholding taxes on his salary due to his RRSP contribution and his employment expenses, Donald was able to reduce his income tax withholding by $575 each month, thereby increasing the family's cash flow. He was therefore able to make up for about half of the lost earnings from Meredith's decision to go back to school.
2. **Almost $2,000 More is Invested from Tax Savings from the New Tax Brackets.** As show in the table in Figure 1-1, Donald saves $1,786 and Meredith saves $62 as a result of the tax changes for 2001. This provides an opportunity to make an RRSP contribution of $1,847. By the time Donald and Meredith retire, if this amount was contributed each year and earned a 5% return, it would grow to $184,000 in their retirement fund. The RRSP contribution should be made to a spousal RRSP to facilitate income splitting.
3. **The Down Payment Fund for the New Home is Started.** By contributing $1,847 to his RRSP, Donald reduced his taxes by just over $800 this year. If this $800 is invested each year and earns 5% before taxes, it will take the Grants almost 18 years to save the down payment. Some other plan will be needed to help achieve the goal of home ownership. Fortunately, by shoring up RRSP contributions, Donald and Meredith are in the position of withdrawing RRSP accumulations on a tax free basis under the Home Buyer's Plan (HBP), when they are ready to purchase a home. Their annual RRSP tax savings from future contributions can then be used to make the HBP repayments.
4. **Over $13,000 is Recovered from Prior Filing Errors.** By adjusting her returns for the last five years (ever since she and Donald got together), Meredith was able to find $3,000 in tax savings, from missed moving expenses, missed medical expenses and errors in calculating her babysitting income. This was enough to pay her first year's tuition. Donald, on the other hand, filed adjustments to his returns for 1999 and 2000 to claim the employment expenses he had missed, reaping tax savings close to $10,000 over the two years. Approximately half of this would be contributed to the RRSP to help with the down payment on their new home.

5. **Almost $6,000 is Added to the Children's Education Fund.** The family chooses to allocate $4,800 of the received tax overpayments to the children's education savings plan. Divided equally, these tax savings of about $1,200 per child per year are added to their RESP. As a result, they also reap an additional Canada Education and Savings Grant of 20% of their investment—an amount kicked in by the federal government. The family therefore saves a grand total of $5,760 for their children's education this year. Invested at 5% and contributed each year for 14 years, this saving would result in accumulations of over $33,000 per child in their education funds. Further, if Donald decides to add his $250 GST rebate to this fund, the accumulated savings increase to almost $34,000 per child.
6. **Saving the Child Tax Benefit can Multiply Intergenerational Wealth.** If CTBs received in the name of each child are invested in non-registered accounts in the name of the child, earnings will be taxed to the child, not the parent. If these savings earn 5% per year, each child will accumulate an additional $20,000 in their non-registered accounts, money that could be used towards their education, a down payment on their future homes or other requirements.
7. **Family Life Insurance Needs are Funded.** By converting the $5,000 in CSBs that the Grants currently own into a Labour-Sponsored Investment Fund, Donald can claim an income tax saving of $1,500 which should cover their insurance premiums for the year.*

The family is well on their way to achieving their dreams, despite tough financial times. This is important in light of the fact that the next few years will be more difficult still, as Meredith goes to school. The family will need to cut back to accommodate the loss of her income in their budget, but the investment in her education, combined with their efficient tax planning, will accelerate their progress toward their goals.

*Note: Converting other investments or other RRSP holdings in future will continue to generate tax savings to pay for premiums. After eight years, no new LSIF investments are required, as rolling over matured LSIF holdings each year will continue to generate savings.

Tax Secrets
For Creating Family Legacies

1. **Know Your Tax Filing Rights.** When you discover errors or omissions on prior-filed returns, ask for an adjustment. CCRA will do so for:
   - Most federal provisions: back to 1985
   - GST provisions: back to 1991
   - Most provincial provisions: current year and two years back
   - Capital Cost Allowance revisions: within 90 days of receipt of Notice of Assessment.
2. **Invest Any Tax Savings You Reap.** Treat them as a windfall that can help you meet your financial goals. This is particularly important in the period 2001 to 2005, when recent federal and provincial tax changes have provided Canadians with significant tax savings over prior years' obligations. The key to benefiting is to first identify those tax savings and then to take action to invest them.
3. **Reap Even More Rewards in Tax Season.** RRSP contributions can put tax-payers in lower tax brackets and increase both refundable and non-refundable tax credits. However, because we expect that taxes will continue to go down in the short term, due to indexing of tax brackets, tax credits and clawback zones, every dollar invested in an RRSP this year will generally reap larger marginal tax gains. So, it is important not to miss the RRSP contribution deadlines.
4. **Meet More than Retirement Needs with RRSP Savings.** Making contributions to an RRSP can help you meet multiple financial needs: first, reap rich, guaranteed returns in tax savings immediately; then leverage your investment by making tax-free withdrawals from the RRSP under the Lifelong Learning Plan and/or Home Buyers' Plan to fund your education or home buying needs. Funds may not be withdrawn for these purposes on a tax-free basis unless a minimum 90-day investment period is met.
5. **Employees Need to Reduce Tax on Employment Income.** The majority of taxpayers in Canada still make their income from employment purposes. Unfortunately many are unaware that they may be able to claim out-of-pocket expenses incurred by virtue of their employment, on Line 229 of the tax return, using *Form T777* as a statement. To do so, it is necessary to keep *Form T2200 Declaration of Conditions of Employment*, signed by the employer, in your files in case of audit by CCRA. The tax savings on these deductions can be lucrative in some cases, freeing up new capital for investment purposes.
6. **Don't Forget about the GST/HST Rebate on Line 457.** Many employees who pay GST/HST on union or professional fees or employment expenses claimed on Line 229 miss applying for a refund of GST/HST paid on those deductible items. Do so using *Form GST370.*

7. **Pay Yourself, Not the Government,** First. Make sure you only pay the correct amount of tax with every pay period. If you qualify for significant tax deductions or credits that your employer may not know about, you can request that tax withholding be adjusted to account for these tax preferences by filing *Form T1213 Request to Reduce Tax Deductions at Source.*
8. **Minimize Quarterly Instalment Tax Payments.** Many seniors, or those who are self-employed, are required to remit their estimated tax obligations on a quarterly basis. This happens when taxes owed at tax filing time exceeds $2,000 in each of the current and immediately prior taxation years. The ideal situation at tax filing time is to find that you owe just under $2,000. If you're making quarterly instalment payments, consult with your tax advisor to recalculate the amount of your instalments throughout the year as your income picture changes. CCRA will allow you to reflect these changes in your instalment payment schedule. This will ensure that you retain as much of your money as possible during the year for your own purposes, without incurring interest costs by underpaying your instalments.
9. **Increase Your Monthly Income from Child Tax Benefits with RRSP Contributions.** RRSP contributions reduce net income and for this reason can create or increase monthly benefits receivable under the newly enriched Canada Child Tax Benefit. In addition, clawback ceilings have been raised making it possible for more middle income families to benefit. If your income picture has changed substantially due to tough times, you may be in the running—for the first time, perhaps—for the CTB, so don't miss out on maximizing benefits because you missed the RRSP contribution deadline.
10. **Consider Using LSIF Share Purchases for Tax Relief.** Tax savings can be further enhanced with Labour-Sponsored Investment Funds. Those extra savings might help fund RRSP deposits, disability or life insurance needs or education savings for young children. In fact, by switching existing investments within an RRSP to LSIF shares, Canadians can create new tax savings immediately without coming up with any extra cash.
11. **Look For Opportunities to Split Income with Family Members.** Our progressive tax system applies higher tax rates to those with higher income levels. Any time you can spread family earnings among family members, you will likely pay lower combined taxes. Taking advantage of a spousal RRSP contribution or putting Child Tax Benefits into an untainted account in the name of your minor child are all good ways to split income and avoid the "Attribution Rules" at the same time. More on this in chapters that follow.

12. **Try to Create Additional Wealth in Non-Registered Investment Accounts.** For most taxpayers it is important to make RRSP investments first, to reap the immediate tax benefits and earn growth on a tax sheltered basis. However, it is also important to start a tax-effective non-registered savings plan to fund other financial priorities. Non-registered investments can also be later transferred into RRSP accounts to create the RRSP deduction. Because interest costs on loans taken to make non-registered investments are tax deductible, borrowing to create new wealth may be a tax-effective option for some families (more on this in later chapters).
13. **Pay Down the Mortgage with Tax Savings.** Buying a family home is an important step that has advantageous tax consequences in that any future gains on the property are tax exempt. Unfortunately, mortgage interest is not deductible. So, while it is important for families to rid themselves of non-deductible debt, in most cases, it makes more tax sense to fund mortgage reduction payments with tax savings received from RRSP contributions, than to forego those savings in favour of the mortgage reduction only.
14. **Be Organized.** One of the main reasons that Canadian taxpayers miss out on legitimate tax deductions and credits every year is that they can't conquer the documentation challenge. Take control! You'll find your ability to save tax dollars rises significantly when you bring order to your financial receipts and records.
15. **Inform Yourself of New Eligibility for Tax Preferences.** Whenever personal circumstances change—births, deaths, disability, marriages, divorces, family moves, new careers, raises, terminations, small business start-up, etc.—you may be in a position to benefit from tax provisions you did not know existed (the most commonly missed provisions include moving expenses, medical and child care costs). Ask your advisor about this before your circumstances change (if you have control over this) or, if you are finding out tax preferences in retrospect, be sure to exercise your right to recover overpaid taxes on prior-filed returns.

CHAPTER 2

Maximizing Your After-Tax Severance Dollars

KEY PERSONAL TAX CONCEPTS:

- Severance from your employer can bump you into a higher tax bracket
- Taking severance over two taxation years can help you keep more
- Tax liability from severance can often be offset with an RRSP rollover based on your eligible years of service
- Tax liability from severance can further be offset with unused RRSP contribution room
- Dramatic changes in income could open up eligibility for refundable tax credits like the Child Tax Benefit
- Terminated employees qualifying for Employment Insurance (EI) may be subject to a clawback if their net income exceeds $48,750*
- Legal fees expended to collect severance may qualify for a tax deduction
- Other tax credits—like Labour-Sponsored Funds Tax Credits—may help the taxpayer decrease tax liabilities
- The transfer of certain provisions between spouses—like medical expenses, charitable donations, tuition and education amounts, pension income amounts—may be possible in times of change
- It is important to look at tax savings options over a period of years for best results

*As at time of writing.

REAL LIFE

Martin, the vice-president of marketing for a small regional airline, received a severance package of $85,000 late in 2001 when his employer's company merged with another. Martin had worked for his employer for 15 years, from 1986 to mid-November 2001, and was grateful for the generosity shown to him.

However, while the parting money was good, the event itself was traumatic, both for him and his wife, Ava, a stay-at-home mother of their three children, aged 12, 16 and 17.

Throughout the year, Martin's $125,000 salary put him in the top federal tax bracket. He had maximized his RRSP contribution at $13,500 during the year. As usual, he put half his RRSP contribution into a spousal plan, with the intent to split income in retirement. Since 1991, Martin had, however, accumulated additional unused RRSP contribution room of $25,000, which he had not yet been able to top up. The family was therefore used to living on net income, after taxes and RRSP contributions of about $6,416 each month ($77,000 annually).

THE CHALLENGE

There are several issues to consider when job termination comes, especially if it is thrust upon you unexpectedly. Significant tax planning opportunities can serve to maximize the after-tax size of the severance package itself, as well as create both monthly cash flow and future security options. However, every situation is different and the true benefits of planning can only be achieved with the help of an astute tax advisor who can prepare actual tax calculations over a period of several years. These numbers will clearly outline the path your severance planning and new career decisions should take.

With the help of his financial advisor, Martin quickly identified his two primary needs: immediate cash flow requirements and anti-depletion strategies. The challenge was to keep the family household running financially in the short term, while minimizing erosion to his savings in the meantime.

FACTORS TO CONSIDER

Martin's scenario is a common one, which can be effectively managed with a little help from newly revised federal and provincial tax systems, as described in the Introduction and Chapter 1 of this book. However, there are also important existing tax provisions which will have a bearing on his plan, including the eight outlined here.

1. Tax Free Rollover of Severance into an RRSP

The amount eligible for rollover into Martin's (not his spouse's) RRSP depends upon when service was provided to the employer:

- For service after 1995, no amount of severance can be rolled over to an RRSP and therefore the full amount is exposed to income taxes.
- For service after 1988 and before 1996, a single limit of $2,000 per year of service can be rolled over.
- For service before 1989, it is possible to roll over $2,000 for each year of service plus $1,500 for each year in which none of the employer's contributions to a company pension plan vested in the employee.

It would be wise for Martin to use his severance to shore up his unused RRSP contribution room and take his deduction against the exposed income. He can then make taxable withdrawals from the RRSP as required, hopefully in a year in which his income falls into a lower tax bracket.

2. Income Deferral

The possibility of taking severance over two taxation years should be explored to determine whether the tax brackets and rates at which the income will be taxed can be reduced and whether eligibility for social benefits, like the Child Tax Benefit, can be created.

3. EI Maximization

The clawback of Employment Insurance benefits Martin may receive throughout the year, which begins when net income is $48,750 or higher, should be avoided.

4. Child Tax Benefit (CTB) Creation

Planning should include the view to creating eligibility for CTB which are maximized at family net income levels around $22,000, but can be paid partially if income is above this, depending on the number of children in the home.

5. Canada Education Savings Grant (CESG) Maximization

Despite tough times, families must find a way to continue education savings plans for their children. One good way to maximize investment opportunities is to contribute to a Registered Education Savings Plan (RESP). Not only are earnings within the plan tax sheltered, but a tax free bonus is earned in the plan from the federal government: up to $400—20% of contributions to a maximum of $2,000 are paid through the CESG. Taxpayers may otherwise contribute a maximum of $4,000 per minor child each year, but should try to contribute at least $2,000 to maximize the grant.

6. Use of Labour-Sponsored Funds Tax Credits

The opportunity exists to shelter taxes on the exposed severance with additional tax credits, including an investment in Labour-Sponsored Funds. See Tip Sheet—Labour-Sponsored Investment Fund in Chapter 1 (Figure 1-6) for details.

7. Business Loss Deductibility

There is a possibility of sheltering the severance income with start-up losses incurred in a proprietorship should Martin decide that is the route to go to earn income in either the short or long term. These losses can offset other income of the year or, if in excess of other income, can be carried back to offset income in the prior three years or up to seven years in the future. This is discussed in more detail in Chapter 5.

8. Medical Expense Deductibility

Taxpayers often forget that group health benefits end with employment. It is therefore important to know that the premiums paid for private health insurance, now required to be financed personally, may be claimed as a non-refundable tax credit.

THE PLAN

The primary goal in planning when there is a layoff or termination is to meet the family's immediate cash flow needs. This generally requires some attention to budgeting and adjustments in the family lifestyle. Couples often discuss the option of sending a stay-at-home parent back to work or of the unemployed parent's opportunities to take part-time work or consulting work on a self-employed basis.

In the case of Martin's family, it was determined that $3,000 per month was a minimum requirement. But in addition, it was clear that tax planning should accomplish more:

- Minimize taxes on any severance unprotected by RRSP deductions
- Create at least partial Child Tax Benefits
- Avoid repayment of Employment Insurance benefits, if possible.

The options for determining the right direction for the family should encompass the following:

- The possibility of splitting income over two taxation years to enable income to be taxed in lower tax brackets and at lower rates
- The possibility of using RRSP contributions to reduce net and taxable income levels, and increase the availability of Canada Child Tax Benefits
- The possibility of using investments in LSIFs to create new cash flow for investment purposes.

The illustrations in the Options below show cash flow, before taxes, available to the family, assuming RRSP and Labour Sponsored Investment Fund contributions are maximized.

Option 1: Take All Severance ($85,000) in 2001

Year	Employment Income	Severance	EI	Total	RRSP Contr.	LSFTC
2001	$125,000	$85,000	None	$210,000	$56,500	$1,500
2002 (a)	None	None	$19,800	$19,800	$7,206	$1,500
2002 (b)	None	None	$19,800	$19,800	$0	$1,500

Assumptions: Severance is offset with RRSP deductions: for the rollover ($18,000), the unused room ($25,000), the current year's earned income ($13,500); total $56,500. Assume the EI benefits were received for the full year in 2002 ($19,800) and that RRSP room of $13,500 is available based on employment income of the 2001 tax year. Given his low income in 2002, Martin may wish to forego making his RRSP contribution to get a bigger bang in a future year when his marginal income may be higher. Such a decision may also assist his family in their immediate cash flow needs.

Option 2: Take Severance Over Two Years: $18,000 in Year 1

Year	Employment Income	Severance	EI	Total	RRSP Contr.	LSFTC
2001	$125,000	$18,000	None	$143,000	$31,500	$1,500
2002	None	$67,000	$19,800	$86,800	$38,500	$1,500

Assumptions: The $18,000 severance taken in 2001 is fully offset by an $18,000 RRSP rollover; with other employment income of the year offset by the $13,500 RRSP contribution. The balance of the severance ($67,000) is taken in 2002, offset by RRSP deductions of $38,500 ($25,000 and $13,500 on the RRSP room created in 2001 and prior years) for a net income of $48,300 ($86,800 – $38,500), a level at which EI benefits repayment is avoided.

Option 3: Take All Severance ($85,000) in 2002

Year	Employment Income	Severance	EI	Total Income	RRSP Contr.	LSFTC
2001	$125,000	None	None	$125,000	$13,500	$1,500
2002	none	$85,000	$19,800	$104,800	$56,500*	$1,500

*contributed in March 2003

Assumptions: Take all the severance in 2002, offset by RRSP contributions of $18,000, $25,000 and $13,500 (Total $56,500). In this year, $19,800 of EI benefits must be reported. Again net income is $48,300 ($104,800 – $56,500), a level at which EI benefits repayment is avoided.

THE RESULTS

This is a very interesting case in which timing, cash flow, the availability of RRSP room and potential Child Tax Benefits all play a role in making the right decision, as illustrated in the three options in Figure 2-1.

Martin can come closest to his current lifestyle if he chooses to take all severance in 2001, as described in Option 1. He would increase disposable income available in 2002 by not making an RRSP contribution at all in 2002; saving his $13,500 in RRSP room for a future year when income is higher. Under this option, Canada Child Tax Benefits are maximized over the period July 2003 to June 2004, leaving Martin and his family with a combined two-year tax bill of $52,840 and an average disposable income of $5,175 per month.

However, in Options 2 and 3 taxes payable are minimized significantly (a total of $12,230: $40,610 vs. $52,840 in the first Option), while Child Tax Benefits are reduced by $4,880 ($7,500 under Option 1 vs. $2,620 under Options 2 and 3). However, both Options 2 and 3 allow Martin to maximize his RRSP contributions at $70,000 and leave him with average monthly disposable income of just over $5,000.

In the final analysis, the ability to receive an immediately reduced tax liability became more important than maximizing the CCTB, which would not begin until 2003. Martin chose to take all of his severance in 2002, to maximize his cash flow in 2002. Doing so saved him a net total of $7,350 in net taxes ($52,840 – $40,610 = $12,230 – reduced CTB of $4,880 = $7,350).

It is worthwhile noting that this scenario depends greatly on the $25,000 unused RRSP contribution room that Martin has going into 2001. Had Martin maximized his RRSP contributions each year, his options on planning to maximize severance would have been significantly different.

Figure 2-1

Average Monthly Cash Flow Under Three Options

Option 1: Take All Severance ($85,000) in 2001

Year	Total Income 2001+ 2002 (a) or (b)	RRSP	Net Income	LSFTC[1]	Net Taxes	CCTB / GSTC	Cash Flow Left	Average monthly income over 24 months
2001	$210,000	$56,500	$153,500	$1,500	$52,650	0	$100,850	
2002 (a)	$19,800	$7,206	$12,594	$1,500	$ –200	$7,500/2 **	$16,524	
Total*	$229,800	$63,706	$166,094	$3,000	$52,450	$7,500/2	$117,394	$4,891
2002 (b)	$19,800	$0	$19,800	$1,500	$ 190	$7,500/2	$ 23,360	
Total*	$229,800	$56,500	$173,300	$3,000	$52,840	$7,500/2	$124,210	$5,175

* Total = 2001 plus 2002 (a) or (b). Scenario 2002 (a) contemplates an RRSP contribution, while scenario 2002 (b) cotemplates none.

** CTB and GSTC payments begin in July of 2002

Option 2: Take Severance Over Two Years: $18,000 in Year 1

Year	Total Income	RRSP	Net Income	LSFTC[1]	Net Taxes	CTB	Cash Flow Left	24 month average monthly income
2001	$143,000	$31,500	$111,500	$1,500	$33,160	$0	$78,340	
2002	$ 86,800	$38,500	$48,300	$1,500	$ 7,450	$2,620/2	$42,160	
Total	$229,800	$70,000	$159,800	$3,000	$40,610	$2,620/2	$120,500	$5,021

Option 3: Take All Severance ($85,000) in 2002

Year	Total Income	RRSP	Net Income	LSFTC[1]	Net Taxes	CTB	Cash Flow Left	24 month average monthly income
2001	$125,000	$13,500	$111,500	$1,500	$33,160	$0	$78,340	
2002	$104,800	$56,500	$48,300	$1,500	$7,450	$2,620/2	$42,160	
Total	$229,800	$70,000	$159,800	$3,000	$40,610	$2,620/2	$120,500	$5,021

In devising the strategy for those taxpayers with no RRSP contribution room, many of the same principles apply. Review the following considerations:

[1] LSIF investment is made within RRSP to create the credit; no new money required.

- Splitting the income between two taxation years could reduce Martin's overall tax bill so some of the severance should be postponed until 2002 if possible.
- The $18,000 transfer of severance payments into Martin's RRSP does not depend on contribution room so this transfer should still be made. If timing is not important for tax or cash flow purposes, the earlier the contribution is made, the more time the investment has to grow, tax deferred, within Martin's RRSP.
- An RRSP contribution of $13,500 is possible in 2002 based on earned income in 2001.
- Clawback of EI benefits should be avoided in 2002 by keeping taxable income below $48,750.
- The Child Tax Benefit is clawed back at 32% of income over about $22,000 so if some of the severance is moved to 2002, net income in 2002 should be ideally limited to about $22,000.

Here's a plan based on these points:

- Split the severance so that $15,700 is received in 2002 and the remaining $69,300 is received in 2001.
- Transfer $18,000 of the severance received in 2001 to the RRSP and contribute $13,500 based on earned income in 2000.
- Contribute $13,500 to the RRSP in 2002 based on 2001 earned income.
- Ensure that $5,000 of RRSP contributions each year are to a Labour-Sponsored Fund to maximize tax savings opportunities.

The tables in Figure 2-2 show the tax consequences of this plan over simply taking all the severance in 2001.

Note how income taxes are reduced by $5,608 by moving the $15,700 to 2002. The tax savings are added to Martin's RRSP while leaving nearly the same average monthly income.

The moral? Each severance situation must be calculated separately to take into account all income sources receivable over two to three years, as well as available RRSP deductions, refundable and non-refundable credits. The results will differ for those who are single, retired, those with families, those running proprietorships and those with a variety of other income sources.

Figure 2-2
When There's No RRSP Room

Option 1: Take All Severance in 2001

Year	Total Income	RRSP	Net Income	LSFTC	Net Taxes	CTB / GSTC	Cash Flow Left	Average monthly income over 24 months
2001	$210,000	$31,500	$178,500	$1,500	$64,250	$0	$114,250	
2002	$19,800	$7,206	$12,594	$1,500	$–200	$7,500/2 *	$16,544	
Total	$229,800	$38,706	$191,094	$3,000	$64,050	$3,750	$130,794	$5,450

*CTB and GSTC payments begin in July of 2002

Option 2: Take Severance Over Two Years: $15,700 in Year 2

Year	Total Income	RRSP	Net Income	LSFTC	Net Taxes	CTB GSTC	Cash Flow Left	24 month average monthly income
2001	$194,300	$31,500	$162,800	$1,500	$56,965	$0	$105,835	
2002	$35,500	$13,500	$22,000	$1,500	$577	$7,400/2	$25,123	
Total	$229,800	$45,000	$184,800	$3,000	$57,542	$3,700	$130,958	$5,456

Looking Forward to 2003

In discussing these options, we've looked at the year of severance and the following year. Let's take this task one year further down the line. In 2003, the situation will be the following:

- The EI benefits will run out
- The oldest child will turn 19 and so the Child Tax Benefits will be reduced by about $2,000
- The oldest child may need funds for college.

Where will the money come from? If Martin is unable to land another job, he may consider starting a small business. Ava may need to seek full- or part-time employment. If these options are not enough, the RRSP contributions made in 2001 and 2002 (and prior years) are available to supplement the family income in 2003. If income levels are sufficiently low, the taxes paid on the withdrawal will be significantly lower than the tax savings in the year they were contributed. This validates the theory behind the RRSP for its younger contributors—its use during early or temporary retirement to bridge the gap to new productivity.

Tax Secrets

For Maximizing Your Severance

1. **Bracket Watch.** Negotiate with your employer to take a severance package over two taxation years to enable taxation of any exposed portion of the package at a lower tax rate.
2. **Prepare Tax Calculations Over a Period of Time.** Finding the most tax-efficient option for those receiving severance usually involves tax calculations that encompass several years: the current year and up to two years in the future. In this way, taxpayers and their advisors can fully understand the implications of income peaks and valleys on taxes payable over time and refundable tax credits receivable.
3. **RRSP Deductions.** Make wise use of unused RRSP contribution room, and tax free RRSP rollover opportunities created by eligible severance payments. Then use the deduction of contributions in a year in which the highest marginal tax rate occurs.
4. **RRSP Withdrawals.** Where cash flow falls short of family needs, withdraw RRSP accumulations in the tax year in which the lowest taxable income occurs. While these amounts will be taxable, tax should be computed at lower marginal tax rates. Later when income rises again upon re-employment or the creation of net business income, RRSP contributions can be replaced, together with a tax benefit at a higher marginal rate.
5. **Labour-Sponsored Investment Funds Use.** Multiply immediate tax savings available by using the Labour-Sponsored Funds Tax Credit, either inside or outside registered accounts.
6. **Revisit Refundable Tax Credit Eligibility.** Especially those who have been employed continuously over a long period of time should review the kinds of refundable and non-refundable tax credits that are available to low and middle income earners. While unemployment for most is a temporary condition, during tough times it is possible that the family will qualify for provisions they normally would not have claimed at higher income levels. This includes eligibility for the Canada Child Tax Benefit, the spousal amount, medical expenses and other provisions commonly claimable only by low or middle income earners. An RRSP contribution can often help to bump up the value of these provisions, especially for those taxpayers who find their net income is on a "bracket border."
7. **Compute the Lowest "Net" Tax Bill.** It is not possible to get an accurate picture of your true marginal tax rate unless the results of your tax calculations take into account both taxes payable and credits receivable. That is, take all refundable tax credits you may be entitled to into account and offset income

taxes payable with these amounts, even if that means projecting taxes forward a couple of years into the future. This gives you a true "net tax picture" that can then be analyzed in relation to cash flow timing so that you can decide whether it is better to forfeit some tax credits available in the future in order to minimize taxes payable today. See Chapter 1 for a discussion of the steep "marginal tax rate spike" to which many families are subject, especially if their net incomes fall between $22,000 and $42,000.

8. **Preserve Your Severance Savings.** A severance package is one of the most significant transactions in most employees' financial affairs lifetime. The more that can be saved immediately within an RRSP and in reduced taxes payable, the greater flexibility the retiree will have to maximize cash flow in that interim period between jobs or new business ventures.
9. **Claim Business Losses Wisely.** When new career choices involve the starting of a new business after termination, start-up losses can be used to offset other income of the current year, three years back and up to seven years forward. Planning to take advantage of these rules can reap even more benefits for the family.
10. **Avoid Paying a Clawback on your Employment Insurance Benefits.** This will happen if your net income for the year exceeds $48,750. For most tax filers, this is a nasty surprise at tax time, causing further and unexpected hardship when family finances are already tight. Often, RRSP contributions can reduce net income below this clawback ceiling level, thereby preserving the EI benefits previously received.
11. **Think "Out of the Tax Box."** Watch for pitfalls in claiming other tax provisions. Remember the following:
    - Child care expenses are usually claimable by the spouse or common-law partner with the lowest net income. If this is the person collecting EI during the year, child care expenses will not be claimable at all, as this is not a source considered to be "earned income" for those purposes.
    - Medical expenses should be claimed by the person with the lowest net income to create a maximum benefit. This is because medical expenses must be reduced by 3% of net income, which permits a higher claim if made by the person with the lower income.
    - Certain provisions are transferrable between spouses: charitable donations, political contributions, tuition and education credits, disability amounts, pension income amounts, age amounts. When the person who usually has the higher income becomes the lower income earner, who should claim these provisions must be reviewed.

12. **Revisit Prior-Filed Returns.** When cash is short, going back over old tax returns can be a worthwhile experience, especially if you find you have missed some common tax provisions, like your safety deposit box or medical expenses, for example. Remember that most errors and omissions on prior-filed returns can be adjusted all the way back to 1985 (federal provisions) or over three years on provincial provisions. See the bonus section "Digging for Gold" at the end of this book, for more information.

CHAPTER 3

Coping with Lost Values in RRSPs

KEY PERSONAL TAX CONCEPTS:

- Recent market losses? Re-evaluate retirement strategies, but don't panic! There is no tax reason to lock in losses within registered funds
- The biggest risk facing investors today is not market risk, but the risk of outliving their savings
- Under-use of RRSP contribution room is the biggest accumulation problem Canadians face today
- Any windfalls—including new tax savings—should be invested in unused RRSP room to enhance diminished portfolios
- Returns from RRSP contributions can far exceed market performance when the deduction is applied to increase other tax provisions
- Cash poor investors can take advantage of RRSP-induced tax savings—simply switch existing non-registered investments into an RRSP
- Further immediate cash—flip investments within an RRSP to Labour-Sponsored Investment Funds
- A minority of Canadians make regular RRSP contributions and maximize RRSP room. With larger accumulations, they face different challenges in tough times—review your strategies
- RRSP contribution levels are increasing for upper income earners—this will help those with diminished portfolios today to catch up

REAL LIFE

Deidre, age 45, a single mother of daughter Diana, 12, earns $55,000 a year employed as an editor with a national publishing company. Over the years, she had accumulated $250,000 in her RRSP. However, with the recession of 2001, much to her dismay, Deidre's RRSP lost one-third of its value. Her recent statement showed total accumulations of only $167,000. Was her goal to retire at 55 now lost to an uncertain economic haze?

Deidre, like many other Canadians, had been unable to maximize her RRSP contribution room over the years; she still had unused room of $50,000. One of the reasons for this is because she had decided to buy a house five years ago. She still carries a mortgage of $100,000 at 6% amortized over 25 years.

Deidre, the only child of now-deceased parents, was the favourite of her Uncle Mack, who recently died of a heart attack. She was the recipient of a $20,000 share of his life insurance policies, a windfall she wanted to invest wisely.

But most of all, Deidre wanted to understand how recent economic conditions would affect her long term retirement goals and how to make up for lost time to ensure the future she had envisioned for herself and her daughter. This was particularly important given continued uncertainty in the marketplace. If Deidre lost her job or was faced with a physical or mental disability unexpectedly, her investments would have to pull her through temporary tough times, and her plans for her daughter's future would need to be in place.

THE CHALLENGE

Like many Canadians, Deidre wonders should action be taken in managing diminished RRSP portfolios in the short term or over the long term? What investment choices should be made with existing funds and with future investments into the plan? Are there any tax consequences to consider?

These are important questions many Canadians have been asking themselves throughout this economic period—the most turbulent in over 60 years. Answers have been difficult, even for the experts, given the uncharted territory recent political and economic events have taken us through.

Many investors have responded with anxiety and some with panic. Uncertainty and the resulting lack of control felt by many who have lost equity in their savings has caused fear ... fear that retirement lifestyles will be dramatically reduced, that retirement will begin later rather than sooner and that investment returns will continue to drop or stagnate.

There are two antidotes to fear: knowledge and action. To take action without knowledge contains significant risk, however. Therefore it is more critical now than in recent history to revisit investment goals and strategies with a qualified financial advisor who can help the investor make a knowledgeable decision, rather than a snap decision based on emotion or fear. The importance of the advisor's role can be well summarized with this quote:

> If you wish to know the road up the mountain, ask the one who goes back and forth on it. (Zenrin)

Within the consultative process, the future of the remaining capital accumulations in the plan should be assessed and decisions surrounding the mix of asset classes—stocks, bonds, mutual funds, etc., should be discussed. One should also be aware of individual corporate investments that may be ready to spike or suffer insolvency.

Are these tough times the prelude to a golden time of opportunity? This is a question we may be asking ourselves five years from now when markets have normalized and rates of return are compared, based on today's investment decisions. Remember that some of the greatest opportunities for success arise in periods of dramatic change. Tough times are temporary. The key to recovery is often persistence, dedication to personal productivity, timing and patience.

Finally, consider this: the biggest drain on productivity in an individual's lifetime is not fluctuations within the marketplace. It is his or her personal tax liability. We pay more in taxes in our lifetime than we do for food, clothing and shelter, and this burden has increased throughout the last half of the last century.

According to the Fraser Institute's Tax Facts #12:

> Between 1961 and 2000, for example, the average Canadian family's tax bill rose from 33.5 percent to 47.5 percent of its income. In 2000, the average family earned $51,174 and paid $24,309 (47.5%) in federal, provincial, and municipal direct and hidden taxes ... taxes have risen much more sharply than spending on food, clothing, and shelter. The tax bill now accounts for more of the average Canadian's budget than shelter, food and clothing combined, a marked reversal from the situation in 1961.

When it comes to income taxes specifically, we know the following: this is the only type of tax that allows Canadians to arrange their affairs, within the framework of the law, so as to pay the least amount of taxes legally possible. It is your right and obligation to pay only the correct amount of tax and not one cent more.

Therefore, one of the worst actions taxpayers can take is to fail to maximize their RRSP contribution room—something that, according to Statistics Canada, 90% of Canadians do. What is certain in these uncertain times is that the RRSP will reap tax savings returns in the double-digits—*22% to almost 50% depending on your tax bracket and whether you are the subject of a social benefits clawback*—and that's a good return on an investment by any measure.

Another mistake is to crystallize losses within an RRSP. This has no immediate tax merit and may have little financial merit overall. That is, losses, like gains generated within a registered fund, lose their normal tax identity and simply decrease or increase the eventual taxable withdrawals from the fund. Losses cannot, however, be claimed against other income reported on the tax return. But to continue your original investment strategy increases the chances that market gains may restore values so quickly lost in unusual times.

FACTORS TO CONSIDER

Strategies to explore to put retirement plans back on track will depend on a number of factors:

- Available and immediate tax savings through reduced marginal tax rates
- Age to retirement
- Availability of new capital for investment purposes
- Asset mix in the short and long term.

These factors should be taken into account in exploring:

1. **Accumulation Strategies:** How much more can I contribute to my RRSP before I reach age 70? What are the tax savings resulting from this contribution?
2. **Withdrawal Strategies:** How much of those accumulations will remain in the hands of the taxpayer and/or the taxpayer's estate on an after-tax basis at the end of life's road?
3. **Investment Strategies:** How can my investment choices best meet my objectives and risk tolerance levels, both inside RRSPs, and later, once funds are transferred to Registered Retirement Income Funds (RRIFs) or annuities?

A reliable, fast and effective way to normalize market risk fluctuations is to look to the Canadian taxation system for support. Taxpayers need to understand the long term accumulation power created with certain tax preferences, like the RRSP, together with other special provisions available within the tax system to assist taxpayers through troubled times.

This is particularly important if tough times bring further complications: job loss, temporary or permanent disability or the need to start a business should gainful employment elude those suffering job loss within a recession.

What investor-driven actions are appropriate in tough times to get control of stagnant or diminishing performance within RRSPs? There are both short and long term strategies to consider to ensure the desired standard of living throughout retirement. A few ideas follow:

1. Accumulation Strategies

Investments should always be made based on their individual merits, according to the investor's risk tolerance level and specific financial and personal goals. No investment should be pursued for tax reasons alone. However, when all other bases are covered, choosing investments with tax benefits can help you to multiply your growth significantly and enhance your financial planning priorities in both the short and long term.

During the accumulation years, and in particular when new capital is tight or non-existent, planning for a tax savings benefit at the time of investment can also work significantly in an investor's favour. To make the choice to leverage investment dollars with tax benefits is therefore a good one, particularly if the investor and his/her family face high marginal tax rates.

Most people understand that marginal tax rates are higher for those at higher income levels. However, as discussed in Chapter 1, high marginal tax rates also result in social benefits "clawback zones," which reduce benefits payable through credits such as the Child Tax Benefit, as income rises. This "benefit bleeding" can be stopped or reduced, depending on income level and number of dependants, using tax preferences that reduce net family income. The RRSP contribution factors into this strategy.

RRSP Contributions Increase Benefits

Making an RRSP contribution can therefore positively affect all of the following provisions on the tax return, which are based on net income:

- **Social Benefits Repayments.** Recipients of Old Age Security or Employment Insurance will have to pay back less of those benefits if an RRSP deduction reduces individual net income to below $56,968 and $48,750 respectively in 2002.
- **Non-Refundable Tax Credits.** When an RRSP is used to reduce net income of the individual, the non-refundable tax credits available are increased, as outlined in Figure 3-1.

Figure 3-1
Increased Non-Refundable Tax Credits

Provision	Claimed by
The Age Amount	The individual taxpayer
The Spousal Amount	The supporting individual
The Amount for an Eligible Dependant	The supporting individual
The Amount for Infirm Adult Dependants	The supporting individual
The Caregiver Amount	The supporting individual
Amounts Transferred from Spouse/Common-law Partner	The Spouse or Common-law Partner
The Disability Amount	Either the individual or the supporting individual
The Tuition and Education Amounts	Either the individual or the supporting individual
Medical Expense Amounts	Either the individual or the supporting individual
Charitable Donations	Either the individual or the supporting individual

- **Refundable Tax Credits.** Federally, the Canada Child Tax Benefit and the Goods and Services Tax Credit are affected by the size of the family (not individual) net income. Provincial child benefits are based on this figure.

The tax savings benefits of the RRSP can therefore be further enhanced:
- By maximizing other refundable and non-refundable tax credits available
- By maximizing the use of Labour-Sponsored Investment Funds (LSIFs)
- By reinvesting tax savings so earned within the RRSP of the taxpayer or his/her spouse
- By choosing value and growth-oriented investments to balance out the investment returns within the RRSP portfolio over time and preserve capital.

Avoid Marginal Tax Rate Spikes

The immediate benefits provided by the RRSP are determined by:
- The taxpayer's available RRSP contribution room
- The current year's marginal tax rate
- That taxpayer's eligibility for refundable tax credits like the Child Tax Benefit
- The taxpayer's exposure to social benefit clawbacks, like Employment Insurance or Old Age Security Repayment.

So if the taxpayer's marginal tax rate is 40%, and we assume that RRSP contribution room exists and taxes are payable, each dollar invested in the RRSP will save 40 cents. However, at certain income levels that marginal rate can be much higher, if refundable tax credits are reduced because the family's income falls within a "clawback zone."

Figure 3-2 provides common clawback zones for 2002.

Figure 3-2
Thresholds for Maximizing Tax Savings from RRSP Contributions

Provision	Maximum Benefits	Clawback of Benefits Begins
Refundable Credits:		
Canada Child Tax Benefit*	$1,151 per child	At family net income level of $32,960
National Child Benefit Supplement	$1,293 for first child $1,087 for second $1,009 for third child	At family net income level of $22,397
Goods and Services Tax Credit	$213 per adult $112 per child	At family net income level of $27,749
Non-Refundable Tax Credits:**		
The Age Amount	$3,728	At individual net income of $27,749
The Spousal or Common-law Partner Amount	$6,482	When spouse's income exceeds $649
Infirm Dependent Adult Amount	$3,605	When individual net income exceeds $5,115
Caregiver Amount	$3,605	When individual net income exceeds $12,312
Social Benefits Payments:		
Old Age Security Benefits	$5,500 (approx.)	When individual net income exceeds $56,968
Employment Insurance Benefits	Based on contributionss	When individual net income exceeds $48,750
Tax Bracket Thresholds:		
Income at which taxation begins	$7,634	The Basic Personal Amount or tax free zone for all individuals
Income at which the 16% federal tax bracket begins	$7,635	
Income at which the 22% federal tax bracket begins	$31,677	
Income at which the 26% federal tax bracket begins	$63,354	
Income at which the 29% federal tax bracket begins	$103,000	

*CCTB rates vary slightly in Alberta.
**The Federal Amounts are shown. Provincial credits vary by province.

To highlight the effect of the RRSP on tax savings and the enhancement of refundable tax credits, study the example in Figure 3-3, which illustrates the significant results—almost $4,000 in savings—obtained by a family of four, supported by a single earner, with net family income of $38,000 and two school-aged children.

Figure 3-3
Marginal Tax Rates Including Child Tax Benefit Clawbacks

RRSP	Net Income	Taxes Payable	Child Tax Benefit	GST Credit	Total Net Tax Liability	Marginal Tax Rate (MTR)
$100	$38,000	$6,914	$1,934	$ 79	$4,901	41.4%
$8,000	$30,000	$4,153	$2,686	$479	$ 988	55.3%

Note that with the effect of the Child Tax Benefit and National Child Benefit Clawbacks, this family's marginal tax rate is actually much higher at lower income levels. The MTR represents how much was clawed back for each $100 of additional income.

This is a little confusing at first glance. However, it is important not to confuse the higher marginal tax rate with the actual tax savings. The higher marginal tax rate at the RRSP-reduced income level does not equate to higher marginal taxes payable, unless you add income. It simply equates to bigger tax and social benefit savings if you can reduce net income.

In the example in Figure 3-3, the $100 contributed to the RRSP saved the family $41.40 but as the net income was lowered to below another clawback threshold, the additional contributions saved even more. The last $100 of the $8,000 contribution saved the family $55.30. These huge tax savings continue until the family's net income reaches about $22,400. After that level, the marginal tax rate drops to about 24%.

Therefore, it can be generalized that within social benefit clawback zones, taxpayers suffer higher marginal tax rates due to the fact that benefits are reduced as income rises. This is particularly so at income levels between $22,000 and $32,000, but depends on both income level and the number of children in the family (see Figure 1-10 in Chapter 1 for income/family size outcomes).

In short, the clawback phenomenon is really an added tax—but only at certain income levels. Therefore, failure to use the RRSP as a way to reduce family net income at middle income levels can significantly increase net taxes, when reductions in such benefits are taken into account.

Focus on Maximizing RRSP Contribution Room

Investors who are panicking about losses within their RRSP portfolios are perhaps focusing their energies on the wrong asset. Should one dwell on the past or take action to create gains in the future?

To illustrate, consider the following common problem: a homeowner locked into a mortgage with a high interest rate, in a period of time in which interest rates were continuously reducing. He worried about the increased costs to his family on such a large sum. However, by making some wise choices, he pulled ahead in the end. He decided to focus on offsetting those costs by accelerating his principal payments. By paying down the mortgage faster, he actually reduced his interest costs by an amount greater than lower market interest rates would have provided.

One could view the diminished RRSP portfolio in a similar way. To enhance the building of capital in the fund and catch up from recent erosion, future contributions must be increased and accelerated. For most Canadians, this is a viable investment strategy as 90% of us do not maximize our RRSP contribution room.

If most Canadians under-contribute to their RRSPs, it follows that the majority are also overpaying their taxes significantly every year. This double-negative can be very costly over the long term.

For example, if the average tax saving available to Maria Smith is 30% of an annual deposit of $5,000, calculated over 20 years, tax overpayments will have amounted to over $30,000 ($1,500 in annual savings times 20 years). This money could have gone a long way to shoring up retirement savings, particularly when tax-deferred earnings growth is factored into the equation.

Such long term "tax overpayment risk" poses a greater concern than market losses within an existing portfolio. Before you buy, sell or withdraw money within your RRSP, think first about bolstering your accumulations within the RRSP, by maximizing RRSP contribution room. Then make a plan to reinvest all your tax savings to get back on track. You'll pull ahead faster focusing on future investments rather than on the losses resulting from the current accumulations.

Make the RRSP Contribution a Priority Now

Aside from the discussion above, there are a number of additional reasons why Canadians should contribute immediately:

- **Taxes are higher today than they will be next year.** Because of previously announced tax changes, Canadians will reap tax reductions in the range of 20-27% in the period 2000 to 2005. That means every dollar invested in an RRSP today is worth marginally more than one invested in the future, all things being equal.
- **The majority of Canadians fall into the lowest tax brackets.** This is an unfortunate fact of life that will impact revenues for governments and taxpayers alike when these people retire in the future. Many will likely live in poverty. However, by missing their RRSP contributions there are also other consequences: refundable tax credits meant for this income class will be understated. So it is most important for lower income earners to maximize their social benefits today and their tax-deferred investment compounding time by contributing to their RRSPs.

- **RRSP Savings are highly achievable.** When broken down into manageable amounts, savings required to maximize available RRSP room for the majority of Canadians are highly achievable as demonstrated in Figure 3-4.

  Therefore average Canadians have the potential to save significant accumulations over their lifetimes as outlined in Figure 3-5.

Figure 3-4
Monthly RRSP Ideal Contributions

Income Level	% of All Tax Filers	Contribution Room: 18% of Earned Income (max. $13,500)	Monthly Savings Required
$10,000 to $20,000	18%	$1,800 to $3,600	$150 to $300
$20,000 to $30,000	16%	$3,600 to $5,400	$300 to $450
$30,000 to $40,000	14%	$5,400 to $7,200	$450 to $600
$40,000 to $60,000	17%	$7,200 to $10,800	$600 to $900
$60,000 to $80,000	7%	$10,800 to $13,500*	$900 to $1,125

*maximum contribution of $13,500 is reached when earned income reaches $75,000.

Figure 3-5
Lifetime Registered and Non-Registered Savings Accumulations Potential

Income Level	Average* Marginal Tax Rate	Contribution Room: 18% of Earned Income (max. $13,500)	Average Tax Savings from RRSP Contribution	Total RRSP Plan Over 40 years @ 6% Return	Comparable Non-registered Savings**
$10,000 to $20,000	24%	$1,800 to $3,600	$432 to $864	$295,000 to $591,000	$204,000 to $409,000
$20,000 to $30,000	24%	$3,600 to $5,400	$564 to $1,296	$591,000 to $886,000	$409,000 to $613,000
$30,000 to $40,000	24% to 31%	$5,400 to $7,200	$1,296 to $2,232	$886,000 to $1,181,000	$613,000 to $736,000
$40,000 to $60,000	31%	$7,200 to $10,800	$2,232 to $3,348	$1,181,000 to $1,772,000	$736,000 to $1,105,000
$60,000 to $80,000	31% to 41%	$10,800 to $13,500	$3,348 to $5,535	$1,772,000 to $2,215,000	$1,105,000 to $1,193,000

*Combined federal and provincial rates in effect at time of writing.
**Assumes return from interest income, which provides a worst case scenario.

Create a New RRSP Deduction

Taxpayers can create RRSP tax savings today, even if they are cash poor. For example, you can switch investments from your non-registered portfolio—

like Canada Savings Bonds and mutual funds—into your RRSP, subject to contribution room and limits. There are tax consequences, though. All interest accrued to the date of the flip must be reported. Also if assets have increased in value since acquisition, the capital gain must be reported as a result of the flip. If assets have decreased in value the capital loss will not be deductible. This is considered to create a "superficial loss." To get around this, the investment would have to be sold to trigger a deductible loss and the cash would then be contributed to a RRSP.

Create More New Capital

While Canadian taxpayers are familiar with RRSPs through significant annual advertising, the Labour-Sponsored Investment Funds (LSIF) are less commonly known. Briefly, the Labour-Sponsored Fund Tax Credit (LSFTC) can have both a federal and a provincial component. Taxpayers can create more new capital by flipping investments within the RRSP into a LSIF.

As discussed in prior chapters, taxpayers can make an investment of up to $5,000 and reap a federal tax credit of 15% of their investment (maximum $750). In many provinces, if the LSIF is registered an additional credit is available. These credit maximums may vary from province to province. In some provinces, like Manitoba, they can provide for a doubling of the credit to a combined maximum credit of 30% (up to $1,500).

Because the LSIF is an RRSP-eligible investment, a single contribution to a LSIF within an RRSP can reap both RRSP tax savings and a LSIF tax credit.

For example, a taxpayer is in a 40% federal/provincial tax bracket. He makes a $5,000 contribution to his RRSP, which provides a return of $2,000. If that $5,000 is invested in a LSIF, registered federally and provincially, a further $1,500 tax credit is created, making the immediate return on this investment through tax savings $3,500 or 70%.

However, a Labour-Sponsored Funds Tax Credit (LSFTC) can also be created without coming up with any new money. Simply reinvest or flip existing RRSP assets into a LSIF, thereby creating a tax credit of up to $1,500 or more, depending on your province of residence. This tax credit can then be deposited as new money into your or your spouse's RRSP or used to make other investments in non-registered accounts, education savings accounts or insurance products.

In another example, David, a high income earner, maximizes his RRSP contribution room every year. He is looking for additional tax savings for 2001, but due to diminished values in his investment portfolios David has little cash with which to accomplish this. His advisor suggests that he consider moving some of the cash accumulations within his RRSP to a Labour-Sponsored Investment Fund. Such a move will create an immediate tax credit of $1,500 in David's home province of Manitoba, money he can use to finance other investment goals.

The LSIF investment (which, like any other investment, must be reviewed with the financial advisor to determine whether its risk and reward factors over the long and short term suit the individual's goals) can in fact influence wealth creation over the short term. To illustrate, in the example in Figure 3-6, a single investment of $5,000 by one spouse creates a new RRSP investment for the other, as well as new education savings through a Registered Education Savings Plan and its bonus from the federal government: the Canada Education Savings Grant.

Figure 3-6

Funding New Capital Creation with Government Money

Assumption: Taxpayer and spouse are at 50% marginal tax rate

Original Capital	Savings from Investment in RRSP	Savings from Investment in LSIF*	New Capital Created	Reinvestment
Spouse 1: $5,000 invested in LSIF within RRSP	$2,500	$1,500	$4,000	In Spousal RRSP: Loan to Spouse: $4,000
Spouse 2: $4,000 invested in LSIF within RRSP	$2,000	$1,200	$3,200	In RESP $2,000 In Mortgage $1,200 Plus CESG $400

*Assumes both federal and provincial tax credit availability totalling 30% of the investment in the fund to a maximum of $5,000.

In Figure 3-6, an original investment of $5,000 creates an increase to net worth of $7,600:

Assets:	RRSP (Spouse 1)	$5,000
	RRSP (Spouse 2)	$4,000
	RESP	$2,000
	CESG	$400
Reduced Liabilities: Mortgage		$1,200
	Total:	**$12,600**
	less original deposit	**$5,000**
	Equals:	**$7,600**

Consider Borrowing Money to Invest in Your RRSP

Interest costs are not deductible when the loan is used to purchase an RRSP, however in today's climate of low interest rates, the tax savings are likely worth it, as illustrated in Figure 3-7.

Figure 3-7

Cost of Borrowing for Your RRSP Contribution

Amount Borrowed	Interest Costs*	Before Tax Dollars Needed to Fund Interest**	Tax Savings @ 31% MTR	Net Benefit
$1,000	$27.29	$39.55	$310.00	$270.45
$2,000	$54.58	$79.11	$620.00	$540.89
$3,000	$81.88	$118.66	$930.00	$811.34
$4,000	$109.17	$158.21	$1,240.00	$1,081.79
$5,000	$136.46	$197.77	$1,550.00	$1,352.23
$6,000	$163.75	$237.32	$1,860.00	$1,622.68
$7,000	$191.04	$276.88	$2,170.00	$1,893.12
$8,000	$218.34	$316.43	$2,480.00	$2,163.57
$9,000	$245.63	$355.98	$2,790.00	$2,434.02
$10,000	$272.92	$395.54	$3,100.00	$2,704.46

*Assume a 5% commercial rate. Loan is assumed to be repaid over a 12-month period. Costs could be reduced by repaying a portion of the loan with the tax refund.

**Because interest on RRSP loans is not deductible, the costs must be funded with after-tax dollars.

Explore Your Borrowing Options

It may be important to consider borrowing options that include your family and your employer given that interest costs on loans taken for RRSP investment purposes are not deductible.

For example, you may be able to obtain a low-interest or no-interest loan from your employer. The difference between the prescribed rate of interest and the rate you negotiate with your employer is a taxable benefit which is added to your income. However, over the short term, the lower interest cost will increase working capital.

For the prescribed interest rates for 2001 and 2002 (first quarter) see Figure 3-8. For the first quarter of 2002, the rates reduce to 7%, 7%, 5% and 3% respectively.

Figure 3-8

Prescribed Interest Rates for Tax Year 2001/2002

Year	Quarter	Overdue Taxes	CPP/EI Premiums	Tax Overpayments	Taxable Benefits Low or No Interst Loans
2001	Q1	10%	10%	8%	6%
2001	Q2	10%	10%	8%	6%
2001	Q3	9%	9%	7%	5%
2001	Q4	9%	9%	7%	5%
2002	Q1	7%	7%	5%	3%

NOTE: The amount of the taxable benefit and the actual interest paid is deductible as a carrying charge if the loan proceeds are used to buy non-registered investments with the potential to produce income from a business or property or a LSIF held outside an RRSP.

Make an RRSP Gift to Your Spouse

In the case of RRSPs, attribution can be avoided by having the RRSP contributor make a spousal RRSP contribution. However, the spouse also may wish to make an RRSP contribution to their own plan. Based on his/her own earned income, the higher income earner should gift the funds used for these purposes. The resulting earnings are not attributed back to the gift giver, as RRSP withdrawals are not considered to be income from property.

Take Advantage of Increased RRSP Contribution Levels

The maximum RRSP contributions taxpayers can make have been stalled at 18% of earned income to a maximum of $13,500 since tax year 1996. The maximum contribution is expected to increase to $14,500 in 2004, based on earned income of the 2003 tax year. To maximize this contribution, earned income of $80,556 must be reported. Another increase is scheduled to take effect in 2005, when the maximum will rise to $15,500. Earned income of $86,111 is required to reach maximum RRSP contribution limit.

For higher income earners, these increases in maximum benefits can further help to catch up prior erosion in RRSP funds, and should be incorporated into today's accumulation plans.

2. Withdrawal Strategies

The idea behind an RRSP is that principal invested in the plan is on a before-tax basis (hence the receipt of a deduction when the money is contributed). In addition, earnings are tax sheltered throughout the time they grow within the RRSP. However, upon withdrawal of the funds from the RRSP, both principal and earnings are included in income in full. The taxpayer pays tax according to his or her marginal tax rate at the time and the addition of the RRSP withdrawal to income could put the taxpayer into a higher marginal tax bracket or could create a clawback of social benefits like Old Age Security, Employment Insurance benefits received or refundable credits like the Child Tax Benefit.

The government will not allow an indefinite deferral of income under the RRSP accumulation plan. Taxpayers must make arrangements to collapse their RRSPs by the end of the year in which they turn 69. At that time, the following options are available:

- The accumulations can be withdrawn as a lump sum (generally not a good idea as the entire amount becomes taxable in the year of withdrawal)
- Funds can be transferred to a Registered Retirement Income Fund (RRIF) (in this case RRSP accumulations are transferred into another registered vehicle that provides for a minimum withdrawal annually and continued tax deferral on the balance of the money in the plan. Those minimal withdrawals increase over time)
- Through the purchase of an annuity contract (in this case an equal amount of income is paid out over a specific term, based on accumulations in the RRSP at the time of conversion. Certain investments may not qualify for this option (i.e., LSIF investments)).

Anticipating the tax liability on withdrawal is difficult if the taxpayer has many years to retirement; it is easier if retirement is imminent. Given recent tax reductions, taxpayers are speculating on the value of RRSP contributions today, in light of potential tax liabilities on withdrawal in the future. Some thoughts on this discussion follow.

Long Term: Invest Inside or Outside an RRSP?

Recent tax changes have introduced reduced taxation rates for middle income earners. Exposure has been increased to those rates by indexing of tax brackets, personal amounts and social benefit clawback zones and, in particular, the reduction of the capital gains inclusion rate to 50% from its pre-February 28, 2000, high of 75%. Taking all this into consideration, Canadians have questioned whether the RRSP is the right retirement savings vehicle when taxation on withdrawal is factored into the picture, in addition to other pressing needs—like saving to pay down a mortgage or for a child's education.

While we discussed that question at length from a tax savings point of view in Chapter 1, the chart in Figure 3-5 answers the accumulation question clearly: you can save up to twice as much inside an RRSP over time than you will investing in non-registered equity accounts.

Because the "tax on withdrawal" issue is more difficult the farther away the taxpayer is from retirement, we have to make an educated guess about the best strategies in the short and long term. Will tax rates, brackets, personal amounts, provincial taxes, capital gains rates be the same? We simply don't know. It is impossible to compare apples to apples in this case. Best to err on the side of maximizing accumulations, with immediate tax savings and long term tax deferral on earnings offered by choosing the RRSP.

Defer Taxes to the Future Over the Short Term

Because we anticipate taxes to be reduced over the period 2000 to 2005, due to recent federal and provincial budget announcements, those who withdraw funds from their RRSP should do so with a view to tax deferral. Here are some examples.

- The taxpayer and spouse wish to take a trip to Florida right after Christmas and will fund this with RRSP or RRIF accumulations. If income levels in the two years will be similar the taxable RRSP withdrawal should be made in January of the new year rather than December of the old to push the tax liability forward into the next tax year.
- The taxpayer wishes to gift to his adult child, the $25,000 down payment required for a new principal residence to be acquired in November of the current year. If possible, taxes should be deferred by making the gift in January of the new year and from non-registered investment deposits before taxable RRSP or RRIF funds are tapped.

3. Investment Strategies

Whether you lost your job, became disabled or lost ground in your retirement accumulations due to political and economic circumstances, you'll need to understand what it takes to pull ahead again. We have discussed some ideas for doing so, using the support of the tax system.

Next it is important for you and your financial advisor to discuss asset selection strategies in your attempt to correct market losses in your RRSP portfolio. We have suggested that, for the majority of Canadians, this is likely best accomplished by focussing on the investment of new capital for the purposes of maximizing RRSP contribution room.

Finally, and probably the most important question of all, you must understand your future retirement needs and build your goals around this objective. Project ahead to the time when your RRSP accumulations must be withdrawn to help you live an appropriate lifestyle in retirement. Do you know how much you'll need? How does that compare to what you have now? Consider the following in establishing your new investment goals.

Will Public Pension Support Be Enough?

While many are of the belief that current levels of public pension support may be unsustainable over the long term, public pension income should be considered in your long term planning, as it will likely provide you with a minimum standard of living, if both the Old Age Security Pension (OAS) and the Canada Pension Plan (CPP) will be available (currently a maximum of about $15,000 annually):

- At present the OAS pays approximately $5,500 annually or $450 a month, with clawbacks of these amounts beginning when the taxpayer's net income reaches approximately $57,000.
- The CPP, which is based on lifetime contributions of you and your spouse, peaks at about $800 a month or $9,600 annually.
- Savings will have to fund any remaining requirements (see Figure 3-8).

Figure 3-8
RRSP Savings Needed to Fund Retirement Lifestyle

Anticipated Retirement Needs	Before Tax Accumulations	Less OAS/ CPP	Shortfall Before Tax	Lump Sum Required at Start of 10 Year Period
$1,500/mo. or $18,000/yr.	$21,300 @ 24% MTR	$15,000	$6,300	$49,150
$2,000/mo. or $24,000/yr.	$29,200 @ 24% MTR	$15,000	$14,200	$110,800
$3,000/mo. or $36,000/yr.	$46,500 @ 31% MTR	$15,000	$31,500	$245,800
$6,000/mo. or $72,000/yr.	$106,100 @ 45% MTR	$15,000	$91,100	$710,700

*Assumes remaining funds grow at 6%, and an available basic personal amount in the $7,400 range. Pension is for 10 years; savings depleted at age 75.

Establish a Plan to Build the Retirement Income Shortfall

This could include a focus on investment performance, but could also require the reality of increased personal productivity. In other words, you may have to plan to work longer than expected to achieve your retirement income goals.

Review Required Rates of Return

Ask your financial advisor to prepare a calculation that shows you the required growth rate in your portfolio to put you back on track with your plans. The chart in Figure 3-9 gives the average rate of return required if you had envisioned an average per annum growth rate (before taxes) of 10% and if you got sidetracked in your goals by losing up to 50% of your portfolio in recent tough times. The balance left after the loss was invested for the remaining years to retirement is shown.

Figure 3-9
Investment Rate of Return Needed in the Remaining Years to Retirement
Projection: Lifetime portfolio growth of 6% annually

If By End of This Year Portfolio Loss is:	4 Years	6 Years	11 Years	16 Years	21 Years	26 Years
5%	7.8%	7.1%	6.5%	6.4%	6.3%	6.2
10%	9.8	8.3	7.1	6.7	6.6	6.4
15%	11.9	9.5	7.7	7.2	6.9	6.7
20%	14.2	10.8	8.4	7.6	7.2	7.0
25%	16.7	12.3	9.1	8.1	7.5	7.2
30%	19.4	13.8	9.8	8.6	7.9	7.5
50%	33.6	21.8	13.6	11.0	9.7	9.0

Review Comfort Levels Regarding Risk and Reward

It is clear that the risks that investors face in the marketplace continue to be multi-faceted in the shorter term. Risk, the potential for loss, is magnified by uncertainty.

Most market watchers have provided similar thoughts on their short and long term outlook. That is, that the short term (under one year) will continue to be burdened by uncertainty and therefore heightened risk. Over the long term, however, most experts are in agreement that the market will rebound and continue its steady upward long term movement.

By staying invested at reasonable rates of return in a balanced portfolio, Canadians still have the opportunity to double and triple their investments over time, as illustrated by the Rule of 72 in Figure 3-10.

Figure 3-10
How Long Does it Take to Double Your Money?
Method: Divide 72 by your rate of return

Rate of Return in Portfolio	Time in Years to Double your Investment
2%	36
3%	24
5%	14
6%	12
10%	7

Review Asset Mix

Obviously, the closer you are to your retirement age, the less time you will have to make up lost values in your retirement portfolio. Therefore the rate of return earned on your accumulations in the short term becomes of primary concern, particularly if you find yourself to be rather risk adverse.

For these reasons it is important to take the time to sit down with your financial planner to review the asset mix in your current portfolio and discuss this mix as it relates to the performance of your future investments. This may, however, be more difficult than it was in the past. As an example, the following quote, from Gordon Pape (in his December 2001 issue of *The Mutual Funds Update*), makes an interesting comment on fixed-income funds, investments that are often held within RRSPs:

> While stock markets struggle to find firm footing, interest rates are at the lowest levels since the 1950s. This has led to a situation that is unexplored territory for most investors. Low-risk fixed-income funds, regarded as safe havens in difficult times, are generating returns that you'll need a microscope to see. Moreover, the possibility that rates will rise in response to a stabilizing economy creates a risk that bond funds could sustain capital losses in the coming months. Even some money market funds could risk recording modest losses. It's an investors' nightmare.

Are You Using the RRSP Accumulations for the Right Reasons?

The RRSP has always been designed to fund the retirement income of Canadians.

Unfortunately, many Canadians think that those RRSP accumulations should also fund their estate planning goals, which is an entirely different need requiring different investment decisions. For example, the use of life insurance products, providing benefits that are tax exempt upon death, should be used to fund estate accumulations. In short, the RRSP is for you, life insurance is for your heirs.

This is an important concept because senior Canadians often live extremely frugal lives in order to leave some of their RRSP savings to children and grandchildren. Unfortunately, if there is no surviving spouse to which unused RRSP/RRIF accumulations can be transferred, the government takes its share of the savings first. That is, the entire accumulations in the registered funds must be added to income in the final return, which means the estate often loses half of the funds before heirs receive the balance. (This will be discussed in more detail in later chapters.)

In fact, if it is possible that the tax rate on the final return will be higher than the taxpayer's current rate, seniors and their advisors should consider making taxable withdrawals early, to generate tax at lower rates. The tax-paid principal can then be reinvested in non-registered investments or inheritances can be distributed during the taxpayer's lifetime.

To drive this home further, consider this true story (names and circumstances have been changed):

Margaret, a 70-year-old widow, had accumulations of over $300,000 in her RRIF, but few other non-registered investments. She had an opportunity to travel to the Caribbean with a friend over Christmas, but didn't know whether she could afford it. This was a luxury she and her beloved late husband Benjamin had never allowed themselves as they worked to support their family throughout their lifetime. Margaret's new financial advisor, whom she had just hired, finally convinced her after several meetings that she could afford the $5,000 it would take to finance the trip. They decided to make a tax-efficient withdrawal in January, to defer the tax liability to the new tax year.

Six months later, Margaret died quite unexpectedly of a heart attack. Her advisor and her family were grateful she had the time to enjoy such a lovely holiday. In the meantime, the balance of her RRIF accumulations were taxable on the final return and subject to a tax rate of close to 50%.

Traditional thinking has been challenged. To make investment decisions with certainty, more knowledge is required. This is not a climate for amateurs. Investors would be wise to seek the advice of financial advisors to make the right investment decisions and survive tough times with a view to maximizing opportunity.

THE PLAN

1. Deidre should top up her RRSP contribution room with the inheritance she received from her Uncle Mack. She can then choose to claim some or all of that amount as a deduction in the current year or carry forward the undeducted contributions for use in the future, if she thinks income will be higher later.
2. Deidre can increase her tax savings by investing some of her RRSP deposits into a Labour-Sponsored Investment Fund.
3. Her tax savings should be used for reinvestment into future RRSP room to reduce her $100,000 mortgage and/or to shore up her education savings plans for her daughter.

4. Deidre can then borrow against the equity in her home to help her create investments in a non-registered account. The interest on such a loan will be tax deductible. If the assets chosen for her non-registered account are poised to earn capital gains, she will benefit from an ongoing tax deferral (see next chapter). The costs of the loan are deductible only if there is potential for income from property—interest, rents, royalties or dividends—or a business.
5. Deidre and her financial advisor should plan to recover lost ground within her RRSP portfolio by re-evaluating her asset mix. With ten years to retirement, under Option 1, and over $80,000 in market losses to recover, rates of returns on the existing portfolio will need to average double-digit returns. Additional contributions to the RRSP, together with tax savings from other provisions available to her can help Deidre comfortably meet her retirement goals.

THE RESULTS

Option 1: Staying the Course

Deidre's RRSP accumulation picture shows a shortfall of over $215,000 over a ten year period to retirement if current market values of her capital accumulations do not improve.

Original Value of RRSP	**$250,000**
Presumed Growth over 10 years @ average rate of return of 10%*	$398,426
Total	**$648,426**
Current Value: RRSP	$167,000
Presumed Growth over 10 years @ average rate of 10%	$266,155
Total	**$433,155**
Anticipated Shortfall	$215,281

*Assume a strong longer term market rcovery.

Option 2: Topping Up RRSP and Creating LSFTC

If she implements her accumulation strategies by topping up her $20,000 RRSP room and creating a $1,500 LSFTC this year, she will add $21,500 to her capital accumulations of $167,000 for a total of $188,500. This makes the following difference to her portfolio.

Current Value: RRSP	$167,000
RRSP Contribution Room Top Ups with LSFTC reinvestment	$21,500
Subtotal	**$188,500**
Continued annual contributions of $5,000 annually for 10 years	$50,000
Presumed Growth over 10 years @ average rate of 10%	$338,076
Total	**$576,576**
Anticipated Shortfall	$71,850

Option 3: Reinvest LSIF Tax Credit

If that $5,000 is made within a LSIF and the $1,500 tax credit is reinvested each year, Deidre reaps further gains.

Current Value: RRSP	**$167,000**
RRSP Contribution Room Top Ups with LSFTC reinvestment	$21,500
Subtotal	**$188,500**
Continued annual contributions of $5,000 annually for 10 years	$50,000
Reinvestment of LSFTC of $1,500 annually	$15,000
Presumed Growth over 10 years @ average rate of 10%	$349,373
Total	**$602,873**
Anticipated Shortfall	$45,553

This shortfall of $45,553 could be overcome by retiring one year later, at age 56. Following this plan for one more year, Deidre's RRSP balance would be $670,310, exceeding her original goal.

Tax Secrets for Coping with Diminished Portfolios

1. **Maximize RRSPs.** Always maximize your RRSP contribution every year.
2. **Never Overpay.** Missing RRSP contributions is the equivalent of overpaying your annual tax bill.
3. **RRSP Contributions can Lead to Bigger Tax Savings.** Increase your monthly income as a result of your RRSP contribution. Your decreased net income, resulting from the RRSP deduction, can help to increase tax savings from:
   - Increase refundable tax credits like the Child Tax Benefit
   - Increase non-refundable tax credits like spouse/common-law partner amounts and tuition and education transfers
   - Decrease social benefits clawbacks like OAS or EI Benefits repayments.
4. **Consider a LSIF.** Multiply the effectiveness of your RRSP deduction by considering a Labour-Sponsored Fund Investment to create a Labour-Sponsored Funds Tax Credit.
5. **Flip Assets from Non-registered Accounts.** Non-registerd accounts, like Canada Savings Bond accumulations, can be flipped into an RRSP to create a tax deduction without coming up with any new cash.
6. **Switch an Existing Asset in the RRSP to a LSIF.** Under the same "no cash" principle, you can switch an existing asset in the RRSP to a LSIF. A tax credit of up to $1,500 may be created in most provinces (see Figure 1-6).
7. **Put RRSP/LSIF Tax Savings to Use.** Use any tax savings from an RRSP/LSIF to meet other financial plans, including:
   - Reinvest in next year's RRSP
   - Contribute to an RESP for your child's education
   - Fund the purchase of life or disability insurance
   - Pay down the mortgage on your home
   - Make new non-registered investments.
8. **Borrow to contribute to your RRSP.** Expenses can be reduced by borrowing from your spouse or employer. Remember that interest paid on money borrowed to invest in your RRSP or RESP is not deductible.
9. **Borrow for Investments.** Leverage your increased value in your home or other non-registered investments by borrowing against this equity for new investment purposes. If those investments have potential to earn income from a business or property held outside a registered fund, the interest will be deductible.
10. **Reconsider whether it is necessary for you to lock in market losses within an RRSP at this time.** History has proven that markets rebound and when they do, you may be happy that you focused your catch up strategy on increasing your investments with RRSP contributions and other tax savings and by averaging into the next bull market, rather than taking the losses of the bear. You can

then spend some time focussing on the tax problems you might have upon the withdrawal of your RRSP funds.

11. **Review Strategies if Nearing Retirement.** If you are close to retirement, discuss your short-term tax savings and accumulation strategies with your advisors immediately. Maximizing RRSP and LSIF contribution room today could pay off handsomely on two fronts: first because we expect taxes to continue to decrease now until 2005, based on provisions introduced in recent federal budgets. In addition, if this proves to be a good time to average back into the marketplace, you'll show impressive gains in your RRSP over the short term.
12. **Reclaim Past Overpayments.** Recover overpaid taxes of the past, stemming from missed tax provisions and then use those funds for RRSP contribution purposes. See "Digging for Gold" at the end of this book for tips and instructions on how to recover prior taxes that were overpaid.

CHAPTER 4

Minimizing Effects of Losses on Non-Registered Assets

KEY PERSONAL TAX CONCEPTS:

- Savings in non-registered investment accounts offer intergenerational income splitting opportunities
- Investments held outside registered plans should be chosen to include tax efficiencies
- Losses from non-registered investments may provide immediate and long term tax benefits—this is different from registered accounts
- Losses incurred in different asset classes may have different tax consequences
- Taxpayers often miss recording their capital losses—these losses may contain important and lucrative tax benefits
- Losses on personal residences cannot be used to reduce income
- Foreclosures can have a nasty tax bite
- Prior capital gains elections can have an effect on capital transactions
- Interest deductibility on loans taken to make non-registered investments may be deductible
- Outlays and expenses incurred in disposing of non-registered assets are often under-claimed or missed
- Investors with significant capital losses are at risk of overpaying quarterly tax instalments
- Income splitting opportunities with lower income earners should be pursued when interest rates and asset values are low
- Non-registered investments can be contributed to RRSPs to create immediate tax savings.

REAL LIFE

Charles, in his mid-40s, and his wife Christina, the stay-at-home mother of their two sons age 17 and 12, had weathered some financial storms during their 25-year union; the family coped well on Charles' income of $75,000 a year. However, recent personal and economic circumstances had caught them off guard.

Charles, an only child, inherited his mother's estate when she died last year. She was pre-deceased by her beloved husband of 50 years. The proceeds from the $300,000 life insurance policy allowed Charles to maximize his RRSP contribution room of $80,000.* He ensured that half of this money went to a spousal plan. While the capital in their RRSP portfolio had remained intact, returns had been stagnant. Before this windfall, the family had been unable to save much outside their RRSP efforts and there was no specific savings for the children's education. Charles had hoped that his stock options and investments in his employer's small business corporation would provide those funds in the future.

The remaining money from the policy had been invested in mutual funds ($120,000), as well as a family cottage at a beautiful lake in northern Ontario ($80,000). The non-registered investment account had accrued some gains and some losses—none of which had been crystallized to date.

What Charles and Christina had never expected was the heart attack that took the life of the company's owner-manager. The company subsequently folded. Not only did Charles, its Director of Employee Training, find himself jobless for the first time in his career, but the money he had loaned the company ($10,000) became uncollectible, and the shares he held as an employee (12,500 purchased at 75 cents per share) were now worthless. There was no severance.

Unable to find work immediately in Sudbury, Charles' best opportunities to date arose with an American firm. He had to make the decision to move to Boston within the next month, but his family was reluctant. Charles needed to consider his options, including how they would make ends meet if he remained unemployed in Canada for a longer period of time. Whether through emigration or for short term survival, Charles faced the taxable disposition of assets.

THE CHALLENGE

For Charles and Christina, tough times have brought tremendous turmoil to the family. In considering his options, Charles became aware that emi-

*Charles carried forward undeducted contributions of $50,000 for use over future years.

gration to the U.S. would bring about a "deemed disposition" of most of the family's assets as of the date of emigration. Therefore, the choice of departure date and the Fair Market Values (FMV) of their assets as of that date, would have a big bearing on their start-up cash in their new environment and the size of their life savings accumulations.

To make that decision—if and when to leave Canada permanently at an advantageous tax time—they needed to know more about both the accrued gains or losses in their asset base and their options in reporting their tax liability on their final return as Canadian residents. That liability, unfortunately, is real not deemed.

Should the couple stay in Canada, they knew they had to tap their savings in the short term to survive until Charles found alternate employment or consulting work. Those efforts would likely be more successful if they lived closer to Toronto and so a family move within Canada was also possible, although not a preference.

The couple's first challenge was to understand those tax consequences and whether the tax system could help them plan to meet their ultimate goals: to stay at home in Sudbury and continue their life as previously envisioned (see The Plan).

FACTORS TO CONSIDER

Fortunately, this family had an asset base that could help them recover in the short term. The following information about the taxation of capital gains and losses would need to be understood by this family in advance of making decisions about career and family moves.

1. Tap into RRSP Accumulations

A monthly withdrawal from accumulated RRSP funds was possible, but that source would be fully taxable. One option would be to withdraw money from Christina's spousal RRSP, but unfortunately the family faced a timing problem here: spousal RRSP withdrawals are taxed in the contributor's hands unless three years from the last contribution has passed. Tapping those funds would have further negative consequences:

- Loss of tax deferred growth
- Loss of funds to be withdrawn, tax free, if necessary to fund a return to school (under the Lifelong Learning Plan) or new home ownership in the future (under the Home Buyer's Plan)
- Loss of leveraging opportunity using Labour-Sponsored Fund Tax Credits (LSFTC).

For couples like Charles and Christina, the RRSP accumulations together with the LSFTC could help in tough times as illustrated in Figure 4-1

Figure 4-1

Fulfill Financial Plans by Tapping into Tax Preferences

Option 1: Fund Insurance Needs with Labour-Sponsored Funds Tax Credit (LSFTC), Created from RRSP Accumulations

Assumption: Taxpayer has previously been unable to fund life or disability insurance coverage. Cash needed to fund insurance is created with LSFTC. No new infusion of cash is needed if existing assets within an RRSP are converted to the LSIF.

Step 1: Insurance premiums are $3,000 annually; $1,500 for each spouse.

Step 2: Taxpayer converts $5,000 of assets within each person's RRSP to LSIF shares.

Step 3: Refund of LSFTC (30% x $5,000 federal + 30% x $5,000 provincial) is paid to cover insurance premiums.

This creates new tax-exempt assets (the insurance policies) for use in estate planning.

Option 2: Use LSFTC to Repay Home Buyer Plan or Lifelong Learning Plan Withdrawals

Assumption: Repayment is $900 annually. The repayment of RRSP funds withdrawn under either of these plans is not tax deductible and must normally be funded with after-tax dollars. Generating the LSFTC will provide repayment with "70 cent dollars."

There are two ways to approach this problem:

1. **With the investment of new dollars into an RRSP.** A contribution of $3,000 to the RRSP, investing in a LSIF and designating $900 of the contribution as a HBP or LLP repayment gives an RRSP deduction of $2,100. This results in a refund of $900 at a marginal rate of 43% as well as a $900 LSF tax credit.
2. **No new cash is available.** If $3,000 of existing RRSP capital is invested in LSIF shares, an income tax refund will result. The $900 cash can then be used to make the HBP or LLP payments.

2. Sell or Leverage Real Estate Holdings

The family's real property would certainly provide new capital upon disposition, but the market was currently depressed. Further, the properties provided a potential income source. Charles could rent out the family cottage (fishing was really good, and there was an excellent American clientele). In fact, the cottage was appreciating in value, while the principal residence was depreciating. The properties could also be used to back an investment loan.

3. Tap into Non-Registered Investments

Taxpayers who accumulate funds outside an RRSP face different tax consequences on their invested capital, earnings and outlays.

As noted previously, when RRSP accumulations are withdrawn, both principal and earnings are fully added to income. However, with non-registered assets, there are important tax consequences:

- On acquisition
- When assets produce income
- Upon disposition.

These are briefly outlined in the following sections.

On Asset Acquisition

When a non-registered investment is made, there is no actual tax consequence. The investment can be made either with after-tax dollars or with borrowed funds. Depending on the choice of the asset acquired, resulting earnings can be in the form of capital appreciation only or income can be realized on an ongoing basis.

Sometimes assets are acquired as a result of "deemed dispositions." This can happen under the following circumstances:

- Upon the death of a spouse
- When an asset is given to another as a gift
- When one asset is exchanged for another
- When an asset's use is changed from business to personal.

When these deemed dispositions occur, the Fair Market Value (FMV) of the property is used to determine the "Proceeds of Disposition" reported by the existing owner of the property. The new owner acquires the asset at that same FMV, but that number now becomes that new owner's Adjusted Cost Base (ACB).

Throughout the period of ownership, the cost of improvements to the asset, such as a new roof or garage to a revenue property, or additions to the property (such as the reinvestment of mutual fund income in new units of the fund) will increase the ACB. These increases in cost base will reduce capital gains or increase capital losses upon later disposition.

Therefore, upon every acquisition, taxpayers will need to record the Fair Market Value of the property as their Adjusted Cost Base for tax purposes and track any additions and improvements as they occur over time. This tax tracking must be addressed each year when tax returns are filed. However, ACB itself, will only have a taxable consequence upon disposition of the asset.

When Assets Produce Income: Taxation of Investment Returns

There are two ways in which investors can make money on their non-registered investments:

- As a result of the income generated by the asset (interest, dividends, foreign income, rents, royalties or business income)
- Through the appreciation of the value of the asset itself (e.g. stock was acquired at $10 a share; after five years its value is $15 a share)

Income generated by the investment during its ownership period falls into two categories:

1. Active business income
2. Income from property.

Active Business Income

In the case of a proprietorship, it is net business profits that are taxed in the hands of the individual proprietor. It is taxed in the calendar year in which the fiscal year of the business ends (for most proprietorships this is December 31). This topic will be featured in the next chapter.

Income from Property

This includes income such as interest, dividends, foreign income, rents, royalties and is generally considered to be passively, rather than actively earned. Shareholders, for example, would earn dividends, generated from a corporation's after-tax profits or later from capital appreciation of their shares. Those who invest in debt obligations, like Guaranteed Investment Certificates or Money Market Funds, for example, would earn interest.

This income from property is taxed in the calendar year in which it is received, except in the case of compounding interest income. Here a special tax rule exists: accrued interest earnings must be reported on an annual basis, even though receipt of the cash is not possible until the asset matures or is redeemed. This provides investors with a tax trap: the interest earnings are eroded over time with both taxes and inflation.

In the case of earnings from foreign investments, all income (and results on disposition) must be reported in Canadian funds, either at the time the income was earned or by using an average conversion rate for the year. This information is available every January for the prior year from the Bank of Canada. If foreign taxes were paid on the income before Canadian investors received it, a federal and provincial foreign tax credit is available to assist in avoiding double taxation. Remaining foreign tax balances can be deducted from income (See TI Schedule 1—Federal Tax in Appendix).

In summary then, the tax treatment for income from property differs according to source:

- **Interest:** Report income in full in the year received or, in the case of compounding investments, in the year accrued.
- **Dividends from Canadian Corporations:** Paid out of the after-tax profits of a corporation, the actual amounts received are "grossed up" by 25% for tax purposes to a "pre-tax level," thereby increasing a taxpayer's net income. This can have an effect on refundable or non-refundable tax credits. Then, the grossed up dividend qualifies for a dividend tax credit of 13.33%, which in the end gives most investors better tax results than interest earnings.
- **Rents:** This income is reported on a "net profit basis." Net rental income qualifies as earned income for RRSP purposes. Capital Cost Allowance (CCA) may be taken on rental property, but cannot create or increase a rental loss. When a revenue property is sold, a recapture of the CCA deduction must be included in income in full, if the level of depreciation has been overstated during the life of the asset. Underclaimed CCA is deductible, on the other hand, in the year of disposition, up to the value of the original cost.
- **Royalties:** This income is reported in full, but in the case of certain resource properties a resource allowance of 25% of the royalties may be deductible.

Asset Disposition

Capital appreciation—increases (or decreases) in the asset's value over its cost base—is never taxed until disposition of the asset. This provides a significant tax deferral. Upon disposition, gains or losses that are realized must be included in income, but at a preferred rate, as shown in Figure 4-2.

Figure 4-2
History of Capital Gains Inclusion Rates

Year	Capital Gains Inclusion Rate
1972-1987 and Oct. 18, 2000 to present	50%(1/2)
1988-89 and Feb. 28, 2000 to Oct. 17, 2000	66.67%(2/3)
1990-Feb. 27,2000	75%(3/4)

Deemed Dispositions

Dispositions can result from outright sale for cash or through a deemed disposition. Deemed dispositions are held to occur when:

- The taxpayer dies
- Property is transferred to a trust or a registered account
- A taxpayer emigrates
- An asset is given to another as a gift
- One asset is exchanged for another
- An asset is stolen, damaged or destroyed
- Property is expropriated
- Shares held are converted, redeemed or cancelled
- Options to acquire or dispose of property expires
- A debt is settled or cancelled
- An asset's use is changed from business to personal
- An asset is donated to charity.*

Grey Areas—Income from Capital vs. Income from Property

Whether a taxpayer reports income on account of a capital disposition or income from property is often the subject of interpretation—that can be expensive from a tax viewpoint. Taxpayers like the preferred income inclusion rates that capital dispositions are subject to. Canada Customs and Revenue Agency, on the other hand, wants to ensure that if the buying and selling of assets amounts to a thriving active business activity, gains are fully taxable as business income. The following are two specific problem areas:

- **Adventures or Concerns in the Nature of Trade**. Sometimes one-time asset sale transactions can be treated by CCRA as income rather than capital in nature, if they consider the transaction to be an "adventure or concern in the nature of trade." Should CCRA interpret that the asset was held for speculation, gains on disposition will be included in income at 100% rather than 50%, even if the transaction is an isolated one. The frequency of similar transactions in the past, the knowledge of the investor, the relationship of the sales transactions to the taxpayer's regular line of

*Gains added to income at only half the normal taxable inclusion rate, under special rules.

work and the intention of the taxpayer at the time of purchase all can point to a commercial activity rather than a passive investment. These factors will be taken into account when assessing the tax status of the transaction.

- **Tax Preferences for Income from Assets.** The income generated from capital assets—income from property—can also be subject to special tax preferences: loan interest deductibility, dividend tax credits, Capital Cost Allowance, the deductibility of resource allowances or the expenses of operating a revenue property. The Income Tax Act specifically states in subsection 9(3) that "income from property" does not include any capital gains from the disposition of that property and "loss from a property" does not include any capital loss from the disposition of the property. This is important for a number of reasons.

  Except as specifically outlined in the Act, interest costs are generally not deductible against taxable capital gains or net capital losses. They are deductible, however, when income from property is earned or there is potential for such income to be earned. In the case of vacant land, interest costs can reduce capital gains or increase capital losses, but only if there was potential for income from the property.

More Tax Preferences on Asset Disposition

Not only do capital assets qualify for the preferred 50% income inclusion rate on disposition, but certain capital gains on assets may qualify for tax exempt treatment. This includes:

- Gains on the shares of qualifying small business corporations or farm properties that qualify for the $500,000 Capital Gains Deduction (CGD)
- Gains in excess of the CGD may qualify for tax deferral if a "replacement property" is acquired within specific time frames.

A family that invests in building a small business, therefore, can significantly increase net worth over the person who is employed by another. Statistics Canada supports this statement. Based on 1999 figures we know the following:

- The median net worth of family units in which the major income recipient was self-employed was three times greater than if that person was a paid worker (net worth of $216,200 vs. $71,300)
- This is because business equity represents 33% of total assets, compared with 8% for paid workers.

However, it must be noted that these statistics do not include accumulations in company pension plans, something which the self-employed must secure for themselves.

Therefore, in assessing future career options, taxpayers in turmoil should consider the tax consequences of starting their own small business corporation: more on this in the next chapter.

4. Understand Marginal Tax Rates on Non-Registered Transactions

Taxpayers have the opportunity—with proper planning—to diversify taxable income sources and defer tax on equity gains, so as to average out market risk as well as tax liabilities.

A tax-efficient portfolio is generally one that minimizes taxes on current income sources generated by capital assets and defers tax on capital appreciation out into the future. The taxpayer should have a good understanding of average marginal tax rates on taxable investment earnings generated during the year, significant income levels that cross tax bracket borders and the rate of tax that will apply both federally and provincially.

Figure 4-3
Average Federal and Provincial Marginal Tax Rates for 2001*

Taxable Income	Federal Tax Rates	Combined Federal and Provincial Rate		
		Interest	Dividends	Capital Gains
$0-$7,412	0%	0%	0%	0%
$7,413 to $30,754	16%	25%	5%	12%
$30,755 to $61,509	22%	31%	16%	16%
$61,510 to $100,000	26%	41%	23%	20%
Over $100,000	29%	45%	29%	22%

* Marginal rates vary slightly by province. This table does not include variations in marginal rates created by clawback of social benefits, non-refundable credits, or refundable credits. However, comparisons of rates for different income sources are valid.

The key is to minimize income distribution, or if this is not possible, to control income source. One can see from Figure 4-3 that taxpayers can accumulate twice as much in capital appreciation and pay the same amount of tax as those who earn interest income.

Further, the holder on non-registered, compounding debt obligations (like Canada Savings Bonds, for example) must report accrued interest earnings annually—even though that income source has not been paid to the investor. Taken together—low interest rates, high taxation and inflation—all present investors in fixed income assets with a negative proposition. Note from Figure 4-4 that after inflation and taxes are applied to the principal of $1,000 and interest of $195.30, the taxpayer has lost $339.20, in real terms, resulting in an overall negative return of 14.41%

Figure 4-4
Real After-tax Return of $1,000 Compounding CSB*

Year	Interest Earned	Taxes	Inflation Adjustment	Principle and Earnings Left**	Real After Tax Return
Principal	$1000.00				
	Plus:	**Less:**	**Less:**		
1	$18.00	($5.58)	($30.00)	$982.42	(1.76%)
2	$18.32	($5.68)	($29.47)	$965.59	(1.71%)
3	$18.65	($5.78)	($28.97)	$949.49	(1.67%)
4	$18.99	($5.89)	($28.48)	$934.11	(1.62%)
5	$19.33	($5.99)	($28.02)	$919.43	(1.57%)
6	$19.68	($6.10)	($27.58)	$905.42	(1.52%)
7	$20.03	($6.21)	($27.16)	$892.08	(1.47%)
8	$20.39	($6.32)	($26.76)	$879.39	(1.42%)
9	$20.76	($6.44)	($26.38)	$867.34	(1.37%)
10	$21.14	($6.55)	($26.02)	$855.90	(1.32%)
Total Taxes	**$1,195.30**	**($60.54)**	**($278.86)**	**$855.90**	**(14.41%)**

* Assumes 1.8% interest rate, inflation at 3% and 10-year hold period. Taxpayer is in 31% tax bracket.
** Amount shown in current-year dollars (i.e. adjusted for inflation from year 0).

Losses on Asset Disposition

When assets are disposed of for an amount greater than their Adjusted Cost Base, plus any outlays or expenses on the transaction, a capital gain results. For the period October 18, 2000, to the time of writing, 50% of those gains had to be included in income. However, when a capital disposition is made from a non-registered account, resulting in a loss, special rules apply, as follows:

- Losses are first used to offset capital gains of the year, with the following two exceptions:
  - *Exception 1: losses on personal use properties* (homes, cars, boats, furniture, etc.) may not be claimed at all. In addition, there is a special "$1,000 Rule:" both the proceeds of disposition and the adjusted cost base are deemed to be at least $1,000 for these properties, so that the need to report small transactions is eliminated.*
  - *Exception 2: losses on listed personal use property* (art, jewellery, stamp or coin collections) may be applied only to listed personal property gains. Again the $1,000 Rule applies to these transactions.
- If there are no gains or excess losses, the net allowable loss can be carried back and applied to capital gains reported in any of the prior three tax years, in any order:

*Note: This figure has not been inflation-adjusted since 1972, meaning that many taxpayers are paying tax on personal use properties at too low a level.

- If excess losses still remain after application to prior years, or if there were no gains reported in the prior years, they may be carried forward to offset capital gains of the future until used up.
- If excess losses remain at death after applying against capital gains in the year of death or the prior three years, those losses can offset all other income of the year of death or the immediately preceding year.

Capital Loss Applications

Because the capital gains inclusion rates have changed over the years, loss carry over applications can be tricky, especially in 2000, where three capital gains inclusion rates existed. Figure 4-5 illustrates calculations used to:

- gross up current year losses for application to prior years and
- gross down prior year losses for application to 2001 and future years in which the 50% inclusion rate exists.

Tax Loss Selling

It can make sense in some cases to generate tax losses in non-registered accounts if, by doing so, resulting tax benefits provide new opportunities, such as:

- The ability to reach back and recover taxes paid on gains reported in the previous three taxation years
- The ability to reinvest proceeds from the loss application in new capital assets (being mindful of the superficial loss rules)
- The ability to offset future capital gains.

Consider the following example which demonstrates the advantages of tax loss selling.

Tanya owns 10,000 shares in XY Telecommunications. She purchased the shares in 2000 for $7.50 per share. In 2002, the shares were selling at $1.50 per share (representing a $60,000 unrealized loss) but Tanya felt that they would begin to recover later in the year so wanted to keep the shares. She had some minor capital gains in 2002 so far, but had a net capital gain of $50,000 in 1999.

Due to the three year carry back limitation, the gains in 1999 will no longer be eligible for offset with losses after 2002. To maximize tax savings opportunities, Tanya might consider:

1. Selling the XY Telecommunications shares at a loss
2. Carrying the loss back to offset the gains in 1999 and recouping taxes paid
3. Repurchasing the XY Telecommunications shares after waiting at least 31 days (to avoid superficial loss rules outlined below).

Figure 4-5
Capital Loss Applications

Example 1—Application of Prior Capital Year Losses to 2001

William has the following capital losses available for carry forward to 2001:

Year	Actual Capital Loss	Capital Gains Inclusion Rate	Allowable Capital Loss
1983	$3,000	50% (1/2)	$1,500
1987	$3,000	50% (1/2)	$1,500
1989	$3,000	66.67% (2/3)	$2,000
1995	$3,000	75% (3/4)	$2,250
2000	$3,000	70%	$2,100

In 2001, he sold a rental property that he purchased many years ago and made a capital gain of $50,000. If he did not apply his prior year losses against this gain, his taxable capital gain would have been $25,000 in 2001.

On his 2001 return, William may apply these capital losses of other years on Line 252 as follows: using conversion rates to reflect capital gains inclusion rates in (a) the year of loss application and (b) the year the loss was incurred.

Year	Actual Capital Loss	Capital Gains Inclusion Rate	Allowable Capital Loss	Conversion Rate	Loss applied to 2001
1983	$3,000	50% (1/2)	$1,500	(1/2)/(1/2) = 1	$1,500
1987	$3,000	50%(1/2)	$1,500	(1/2)/(1/2) = 1	$1,500
1989	$3,000	66.67%(2/3)	$2,000	(1/2)/(2/3) = 3/4	$1,500
1995	$3,000	75%(3/4)	$2,250	(1/2)/(3/4) = 2/3	$1,500
2000	$3,000	70%	$2,100	50%/70% = 5/7	$1,500
Total	**$15,000**		**$9,350**		**$7,500**

Note how, in each year, the amount applied to 2001 is the same as if the actual loss had occurred in 2001. On William's 2001 return, he includes in income $25,000 as a taxable capital gain on Line 120 and claims $7,500 of capital losses of other years on Line 252. The net amount included in income as a result of his capital gains and losses is $17,500. This is the same result as if he had experienced the $50,000 gain and the $15,000 loss in 2001 ($25,000 – $7,500 = $17,500).

The capital loss application could save this taxpayer over $3,500 (depending on other income levels).

Figure 4-5 . . . *continued*

Example 2—Application of Capital Losses in 2001 to Prior Years

Mary had done reasonably well with her capital investments in prior years but she did not fare so well in 2001. The table below shows her net gains for 1998 to 2000:

Year	Actual Net Capital Gains	Capital Gains Inclusion Rate	Taxable Capital Gains
1998	$3,000	75% (3/4)	$2,250
1999	$3,000	75% (3/4)	$2,250
2000	$3,000	60%	$1,800

In 2001, she lost $10,000. This results in an allowable capital loss of $5,000 (50% inclusion rate for 2001). This loss is not deductible against other income in 2001, but Mary can file *Form T1A* with her 2001 return requesting that her losses be applied to prior years. The following table shows how $4,500 of the $5,000 allowable capital loss may be applied to prior years to maximize its effectiveness:

Year	Actual Capital Gains	CG Inclusion Rate	Taxable Capital Gains	Portion of 2001 Loss	Conversion Rate	Gains Offset in Prior Year	Unapplied Loss Remaining
1998	$3,000	75% (3/4)	$2,250	$1,500	(3/4)/(1/2) = 1.5	$2,250	$3,500
1999	$3,000	75% (3/4)	$2,250	$1,500	(3/4)/(1/2) = 1.5	$2,250	$2,000
2000	$3,000	60%	$1,800	$1,500	(60%)/(50%) =1.2	$1,800	$500

After applying $1,500 of the loss to each of the three years, effectively erasing the $3,000 actual gains reported in each of the years, Mary has a $500 Allowable Capital Loss to carry forward and apply against any gains in future years.

This loss carryback will result in an income tax refund of over $1,300. Properly invested into an RRSP earning 9% for the next 25 years, this could add up to over $11,000 in her retirement fund or if placed in an RESP, accumulate over $8,000 for her newborn's education fund.

This plan to utilize the $60,000 loss has the following tax consequences:

- Generate refund from 1999 of about $17,000 in taxes paid on the $50,000 gain
- Use the remaining $10,000 loss to reduce taxes in 2002 on any gains generated.

The downside is that the Adjusted Cost Base of the XY Telecommunications shares is now $1.50 per share so the capital gain when the shares are sold in the future will be significantly higher. But remember that without the transaction the tax savings from carrying the loss back to previous years would be lost. In particular, if adjustments are made to offset gains reported in 1998 and 1999, the adjustment will likely save more tax than the tax on additional gains in future years will attract. This is true because in those years, the capital gains inclusion rate was 75%, the top marginal rate was reached at $60,000 income level rather than the current $100,000 and because the federal individual surtax was still in place.

Tax Consequences of LSIF Share Dispositions

Investing in LSIF shares held outside of an RRSP should be considered to reduce tax burdens in the following cases:

- For students, farmers and business owners who may not have contribution room based on prior year earnings
- For seniors over the age of 69 who are not eligible to make RRSP contributions but who wish to shelter pension or investment income.

However, the higher risk and reduced liquidity of the LSIF investment must be considered in these transactions and therefore will not be suitable for all investors. As with all other scenarios it is suggested that the taxpayer consult with a financial advisor.

Also, capital losses resulting from dispositions of Labour-Sponsored Investment Funds (LSIF) held outside registered accounts must first be reduced by any tax credits previously received. The balance is then applied in the normal manner to capital gains. This adjustment is not required when there are gains.

Mutual Fund Transactions

Taxpayers who own mutual funds outside an RRSP must be aware of a number of tax measures, as summarized below:

- **Upon Acquisition.** Record the cost of the units acquired for use in calculating the Adjusted Cost Base (ACB).
- **Upon Receipt of Income.** Mutual funds are required to distribute all interest, dividends, other income and net capital gains or losses to their unit holders at least once every year. These distributions are taxable. This is so whether they are distributed in cash (which is rare) or whether distributions are reinvested in additional units (which is common). A T3 slip (from a mutual fund trust) or a T5 slip (from a mutual fund corporation) will report these distributions in the proper income categories. Those amounts are added to the ACB of the units held by the taxpayer and therefore decrease capital gains (or increase losses) in the future. While many mutual fund companies will track the ACB figure on an ongoing basis for the investor, if they do not, it is up to the investor to keep track of all additions to the original acquisition.
- **Upon Switches within Fund Families.** In general, when you switch your investment from one fund to another (e.g. an equity fund to a balanced fund), a disposition is considered to have occurred, with normal taxable consequences.
- **Upon Disposition of the Units.** When an investor sells his or her units of a mutual fund, they are considered to have disposed of an "identical

property," subject to special rules that also apply to the sale of the same group of shares held by a taxpayer. In such cases, the average cost of the shares/units must be calculated each time there is a purchase. The cost per share/unit is calculated by dividing total units owned into the cost of the assets including all reinvested earnings.

Superficial Losses

A superficial loss is a loss on the disposition of property in circumstances where, in the 30-day period before disposition and the 30 day period after the disposition, the taxpayer, who disposed of the property acquired, owned, or had the right to own, identical property. Such losses will not be deductible against capital gains in the normal manner. However, if denied by virtue of this rule, they can be added to the cost base of the property that is re-acquired so that the amounts are eventually claimable. The result of this rule is as if the shares were never sold (except the addition of the brokerage fees to the cost base). There is no parallel rule, however, if the transaction results in a capital gain.

Losses on Flips to RRSPs

When a non-registered investment is flipped into an RRSP, thereby generating a capital loss, the loss will not be allowed. However, in these cases, the losses that are denied cannot be added to the cost base of any substituted property. Generally, if you want to move a losing investment to your RRSP, you should first sell the asset, contribute the cash to the RRSP and then purchase the investment in your RRSP. In this situation, the superficial loss rules do not apply.

5. Understand the Special Departure Tax Rules on Emigration

Taxpayers who emigrate from Canada must reconcile their tax obligations with CCRA by filing a final return, due on April 30 after the date of departure. Accrued gains on most capital property held at departure will be taxed, even if they continue to be owned at departure. All such property is deemed disposed of at its Fair Market Value (FMV) as of the date of departure and then deemed immediately reacquired at this value thereafter.

There are a couple of exceptions to this rule: real property situated in Canada, capital property used in a business situated in Canada, and excluded rights (such as accumulations in RRSPs, RRIFs, RESPs, employee profit sharing plans, superannuation and other private and public pension plans, retiring allowances, and rights under stock options) will not be subject to the departure taxes.

Also, there are no tax reporting requirements on the disposition of the principal residence or on personal use property with a value under $10,000. Emigrants who hold property with a value of more than $25,000 must complete a prescribed form by April 30 after departure: *Form T1161 List of Properties by an Emigrant.*

Emigrants may choose to post security in lieu of paying the departure taxes on these deemed dispositions so that they can pay the taxes when they actually sell the property. Interest on the outstanding taxes will not be charged. On amounts equal to taxes payable on the first $100,000 of capital gains, security is not required.

Taxpayers who return to Canada may request that departure taxes be refunded to them. Also, if, after emigration, the property declines in value, emigrants will have paid taxes on paper gains that did not materialize. In that case, a special loss carry back will be allowed at the time of actual disposition to recover overpaid taxes at departure.

6. Understand Asset Transfers Between Family Members

When assets are transferred to family members, special rules exist to deny the opportunity of splitting of income resulting from the transferred asset. These rules are called the Attribution Rules and can be briefly summarized as follows:

- **Property Transferred Between Spouses is Subject to Attribution.*** If the higher earner transfers property to the lower earner for investment purposes, resulting dispositions are reported by the transferor. The following exceptions exist:
  - Spousal RRSP contributions
  - Income resulting from investment of bona fide loans drawn up between the spouses if interest is actually paid within 30 days after the year end
  - Profits resulting from investments in a business
  - Reinvestments of attributed income
  - Transfers resulting from marriage breakdown.
- **Property Transferred to Minor Children.** Income in the form of dividends or interest will be attributed back to the transferor; however, capital gains will be taxed in the hands of the minor. In addition, a "tax on split income" is levied, on taxable dividends and certain other income received by minors from private corporations owned by the parents. This tax is levied at the highest marginal rate. Other exceptions to the attribution rules include:

*Note: Assets are transferred at Adjusted Cost Base, but by election, FMV can be chosen. Discuss planning strategies with your tax advisor.

- Income earned on CCTBs held in an untainted in trust account for the child
- Reinvestments of attributed income (second generation income)
- Employment income actually earned by a child working in a parent's business
- Contributions to RESPs.

- **Property Transferred to Adult Children.** There are no restrictions on the type of property that can be transferred to adult children, and all resulting income will be taxed in their hands except if CCRA invokes subsection 56(4.1): income will be attributed back to the transferor if the main reason for the loan was to reduce or avoid taxes by including the income on the adult child's return. The rules will not apply if:
  - Amounts transferred are used for non-taxable investments: in a principal residence, in the costs of education, car purchases, etc.
  - A bona fide investment loan is drawn up, with interest actually paid at least once a year within 30 days after year-end
  - Transferred funds are used to start a business.

Recent tough times may provide a golden opportunity to transfer assets—like the family cottage—to adult children, given low market values. This should be discussed with your tax and legal advisor.

7. Capital Gains Elections

The $100,000 capital gains deduction available on disposition of taxable capital property, other than qualified small business corporation shares or qualifying farms, was repealed on February 22, 1994. However, the federal government gave Canadian taxpayers a one-time opportunity to pre-report accrued values in property held as of this date, by way of the Capital Gains Election, which was claimed on *Form T664*.

This election, which increased the cost base of assets to their FMV at February 22, 1994, will serve to reduce taxes owing on actual dispositions of the elected asset. Or, if values have diminished since that time, the increased cost base due to the election will serve to increase capital losses.

Taxpayers who forget about these elections or executors or other family members who are responsible for preparing returns of sick, disabled or deceased relatives may over-report the gains on elected assets. It is important to store a copy of *Form T664* with the will or other historical documents for these reasons.

8. Deemed Dispositions at Death

This will be discussed in more detail in a later chapter.

9. Situations Arising in Tough Times

When times are tough, unusual losses may arise from circumstances beyond an individual's control. This can include the following:

- **Uncollectible Debts.** When it becomes clear that a debt will be uncollectible, the creditor may elect a deemed disposition and consider the debt to be disposed of at the end of the tax year. The proceeds are deemed to be nil in that case and it is deemed that the debt is reacquired immediately after the disposition at a value of nil. A capital loss will generally result. This treatment will only be allowed, however, if it can be shown that the debt was acquired for the purposes of earning income.
- **Losses Arising on Loans.** Taxpayers who find that loans they have extended to others will not be repaid may be subject to varying tax treatment, depending on the purpose of the loan. If the loss arises from a loan that was non-interest bearing or that bore interest at a rate below commercial or prescribed rates, losses will generally not be deductible unless the loan was made for a bona fide business purpose.
- **When Guarantees Must be Fulfilled.** Capital losses may be deducted in cases where a guarantor must pay the obligation, again if it can be established that there was a bona fide expectation that income would be earned from the transaction.
- **Shares of Insolvent Public Corporations.** When a public corporation goes bankrupt, shareholders are deemed to have disposed of their shares in the company as of the end of the year for proceeds equal to nil, which results in the reporting of a capital loss. If there is a sale of the shares later, proceeds will have to be reported, using an ACB of nil, with the result being the reporting of a capital gain at that time. This tax treatment is possible even if the corporation is not formally bankrupt, but simply insolvent.
- **Shares of Insolvent Small Business Corporations.** Insolvency of a Canadian-controlled private small business corporation which results in losses due to uncollectible debt, guarantees paid or worthless shares will also qualify for a deemed disposition at a value of nil. However, the resulting loss is considered to be a Business Investment Loss (BIL), a portion of which is deductible against all other income of the year on Line 217 of the return. The deductible amount is based on the capital gains inclusion rate in effect at the time of disposition.

  This deduction reduces net income, which in turn can increase benefits from refundable and non-refundable tax credits. Excess BIL can be carried back and applied against income of the previous three years or carried forward and applied to income in the next six years. Excess losses become normal capital losses in the seventh year, which can only be used to offset capital gains in the future.

To qualify for this special tax treatment the assets of the private small business corporation must have met certain criteria, including the following:

- Substantially all of the assets must have been used in an active business in Canada
- This definition must have been met within the 12 month period before insolvency or bankruptcy
- In the case of losses due to the payment of a guarantee, the debt is not required to be repaid within 12 months of insolvency, but it must be called within that period
- BILs must be reduced by any capital gains deduction claims in the past. When this rule is applied and BILs are subsequently offset, disallowed amounts become normal capital losses.

- **Foreclosure.** Foreclosure will occur when a taxpayer who holds a debt, like a mortgage, cannot pay amounts owing to a creditor. The property is generally transferred back to the original owner in that case and a taxable disposition occurs. The proceeds of disposition to the person who defaults is the amount of the unpaid debt at the time of the foreclosure and, in some cases, often to the shock of the debtor, this can result in a capital gain. If the debt is subsequently repaid in the future, the repayment is considered to be a capital loss to the payor.
- **Debt Forgiveness.** Section 80 of the Income Tax Act was introduced as a result of the last recession in the early 1990s and became effective for transactions after February 21, 1994. The new rules required that in cases where debt is extinguished, forgiven or settled, the person who received the benefit of the forgiveness would have to reduce other tax preferences he or she may be entitled to, including, in the following order:
  - Non-capital losses or preceding years
  - Net capital losses or preceding years
  - The capital cost and undepreciated capital cost balances of depreciable property
  - Cumulative eligible capital, resource expenditure balances
  - Adjusted cost base of certain capital property, excluding personal use properties and certain other properties of the debtor
  - Current year capital losses.

  After this, balances of forgiven amounts can be transferred to another taxpayer who may be paying the transferee's taxes, interest and penalties. Balances remaining after this are included in the taxpayer's income, but a reserve to spread out the liability can be claimed over a five year period.

10. Interest Costs on Assets of Diminished Value

For interest costs to be deductible as a carrying charge on Line 221, there must be the potential for income from property (interest, dividends, rents, royalties or other income, but not including capital gains).

Special rules introduced on August 30, 1993, allow for the continuation of interest deductibility on outstanding loans in cases where the income-producing source no longer exists (i.e., when there has been a significant decline in the value of the property). The portion that has been lost is "deemed" to continue to be used for income-producing purposes. This ensures that interest on the loan will continue to be deductible.

THE PLAN

Charles and Christina, profiled earlier, needed professional guidance surrounding two primary financial issues: cash flow requirements while Charles worked to find a new job or start a business in Canada and the potential for emigration and its tax consequences. In both of these circumstances, the disposition of assets and their subsequent taxation would require planning to assess the timing of each option. Any taxpayer considering a disposition of capital assets held outside an RRSP or RRIF should begin this planning process by:

- Ensuring the adjusted cost base of all assets owned is updated to reflect improvements to the asset and additions, such as new units of a mutual fund due to reinvested income distributions
- Providing receipts for outlays and expenses, including brokerage fees, real estate commissions, appraisal fees, certain legal fees and advertising costs relating to the sale, etc., used to offset capital gains transactions
- Ensuring unused capital loss balances are available. In our example, Charles, unfortunately, did not know about the carry forward rules, but was able to request an adjustment for capital losses he had incurred in 1986, 1987, 1988, 1990 and 1991 for use in 2001 and future years. The allowable losses were $1,000, $535, $2,515, $2,750 and $1,250 respectively (Total $8050).
- Providing information about the capital gains election taken on the 1994 return. In Charles' case, he had made no election
- Claim carrying charge costs: interest paid on investment loans, safety deposit box charges, investment counsel fees on non-registered portfolios and tax preparation costs relating to the calculation of investment tax consequences.

As the couple outlined their immediate priorities, the following options were discussed with the couple's financial advisor:

1. **RRSP Deposits.** The couple's RRSP deposits should remain intact. A LSIF contribution could be considered to provide cash to fund immediate needs, like insurance or a medical plan for the family. A conversion of existing investments in the RRSP to the LSIF would create a tax credit to cover such premiums, without the need for new capital. In addition, if either Charles or Christina decide to upgrade their post-secondary education to increase their income-earning potential in the future, the RRSP could provide tax free access to capital through the Lifelong Learning Plan.
2. **Loss Carryover Application.** Charles had scored in the marketplace in 1999, reaping taxable capital gains of $9,000. He paid taxes of over $4,000 on this sum which he now should recover by applying his previous capital losses. This recovery could help to fund the children's education savings within an RESP which would reap a further tax credit of 20% of the investment to a maximum of $2,000 (or $400) for each child under the Canada Education Savings Grant.
3. **Non-Registered Asset Liquidation.** If cash was tight in the meantime, Charles could generate funds needed by the family by selling shares or by making a systematic withdrawal (part return of capital, part income) from one of his mutual funds. The most tax effective strategy would include the generation of capital gains from these sources. Only 50% of gains would be included in income. Also, that income could be offset by capital losses available, including those new ones incurred on the folding of the company (lost loan repayment and worthless shares in the amount of $19,375 in total). In this way Charles turns his financial misfortune into a tax free income withdrawal.
4. **RRSP Deduction Maximization.** Charles should factor in the effect of Child Tax Benefits receivable in his net results. He does have undeducted RRSP contributions available to reduce net income.
5. **Leveraging for New Opportunities.** Charles could consider borrowing against equity in his home or other assets for business or investment purposes to build equity today when the market is down. Interest costs in those cases would be tax deductible.
6. **Creation of Revenue Property.** Charles should consider renting out his cottage to increase family income over the summer months. If a profit motive exists, he may even be able to write off some operating expenses on a prorated basis.

THE RESULTS

The following two plans helped Charles and Christina understand the tax consequences of moving to the U.S., bearing in mind that emigration would require the reporting of a deemed disposition of most assets. The tax system, in the meantime, provided assistance, if they decided to look for a new opportunity in Canada.

Plan 1: Moving to the U.S.

1. **The Cottage.** Although the cottage could bring in some income, managing it from the U.S. would be problematic. The family would sell the cottage if they emigrated. Because it was increasing in value, it would be declared their tax exempt principal residence since acquisition last year. After real estate costs, the proceeds of almost $90,000 will be available to finance the move and short term cash requirements.
2. **The Residence.** Moving to the U.S. would also require selling of the family home. It would be declared their principal residence for five of the six years that it was owned, with the result that its $25,000 increase in value will not be taxable. (The exempt gain, calculated on *Form T2091* would equal (1+ 5)/6 x $25,000. A "bonus year" is allowed in the exempt period, which works to the family's advantage in this case). The proceeds from the sale of the family home would then be used to purchase a new home.
3. **Non-Registered Investment Accounts.** Deemed disposition of equities and mutual funds would result in a loss of $8,200, if the current date was used as the emigration date. The Fair Market Value on the actual emigration date is used to compute the deemed proceeds of disposition.
4. **The RRSPs.** RRSPs would remain untouched even after the move. There are no immediate tax consequences on emigration for RRSP deposits. To continue the tax-deferred treatment within the RRSP, non-residents living within the U.S. must file an election when filing their U.S. returns (under Revenue Procedure 89-45). Later, on withdrawal, the only Canadian tax consequences of removing funds from the RRSP will be a 25% withholding tax.
5. **Previously Undeducted RRSP Contributions.** These would be used this year to minimize net income, but a large balance of undeducted contributions would remain. This was problematic under the emigration scenario, as the undeducted amounts would be subject to double taxation in the future. A solution would be to withdraw the funds under subsection 146(8.2) of the Income Tax Act. This could be done on a tax free basis, if the withdrawal was made within one year following the year the

contributions were made or the Notice of Assessment in which they were reported was sent.

6. **The Numbers.** For 2001, Charles' return would show the following income:
   - $30,000 employment income
   - $14,000 EI income
   - $10,000 capital loss (from uncollectible loan)
   - $9,375 business investment loss (reduces other income by $4,688)
   - $8,200 capital loss on deemed disposition of non-registered assets.

Based on the tax preferences available to this family, a refund would likely result on the final return upon emigration, assuming tax was deducted from the employment and EI income and provided undeducted RRSP contributions were used to reduce income. This would provide a tax argument in favour of the emigration under similar market conditions. However, the family could not benefit from many tax preferences available: the Child Tax Benefit and GST Credit (over $5,000) would be lost as it is payable only to residents of Canada, and the lucrative unused current year capital losses would also be lost unless the family moved back to Canada in the future.

Plan 2: Staying in Canada

In this year of unexpected change, the decision to stay in Canada to take advantage of future opportunities here had some interesting tax consequences:

1. **The Cottage.** To offset insurance, maintenance, and property taxes, the cottage would be rented as much as possible in the summer months. This is projected to provide $1,000 in net income in the first year.
2. **The RRSP.** A deduction would be possible based on the undeducted contributions of the prior year and more cash flow could be generated by transferring some of the invested capital in the RRSP to a Labour-Sponsored Income Fund to generate the $1,500 LSF tax credit.
3. **Non-Registered Savings.** To shore up cash requirements while Charles looks for work, his advisor would generate gains from his non-registered account. These gains would offset current losses.
4. **Leveraging Opportunities.** After discussion with his advisor Charles would consider borrowing against the equity in his home or cottage to invest in the marketplace to create new investment income or to start his own small business. Interest paid would be deductible in that case.

5. **The Numbers.** For 2001, Charles' return would show the following income in this case:
   - $30,000 employment income
   - $14,000 EI income
   - $10,000 capital loss (from uncollectible loan)
   - $9,375 business investment loss (reduces other income by $4,688)
   - $1,000 net rental income.
6. **The Results on Charles' 2001 Tax Return are the Following:**
   - An income tax refund of $5,833 after claiming an RRSP deduction of $18,165
   - A tax refund of over $4,000 on application of recovered losses to gains in 1999
   - A Child Tax Benefit of $4,543 and a GST Credit of $650
   - A possible capital loss carryover on current year liquidation results
   - Total tax planning benefits: over $15,000.

The family and their advisor found a way to finance current cash flow needs on a tax free basis—fund insurance and education savings with prior year tax adjustments and current year Labour-Sponsored Fund Tax Credits, create a supplementary monthly income in the future with Child Tax Benefit eligibility, and generate new investment income with an investment loan. Further, their unused RRSP contributions continued to earn tax-deferred income and was available to be tapped if it took longer than expected to get re-established.

Tax Secrets

For Minimizing Losses on Non-Registered Accounts

1. **Preserve RRSP Accumulations Early in Life.** Losses of income or capital are usually temporary. Losses on tax savings or tax deferrals can be permanent. Therefore, it is generally not a good idea to cash in RRSP accumulations to support periods of insufficient earnings, unless there are no other alternatives. Look to creating new capital from tax savings, including increased refundable tax credits, recovery of missed tax provisions on prior-filed returns, capital loss applications and others, first. If it is determined that withdrawals from RRSPs will be necessary, do so in low income years, or in the hands of the lower income earner, if possible, and in January rather than December to maximize tax deferrals.
2. **Withdraw RRSP Funds Early in Retirement if Net Worth is High.** If income in the future or upon death will be taxed in higher brackets and at higher rates than it is today, consider making taxable withdrawals now. Then reinvest tax-paid dollars into non-registered accounts, reaping benefits from income diversification: lower capital gains inclusion rates, capital loss applications, or dividend tax credits. Or provide inheritances to adult children while living to help them pay down mortgages, top up RRSPs, fund education, etc.
3. **Fund Insurance Needs, Repayments of Home Buyers Plan or Lifelong Learning Plan Withdrawals.** Withdrawals with tax credits earned from a Labour-Sponsored Investment Fund, if the risks of the investment are offset by the tax rewards, can be used to finance these financial plans. This should be discussed with your financial planner.
4. **Always Report Capital Losses Incurred in Non-Registered Accounts.** These can be used to offset capital gains of the current year, of the previous three years or indefinitely into the future. If you have missed reporting prior losses, request an adjustment to prior-filed returns (you can go back as far as 1985—see Digging for Gold at the end of this book).
5. **Borrow to Invest in Non-Registered Accounts.** If there is potential for income from investments—interest, dividends, rents, royalties, foreign income, other income—interest costs will be deductible.
6. **Build Equity in a Small Business Corporation to Maximize Use of $500,000 Capital Gains Deduction.** Each family member has a lifetime deduction of $500,000 to use up … if you are starting a new business to feed your one-time option, discuss how many family members should own shares to maximize the tax free capital gains opportunity in the future.
7. **Diversity Your Taxable Income.** Remember that tax is deferred on accumulations in registered funds and on capital appreciation on assets held in non-registered accounts. By diversifying your holdings and generating the least

amount of taxable income possible from these assets in the short term, you'll pay less tax. That's because over the next several years, recently announced tax changes are expected to bring tax reductions for most Canadians.

8. **Apply Capital Losses Back First.** While capital losses can be applied to capital gains in the carryover periods (three years back and indefinitely forward) in any order of preference, it makes sense to apply back first, if gains occurred prior to October 18, 2000. That's because capital gains inclusion rates were higher; so were tax brackets, rates and surtaxes. The ability to offset gains incurred in 1998 ends in the 2001 tax year.
9. **Do Some Tax Loss Selling to Generate Cash Flow.** It might make sense in some cases to sell off losers in your non-registered accounts, generating capital losses to offset prior or future capital gains income. Assets sold can be repurchased, but beware of the superficial loss rules that block out the 60 day period around the loss transaction.
10. **Offset Taxes for Seniors Over 69 with LSFTCs.** Seniors who are disqualified by age from investing in RRSPs may wish to consider sheltering pension or investment income with a Labour-Sponsored Tax Credit, if they are comfortable with risks and restrictions. This is also true of other taxpayers who have not accumulated RRSP contribution room: students, farmers, homemakers who have gone back to work and investors whose income are not "earned" for RRSP purposes.
11. **Plan Emigration Carefully to Minimize Departure Taxes.** Picking the right departure date—when markets are down, if possible—will save money on the taxes created by the deemed disposition of capital assets at that time. Current tough times may be ideal for such a move, but consider all tax costs carefully.
12. **Transfer Assets to Adult Family Members in Down Cycles.** When market values are low is the best time to do some estate planning. If you want to transfer the family cottage or other assets to adult family members, consider doing it sooner rather than later if you believe this will be advantageous from a tax point of view. For example, low fair market values, coupled with the ability to offset gains on the transfer with capital losses otherwise incurred, may make tax sense.
13. **Put Estate Planning into Perspective.** RRSPs are for your enjoyment; life insurance is for the kids. If costs are affordable, review your life and disability insurance requirements with your advisor, including the tax-sheltered opportunities universal life insurance policies may provide to high net worth individuals and/or their children. The policies' premiums could be funded from tax savings on preference provisions like LSIF investments, capital loss applications, Child Tax Benefit receipts, etc.
14. **Claim Tax Losses Due to Investments Ending in Insolvency.** Capital losses can be claimed when guarantees are called for worthless shares of public and

private corporations, when funds loaned are not repaid, when debts are uncollectible, provided these investments were made with an intent to earn income. Interest costs on loans taken for investments, whose value has now diminished or disappeared, continues to be deductible.

15. **Review Instalment Payment Obligations and Invest All Tax Savings if Possible.** In tough times, when income drops, be sure to reduce quarterly tax instalments to reflect your true income picture for the year. Then, top up RRSP room, pay down non-deductible debt, save for your child's education, create new wealth for your anticipated lifestyle with the savings.

CHAPTER 5

Buying Yourself a Job with a Home-Based Business

KEY PERSONAL TAX CONCEPTS:

- Unemployment due to tough economic times can lead to new entrepreneurial opportunities with significant tax benefits
- Start a business on an unincorporated basis, to write off start-up losses—tax savings could finance further investments
- Non-capital losses from a proprietorship with a reasonable expectation of profit can offset all other income of the year
- Start-up losses are significant—can be carried back three years or forward seven to offset other income in those periods
- Loss carry-back rules help taxpayers reach back and recover taxes paid while employed or when investment gains were realized
- Home workspace expenses can offset business income, but cannot create or increase a business loss
- Car costs can be written off, but only if distance travelled is broken down to reflect business and personal driving
- Asset acquisitions can decrease net business income with an optional deduction for Capital Cost Allowance, which can create past and future tax savings
- Canada Pension Plan premiums are rising and can be particularly onerous for proprietors

REAL LIFE

Alex is a single 50-year-old woman living in Toronto with her common-law husband, John, in the home they own together. On March 31, 2001, Alex lost her $60,000 managerial job, receiving no severance, when her employer went into receivership. John, fortunately, had a long-standing job as a grocer, earning $45,000 annually.

Alex had earned $60,000 in each of the previous three years of her employment. In 1999, she even won a bonus of $5,000 when she was selected "Employee of the Year." In addition, she had made significant capital gains in the marketplace that year, reporting $10,000 in capital gains and then reinvesting that into an RRSP in the same amount. The RRSP deduction was taken in 2000. She had $8,000 in RRSP room available for the current year. John always maximized his RRSP contribution every year.

Employment Insurance Benefits of $450 weekly helped the family transition and adjust temporarily, but Alex knew she soon needed more to sustain her lifestyle. With few other alternatives, she started a small business in August.

A former meal planner for an airline, Alex managed to strike an alliance with a national chain of food outlets in airports and began to deliver fresh meal snacks through this distribution chain. Her first deliveries were to begin in January in a pilot project at the Toronto airport. If successful, the service would later be expanded throughout the chain's Canadian outlets.

Her business start-up costs, which she funded with a bank loan, included interest costs, legal fees, accounting fees, home workspace and car expenses, promotional expenses, costs of producing the products, liability insurance, packaging and shipping. As her business expanded, she would need to buy or lease a delivery van, refrigerators, stoves and computers and invest in software development for her administrative systems. She would also need to hire staff to prepare the product in the new year and keep the books.

While Alex knew she should incorporate at some time, she wondered about the best time to do so, given the fact that she had incurred nothing but losses so far totalling over $35,000. She also was using the whole main floor of their three story house for the business. Her total cost of utilities were $6,000, taxes were $2,500, mortgage interest was $8,000, insurance $800 and maintenance and repairs $2,000.

THE CHALLENGE

Alex wanted to understand her tax position under this new financial circumstance in her life, whether or not to incorporate her business and, if so, when and how to plan her asset acquisitions in order to maximize all of her tax preferences in the current year. Given that she was no longer the main breadwinner, she also needed to know how the new circumstances would affect family tax-filing options, RRSP contribution plans and options for splitting income with her common-law partner.

Finally, she was hoping that the tax system would provide some immediate miracle to help her and John with their immediate cash flow difficulties. Their credit card balances were growing and they wanted to rid themselves of non-deductible debt.

FACTORS TO CONSIDER

When an unexpected job termination arrives, most employees will be able to tap into the Employment Insurance fund to meet minimum needs. However, for most this is only a stop-gap measure, particularly if a family is depending on an ongoing income flow. In tough times, when unemployment statistics rise, many people take on work on a freelance, part-time or consulting basis that can lead to the establishment of new and viable business enterprises.

While the focus of the day-to-day operations of any small business is the generation of income and profits, the added bonus of your own sweat equity and financial investment is the equity that can build within the enterprise. Sometimes when the right factors combine—hard work, business acumen, market conditions, timing and a little luck—a future buyer could pay a premium for the right to take over your client base, income stream or business assets.

A business begins when an income-producing activity shows a reasonable expectation of profit. That is, if you are pursuing a hobby (carpentry, writing music, making perogies) from your basement, the costs of doing so exceed the revenue earned and there is no reasonable expectation of profit in the future, the activity is not considered to be a viable commercial activity. Therefore, if after applying all legitimate tax provisions, including the expenses of an automobile and home workspace, losses incurred would not be tax deductible. In fact, the activities may not need to be reported at all until such time that a reasonable expectation of profit exists.

However, if any of those activities develops into a business with a reasonable expectation of profit in the foreseeable future, net income or net losses from the activity are claimable on the personal tax return.

The topic of small business enterprises and their specific tax provisions and audit-proofing requirements is discussed in detail in *Make Sure It's Deductible* (Evelyn Jacks), a Canadian best-seller. However, the tax saving factors discussed in the sections following should be considered when unemployment, resulting from tough economic times, leads to entrepreneurship.

1. Forms of Business Organization

Most small business ventures take one of three forms:

- **An Unincorporated Small Business or Proprietorship.** Net profits are reported on the return of the business owner and losses, if any are deductible, against all other income reported in the year (including employment income, pension income, Employment Insurance benefits, investment income, etc.). The individual taxpayer is also required to submit, via his/her personal tax return on an annual basis, both the employer's and employee's portion of Canada Pension Plan premiums based on the net income of the proprietorship.
- **A Small Business Corporation.** This is a separate legal entity in which the business owner holds shares and receives taxable compensation in the form of either salary or wages, dividends or capital gains on the eventual disposition of the shares or other assets in the company. Losses incurred within a corporation cannot be applied to the individual's personal income tax return.
- **A Partnership.** Unincorporated partnerships share common business income and expense statements, with each partner reporting a share of the partnership's net profits or losses on his/her personal tax return. Often adjustments are made to that profit or loss, like when individual partners have additional expenditures pertaining to the enterprise (home office, car or computer costs).

Which form a new enterprise takes should be carefully discussed with professional advisors, but from a tax point of view, there are a number of factors to consider:

Start-up Losses

In most small businesses, start-up costs exceed revenues produced for a period of time. Due to the rules outlined above, it is generally best to try not to incur those losses within a corporation, in order to take advantage of the opportunity to offset other income for the year on the personal tax return. If there was little or no other income for the year, and therefore unapplied losses, these amounts can be carried back three years and applied to income sources in those previous years or carried forward to offset income from all other sources in the next seven years.

These rules provide for interesting planning opportunities, particularly if income and taxes paid were high in the past. In the example above, Alex had been earning a salary at the highest marginal tax rate in 1998 and 1999, and the second highest rate in 2000.

Assume her small business start-up activities had resulted in a loss in 2001. She would first use that loss to offset other income of the year (Employment Insurance Benefits). If a net loss then still occurred on Line 236 of her return (net income), she could apply those losses back to 1998, 1999 and 2000, using *Form T1A Request for Loss Carryback.*

Because her income was unusually high in 1999, she would likely choose to offset that year's results with the losses first. In this simplified example, her tax savings would be as set out in Figure 5-1.

Figure 5-1

Tax Savings from Applying a Non-Capital Loss to Prior Years

Assumption: Non-capital loss of $20,000 in 2001 is applied first to 1999, then to 1998.

Tax Year	Total Income	Taxes	Loss Applied	Taxes	Savings
1998	$60,000	$16,908	$9,150	$13,160	$3,748
1999	$73,500	$17,874	$10,850	$13,305	$4,569
2000	$60,000	$15,303	N/A	$15,303	$0
Total	$193,500	$50,085	$20,000	$41,768	**$8,317**

In this case, losses were applied in each year to minimize the income subject to tax at the highest marginal rates, taking into account both federal taxes and provincial tax (Ontario) and all related surtaxes. This brought the greatest tax savings. The choice of the amount of loss application may have been somewhat different, had the taxpayer lived in another province.

It is clear that by using legitimate tax provisions available through the tax system, entrepreneurs can reach back and recover "gold" from prior tax returns and use that money to reinvest in their business, RRSPs or other investment priorities.

Therefore it is important to plan your business organizational structure carefully to ensure the maximum in tax benefits are received before incorporation. This should be discussed with your tax advisor well in advance of the tax filing deadline.

Tax Filing Deadlines

That tax filing deadline, by the way, is April 30 for most taxpayers. However, those reporting activities within a proprietorship have an extended deadline to June 15. This may be a welcome reprieve for shoe-box fanatics, but not necessarily a benefit. That is, if the result of tax preparation shows that the proprietor has a balance due, interest will be charged back to May 1 of that year. It always pays to file the return on time, but to prepare a preliminary tax calculation early to maximize carryover provisions, RRSP and LSIF contributions and discuss changes to business organization with your advisor.

2. Opportunities to Save Tax with Depreciable Asset Purchases

While operating costs—like rent, wages, promotional expenses, administrative costs and professional fees—are fully deductible on the business income and expense statement, when assets are acquired in a business, their costs must be written off over time to reflect a depreciation in their value due to their income-producing use. The deduction for such depreciation, for tax purposes, is called Capital Cost Allowance (CCA) and this provision's basic characteristics, as detailed in the following sections, deserve consideration.

Claiming the CCA Deduction is Optional

If not needed, the CCA deduction can be saved for use in offsetting future income. This is particularly important if income for the year is so low that personal amounts (like the Basic Personal Amount or the Age Amount) are wasted.

Because non-refundable tax credits cannot be carried forward for use in the future (except for medical expenses and charitable donations), it's likely best to forego making the claim for the CCA deduction, leaving a higher undepreciated balance and deduction for use in the future. Figure 5-2 compares the choices.

There's More than Meets the Eye

In the example in Figure 5-2, the Basic Personal Amount available to the taxpayer wipes out any tax liability, so the CCA deduction, if taken, would be completely wasted. This mistake can result in tax overpayments in future years when taxable income, marginal tax brackets and rates (federal and provincial) are significantly higher. Assuming this will be the case, the tax savings from the decision not to waste the CCA claim in 2001 will be between $1,000 and $2,000 over the life of the asset (at current tax rates). That is, approximately 22% to 45% of $4,500, depending on your province of residence.

Only One-Half Normal CCA Rates Allowed in Year Asset Acquired

Therefore, if you anticipate the acquisition of an asset early in the new year and acquire it in the last half of the current fiscal year instead, your expen-

Figure 5-2

Plan CCA to Maximize Non-Refundable Personal Amounts

Assumption: Proprietorship has net income of $4,500; possible CCA deduction is $4,500. Taxpayer qualifies for Basic Personal Amount of $7,412.

Option 1: Take CCA in 2001

Year	Taxable Income (before CCA claim)	CCA Claim	Income Taxes
2001	$4,500	$4,500	$0
2002	$20,000	$3,600 *	$2,850
Total			$2,850

Option 2: Don't Take CCA in 2001

Year	Taxable Income (before CCA claim)	CCA Claim	Income Taxes
2001	$4,500	$0	$0
2002	$20,000	$4,500	$2,595
Total			$2,595
Total Tax Savings in first yer if no CCA claimed in 2001			**$255**

*Second year claim reduced by claim in 2001

diture will reap a tax reward sooner, and put into place a higher CCA deduction in the new year, when income may be higher. The result is that you have positioned your expenditure to be more tax-efficient and to produce tax savings sooner. This may be even more significant in today's tax climate. If taxes are expected to reduce over time (due to indexing for example), it is important to crystallize tax savings in years in which income is taxed in higher brackets and at higher rates. Figure 5-3 illustrates this factor.

Other Timing Factors to Consider

Always weigh tax-driven decisions with other options. If the taxpayer can receive a higher return on capital by investing capital elsewhere, s/he may wish to postpone the depreciable asset purchase decision. This will depend on the taxpayer's tax bracket in the current year, and the foreseeable future, and the income-producing potential of each asset. Clearly the higher the taxpayer's income bracket, the more tax savings will result from an early acquisition of the depreciable asset. Those tax savings can then be reinvested in other capital assets for future growth.

Figure 5-3
Benefit of Acquiring an Asset in Last Half of Year

Assumption: Computer system purchase of $25,000 is contemplated. When is the most advantageous time to buy from a tax viewpoint?

Assume $15,000 Income

	Year of Purchase	CCA Claim	Tax Savings	Total Tax Savings
Purchase in November 2001	2001	$1,575	$372	
	2002	$2,667	$646	$1,018
Purchase in February 2002	2001	$0	$0	
	2002	$1,575	$372	$372

Assume $50,000 Income

	Year of Purchase	CCA Claim	Tax Savings	Total Tax Savings
Purchase in November 2001	2001	$1,575	$545	
	2002	$2,667	$923	$1,468
Purchase in February 2002	2001	$0	$0	
	2002	$1,575	$545	$545

Assume $110,000 Income

	Year of Purchase	CCA Claim	Tax Savings	Total Tax Savings
Purchase in November 2001	2001	$1,575	$753	
	2002	$2,667	$1,276	$2,029
Purchase in February 2002	2001	$0	$0	
	2002	$1,575	$753	$753

Use CCA Deduction to Reduce Net Income

Reducing net income is especially beneficial as it is the figure on which CPP premiums are based. Because the proprietor must remit both portions of CPP premiums on his/her own behalf based on net income of the proprietorship, the acquisition of assets before year end can have the unexpected benefit of reducing CPP premiums. This is particularly important if the net income of the business is between $3,500 and $39,000, the point at which the maximum CPP premium is achieved. Every dollar the net business income is reduced within those net income ranges is worth marginally more. (When net income is above the maximum $39,000 threshold, there is no CPP premium savings effect.)

Therefore, by maximizing CCA in those income ranges, the deduction can have a bigger marginal impact as outlined in Figure 5-4.

Figure 5-4
Impact of CCA Deduction on CPP Premiums

Assumption: $20,000 is invested in Class 10 Assets (Computer Equipment) before year end. Net income from the proprietorship is $39,000.

CCA Deduction	Net Income	CPP Payable	Tax Liability	Total Liability*
$0	$39,000	$2,992.80	$6,945.87	$9,938.67
$3,000	$36,000	$2,795.00	$6,062.06	$8,857.06
Savings:		**$197.80**	**$883.81**	**$1,081.61**

*Includes CPP and federal/provincial (Ontario) taxes payable

It will become evident that decisions on whether to invest in income-producing assets this year or next, should be considered carefully in light of the cash flow savings that proper expenditure timing can reap.

3. The Company Car

Every new entrepreneur needs to brush up on the rules of tax deductibility when it comes to expenditures of "mixed use"—that is part personal and part business.

Heading up this list is the most common audit problem—a slam-dunk for the auditor one could say—the company car.

The costs of operating a vehicle used in the pursuit of business income are deductible, provided that any personal use component of the costs is removed from the deduction. Unfortunately, the way this is accomplished—and most people find this onerous—is to record all driving of the year, and then deliver accurate records of which were personal and business trips.

This effort provides your tax preparer and the tax auditor with a fraction with which to prorate the expenses incurred. In short, the following equation is used:

$$\frac{\text{Total distance driven for business purposes}}{\text{Total distance driven in the year}} \times \text{Eligible expenses} = \text{Deductible Expenses}$$

It is necessary, not optional, that a log be kept of business driving for use in a tax audit.

There are two types of expenses that can be claimed—fixed or operating. The fixed expenses are subject to deductibility restrictions in some cases, if you drive a "luxury vehicle." This is also known as a "passenger vehicle" in tax jargon.

Fixed Expenses

The maximum claimable amounts have been increased from time to time since 1987 and changes are usually announced in December for the following year. These amounts include:

- Capital cost allowance (subject to a maximum cost of $30,000 plus taxes at the time of writing)
- Leasing costs (subject to a maximum of $800 a month plus taxes)
- Interest costs (subject to a maximum of $300 a month).

The restrictions apply to "passenger vehicles"—cars that are designed to carry no more than nine individuals and which are considered to be "luxury vehicles" by virtue of their costs and their use. Each passenger vehicle is listed in a separate Class 10.1 and qualifies for a 30% CCA rate. All other deductibility rules are similar, including the half year rule on acquisition. However, on disposition, there is another "half year" CCA calculation and no further terminal loss write-offs are allowed.

This restricted classification can be avoided, if the vehicle is used more than 50% of the time to transport goods or equipment, in the case of a pick-up truck which seats one to three people. In the case of a van that seats four to nine people, the vehicle must be used 90% of the time to transport goods, equipment or passengers to avoid the restrictions. Keeping good records, therefore, can increase the claims you can make for your fixed expenses.

Operating Expenses

Operating expenses include the following items:

- Gas, oil, tires, maintenance and repairs, car washes
- Insurance, license fees, auto club memberships
- Parking (generally this is fully deductible and not subject to a proration for personal component).

Most taxpayers have little trouble keeping the receipts for those expenditures. They have more of an issue with a broader question—to buy or lease.

Should I Buy or Lease?

Whether a taxpayer should buy a car (and claim CCA and interest costs as a deduction) or lease a car is often a difficult decision because it is not always possible to make an "apples to apples" comparison.

In making the evaluation, both leasing costs and interest costs must be taken into consideration, and these factors are always changing. The question is further complicated if the "passenger vehicle restrictions" described above must be factored in. Finally, the taxpayer's income picture can vary significantly from year to year, which affects the tax savings outcome.

Leasing costs are written off equally throughout the life of the lease, and there is no option to postpone those deductions to future years when income is higher, except perhaps through non-capital loss applications.

Capital Cost Allowance, on the other hand, can be taken at the taxpayer's option and interest costs can be capitalized. So deferring these deductions to a future year in which income is higher can give the entrepreneur the biggest tax bang for the buck.

Figure 5-5 clarifies the comparison through an example.

Figure 5-5

Buy vs. Lease Option

Assumption: Taxpayer, living in Ontario, has a business loss in current year, but expects to earn net profits next year, putting her in the 22% federal tax bracket. The same vehicle (a delivery van) costs $35,000 to buy, with interest on a car loan of 3%, or $717 a month plus taxes to lease. The lease/financing costs run over five years. There is no personal use component and so the van is not considered a passenger vehicle subject to CCA/leasing or interest cost restrictions.

Year	Lease Costs	Tax Deduction	Tax Savings	Purchase Costs	Tax Deduction	Tax Savings
1	$4,302 *	$4,021	$0	$4,302 *	$0 **	$0
2	$8,604	$8,041	$2,595	$8,603	$12,389	$4,227
3	$8,604	$8,041	$2,595	$8,603	$8,734	$2,855
4	$8,604	$8,041	$2,595	$8,603	$6,100	$1,904
5	$8,604	$8,041	$2,595	$8,603	$4,177	$1,304
6	$4,302	$4,021	$1,297	$4,302	$9,167 ***	$3,017
Total	**$43,020**	**$40,206**	**$11,677**	**$43,016**	**$40,567**	**$13,307**
After Tax Costs			**$31,343**			**$29,709**

*Assumes 6 payments in first year, security deposits and down payments ignored
**Interest in first year is capitalized
*** Assumes vehicle is disposed of in year 6 (zero value)

In the scenario in Figure 5-5, the lease payments in the first year provide no tax savings because the individual is not taxable. If those payments increase or create a non-capital loss, savings may result from application of the loss to other income of the year or income of prior or future years in the carryover period.

This illustration highlights one of the drawbacks of leasing—leasing costs must be claimed in the year incurred and so there is less flexibility in claiming expenses to match economic changes in the taxpayer's business. When considering a vehicle purchase, discuss the following provisions with your advisor.

- Should interest expenses be added to the cost base of the car if deducting them is not beneficial?
- Should Capital Cost Allowance claims be reduced or not claimed at all if it is not beneficial to make the claim this year?

Remember, depending on circumstances, leasing costs can increase or create a non-capital loss that may offset other income of the year or other years in a carryover period.

Also, consider what are your after-tax results at the end of the ownership period? To compare "apples to apples," assume this is a lease with no residual value at its end and that the purchased vehicle is disposed of for a value of nil and therefore completely written off. What we see is that the purchased vehicle will provide a slightly better result, in this case. (Results will vary with classifications.)

Given the same pre-tax costs for a lease and the purchase of a motor vehicle used 90% or more for business use, the major tax differences in making the decision to lease or buy are in the timing of the deductions relating to size of income.

The moral? The decision to buy versus lease cannot be made without discussion with your tax advisor, without an understanding of the tax bracket and tax rates that will be applied to income from the business and without the actual crunching of the numbers to get the best result for your individual situation.

4. The Home Workspace

The self-employed may claim the costs of the home workspace used to run their business if one of the following conditions exists:

- The space is used exclusively to earn business income on a regular and continuous basis for the purposes of meeting clients of the business
- It is the principal place of business.

An area must be set aside to separate the workspace from the rest of the living area in the home and all expenses are then prorated by the following fraction:

$$\frac{\textbf{Square footage of the home}}{\textbf{Square footage of whole home*}} \times \textbf{Total Eligible Expenses} = \textbf{Deductible Expenses}$$

*all the living areas

The self-employed may claim the expenses listed, provided that they do not increase or create an operating loss. If they do, they must only be used to reduce net income to zero and the balance must be carried forward for use next year. Deductible home workspace expenses include the following:

- Utilities
- Maintenance and repairs including cleaning supplies
- Property taxes, insurance, mortgage interest
- Capital Cost Allowance (CCA) (not recommended as the exempt status of the principal residence is lost on the portion of the home on which CCA is claimed).

Start-up businesses should therefore partition the home workspace from other living areas of the home and provide receipts for the deductible expenses above.

6. Maximizing Income Diversification Opportunities

When a start-up takes flight and revenues begin to materialize on a regular and consistent basis, some planning is required to ensure that the business structure is still sound. Some factors to consider in that case are discussed in the following sections.

Retirement Savings

Entrepreneurs are responsible for their own pension plans. For this reason, once the business is generating revenues, compensation for the owner-manager should focus on maximizing RRSP contribution room. Within a proprietorship the net business income must be $75,000. Within a corporate structure, employment income of $75,000 must be paid in order to contribute $13,500 to an RRSP (the maximum contribution level until 2004, according to rules in effect at the time of writing).

Benefits of Incorporation

When is the best time to incorporate? Generally once the carry-back benefits of start-up losses are absorbed personally and revenues begin to flow, incorporation can provide an opportunity to diversify income sources (salary, dividends and capital appreciation) as well as to provide lower tax rates on the income itself, providing taxable income does not exceed the small business deduction level. In addition, incorporation provides limited liability to shareholders.

All forms of business organization—proprietorships, corporations and partnerships—provide an opportunity for income splitting with family members who work in the business. That is, provided that the family member is hired to do work a stranger would be hired to do and at the same compensation levels, the business can take a deduction for the amounts paid and the family member is allowed to report income earned without attribution.

Further, shareholders may receive dividends paid out of the after-tax earnings of the company. Dividends receive preferential tax treatment on the personal tax return in most provinces, particularly when taxpayers are in low tax brackets. It may be advantageous, for these reasons, to have adult children hold shares and to distribute dividend income to them, to pay for education costs. Distribution of dividends to minor children, however, is subject to a special "tax on split income," which taxes such distributions at the highest marginal rates.

However, there is also an important opportunity to split income on capital appreciation with family members who are shareholders of a small business corporation, which is an advantage over an unincorporated structure. That is, each individual may claim a lifetime $500,000 capital gains deduction on the gains realized on shares of a qualifying small business corporation.

Therefore, if properly set up, the ownership structure within a family business can provide for income splitting and capital splitting opportunities that will greatly increase the wealth of the family unit when the company is sold in the future.

Further, through the use of a planning technique known as an "estate freeze," the future capital appreciation of a corporation can be transferred to family members, while the current value of the corporation is frozen in the hands of the original owner. This limits the tax liability on deemed disposition of the company to other family members and later, upon the death of the original owner, to the current value of the company and maximizes everyone's use of the capital gains deduction.

These issues and other benefits of incorporation and business ownership should be discussed with the family tax lawyer and accountant because tough times can turn into lucrative times for many who find they must "buy themselves a job" by starting their own company.

THE PLAN

There are numerous tax planning options for Alex to consider in maximizing her opportunities to save taxes in the year her business starts, particularly with a $35,000 loss from the business before claiming her home workspace expenses.

1. Home Workspace Expenses

Alex cannot claim the expenses this year because a loss cannot be increased or created with this type of expense. However, expenses incurred this year can be carried forward to reduce her business income in 2002.

2. Excess Business Loss

Since her business loss also exceeded all of her other income ($15,000 from employment , $16,650 from EI and $400 interest), Alex has a net capital loss of $2,950 for the year. This net capital loss has several consequences for the family this year:

- **Spousal Amount.** With no taxable income of her own, Alex may now be considered dependent on John for tax purposes. Therefore, John may claim the spouse or common-law partner amount for her for the first time in many years.
- **Loss Carry-back.** Alex may carry the non-capital loss back to any of the prior three taxation years or carry it forward (for up to seven years). Three factors made Alex decide that carrying the loss back to 1999 was the most appropriate course of action:
  - Her 1999 income was higher than 1998 and 2000
  - The tax brackets in 1999 put Alex in the top marginal rate (29% federally)
  - The federal surtax was still in place in 1999.
- **Medical Expense Claim.** For the first time, Alex had medical expenses that were not covered by a group insurance plan. Unfortunately, with no taxable income, she could make no claim for these expenses. Had they exceeded 3% of John's income, John could have made a claim, but since they did not, no claim could be made in 2001. However, Alex will retain the receipts and possibly make a claim on her 2002 return.
- **Alex's RRSP Contributions in 2001.** These seem to have no beneficial effect for Alex since there is no taxable income. However, if funds had been available, an RRSP contribution would have increased the non-capital loss for the year, increasing the refund possible from applying the loss to 1999. Unfortunately, no funds were available in 2001 or early 2002.

3. Additional Tax Savers Using LSIF Strategies

For Alex, further options to increase tax refunds in 2001 are limited. As no taxes are being paid, deductions and non-refundable credits, including a Labour-Sponsored Fund Tax Credit cannot increase the refund. However,

John can use a contribution to a Labour-Sponsored Investment Fund (LSIF) as a strategy to increase cash flow for the family. By transferring $5,000 of his existing RRSP assets into a LSIF, John was able to increase his tax refund by $1,500.

4. Working with Capital Acquisitions

In 2002 Alex will need capital equipment. If she purchases the equipment in 2002, the half-year rule will reduce her claim to one-half of the normal amount. If that same equipment was purchased in 2001, the half-year rule would apply to 2001 and the full deduction would be available in 2002 to offset her projected business income for the year. With no taxable income in 2001, Alex could elect to include the interest costs in the capital cost of the assets and not claim any CCA in 2001 thereby increasing her available CCA claim for 2002.

However, after the $2,950 loss is carried back to 1999, there is still $1,370 of income in 1999 which is subject to the 29% rate and the federal surtax. Alex could decide to borrow money to purchase the new equipment late in 2001, deduct the small amount of interest payable on the loan and claim enough CCA to bring the non-capital loss to $4,320.

THE RESULTS

1. Carrying back Alex's $4,320 non-capital loss to 1999 results in a refund of $1,988 upon reassessment of the 1999 return.
2. When Alex's 2001 return is assessed, she will receive a tax refund of all taxes withheld from her employment income and Employment Insurance. This amounts to a refund of $3,161.
3. Claiming the common-law partner amount for Alex increases John's tax refund by $1,395. John's investment in a LSIF also increases his refund by $1,500. Along with the tax benefits of the monthly RRSP contributions John was making until Alex was laid off, John's refund is $3,246.
4. Total tax refunds of almost $8,400 will go a long way to reducing the mounting credit card debt in this year of change.

Tax Secrets

For Surviving Job Loss by Starting a New Business

1. **Maximize Tax Benefits on Start-up Losses.** As most start-up businesses lose money in their establishment, those losses can reap significant cash benefits if they are earned outside of a corporation. This is because non-capital losses can offset all other income of the year and if an excess loss occurs, it can be carried back to offset all other income of the prior three years or seven years into the future. This requires some important decision-making. For example, if you were employed at a high salary over the past three years and can apply non-capital losses to any one of them, you'll be able to recover taxes previously paid at old tax rates and brackets, which were higher than those we are subject to today. But if you expect to be in a higher tax bracket next year than you were this year or over the prior three years, it may make more sense to carry the losses forward.
2. **RRSP Contributions can Increase Non-Capital Losses Available for Carry-overs.** All self-employed taxpayers should focus on maximizing RRSP contributions. However, their tax benefits may allow the business owner to increase marginal tax benefits this year, particularly if the resulting non-capital losses are applied back to previous three taxation years, when taxes were higher than they are today. Remember not to waste RRSP contributions to reduce income that falls within tax free zones. Watch for potential to transfer personal amounts to supporting individuals if income is low.
3. **Increase Losses with Capital Cost Allowance Claims.** By acquiring assets at opportune times, losses claimable for tax refunds in current, prior or future years can be increased. Or, at the taxpayer's option, CCA deductions can be deferred for use against higher income in the future, while income-producing assets are put to work immediately. Finally, interest costs incurred to acquire capital assets can be capitalized at the taxpayer's option, thereby saving tax deductions for future use against taxable income.
4. **Never Waste Your Personal Non-Refundable Tax Credits.** Because CCA can be claimed at the taxpayer's option, it should be deferred in cases where personal amounts are unused due to low income. In such cases, also be sure that transferable provisions are used by a supporting person: the spousal amount, medical expenses, disability amounts, pension income amounts, tuition and education amounts, political contributions and charitable donations.
5. **Reduce Exposure To Social Benefits Clawbacks With CCA Claims.** If the taxpayer is close or over an income threshold which requires a repayment of a provision on the tax return or a benefit payable—Age Amounts, Old Age Security, Employment Insurance, Child Tax Benefits—use the CCA deduction to increase business losses or decrease net business income—to avoid these tax penalties.

6. **Acquire Assets at Year End to Accelerate CCA Deductions.** If you know that you must acquire new equipment, a new business vehicle or other assets for the business in the new year, it is often tax-wise to make that acquisition just before year end to accelerate the use of the CCA deduction and reap tax benefits one year sooner.
7. **Write Off as Much of Home Workspace as Possible—But Remove All Personal Use Components.** It is legitimate to write off certain costs of home ownership if this asset is used in the business to earn profits. However, it must be shown that no expenses for personal use are written off. In the case of the home workspace, that involves confining deductible expenses to the square footage of the space itself over the total square footage in the home. Remember also that home workspace costs cannot create or increase a loss, but if the costs exceed net business income, the balance can be carried forward for use next year.
8. **Deduct the Costs of the Company Car.** In the case of the vehicle, a distance log must be maintained to ensure that expenses are prorated according to business kilometres driven over total kilometres driven. Certain fixed costs are subject to annual or monthly maximum claims, therefore buying decisions should be made to capitalize on, but not exceed these maximums.
9. **Diversify Family Income with Incorporation.** Besides the limited liability that incorporation provides for the protection of personal assets, incorporation of a business whose revenues are growing over time can provide significant opportunities for preferential tax treatment. Future capital appreciation in the company can also be transferred to family members in order to maximize the use of each individual's lifetime $500,000 capital gains deduction. It is therefore important to speak to tax advisors about the future structure of the business to maximize tax savings opportunities through incorporation or the creation of a family trust, or both.
10. **Save Money on Sale of Business.** Every taxpayer may take advantage of one lifetime capital gains exemption of $500,000 on qualifying small business corporations or farms. By incorporating your business and naming family members as shareholders, it is possible to multiply that exemption to be worth millions of dollars in tax free gains in the future when the qualifying small business is sold.
11. **Business Acquisitions are Attribution Free.** A higher income earning spouse can provide an interest-free loan or gift of money to the lower earner to buy a business or start a business and the resulting income will be taxed to the lower earner, thereby circumventing normal attribution rules on the transfer of money between spouses.

12. **Borrow from Spouse or Non-arm's Length Lenders and Deduct Interest Costs.** The cost of money borrowed to finance business enterprises is deductible but borrowing from your spouse presents some interesting opportunites. Interest must be paid at prescribed or commercial rates at least once a year and no later than 30 days after year end. Interest costs on money borrowed to acquire assets can be capitalized, if the full interest deduction is wasted in a year of low income or unused non-capital losses.
13. **File Your Taxes Early and Do Some Planning.** April 30 is the tax filing deadline for most taxpayers. However, those reporting activities within a proprietorship have an extended deadline to June 15. But, if the proprietor has a balance due, interest will be charged back to May 1. It always pays to file the return on time, but to prepare a preliminary tax calculation early to maximize carryover provisions, RRSP and LSIF contributions and discuss changes to business organization with your advisor.

CHAPTER 6

Tax Breaks for Critical Illness

KEY PERSONAL TAX CONCEPTS:

- Most people are unprepared financially when critical illness strikes
- Taxation of wage loss replacement premiums/benefits is often misunderstood and over-reported, costing unnecessary tax dollars
- Income assistance from EI and CPP may aid the sick and the disabled—interesting tax consequences to know
- When private and public benefits collide, tax timing can leave taxpayers cash poor
- For those with a severe and prolonged impairment, the Disability Amount can be very lucrative
- Claiming medical expenses can be tricky—claim them all in the right year and on the right spouse's return
- Transferable provisions within the family can multiply benefits
- Think outside the normal "tax box"—tax role reversal is possible and beneficial for certain provisions on the return
- Caring for the disabled can reap tax rewards, including claims for non-refundable tax credits
- Attendant and nursing home care can be claimed to reduce taxes

REAL LIFE

Taxpayer, Tom Hardy age 40, is the owner of a small business corporation. He is married and his spouse, Emma, is a nurse earning $30,000 annually. She pays professional fees of $400 a year (GST included) and contributes to a company pension plan. (Emma was unaware that the GST portion of her fees qualified for a GST Rebate on Line 457 of her return.)

The Hardys are parents to one daughter, age 16, who has part-time earnings of $4,000 a year from various jobs. The family also looks after grandma, age 75, who is confined permanently to a bed and whose income is comprised of OAS, CPP survivors' benefit and RRIF withdrawals, all totalling $14,500. Her prescription costs are $1,000 and she qualifies for the Disability Amount.

Tom earns a salary of $75,000 from his job as a pharmacist and he maximizes his RRSP contributions. Tom has an emergency fund of six months salary invested in his non-registered account, following the advice of his financial planner. This turned out to be a good strategy. In July of 2001, Tom was involved in a serious car accident, leaving him confined to a wheelchair with spinal damage and chronic pain.

Tom has been contributing to a wage loss replacement plan as an employee through his company. The premiums payable each year were $1,000, funded 50% each by employer and employee. This plan has been in effect since Tom started working at the company, five years ago. Its long term disability benefits became available after 120 days, in the amount of 85% of his salary.

In the interim, Tom's wife was able to apply for CPP disability benefits, which were approved and received in January of the new year in the amount of $750 a month. This caused a repayment of wage loss replacement benefits which have to be reduced by the amount of the CPP benefits. Tom noted that CPP disability payments qualified to create RRSP contribution room, which Tom intended to make up once he recovered.

His medical costs for prescriptions and his wheelchair, together with ambulance costs totalled $1,650 and were covered by his group health plan. Eighty percent of his required new dental work was also covered. He suffered substantial damage to his teeth due to the accident, resulting in the need to cap front teeth at a cost of $2,000. However, home renovations to accommodate the wheelchair, for the whirlpool to accommodate treatments for chronic pain and the changes required to a new van purchased by the family were not covered. The total expenses here amounted to $15,000.

EI benefits were $418 a week and they began within a month of the accident and ended when wage loss replacement started after 120 days.

THE CHALLENGE

When tough times descend upon us, we are often forced to realize that from the moment of the occurrence, a new chapter in our life has begun and our future path must be re-evaluated. For many—letting go of the past—is the single most difficult concept to comprehend about change.

When the uncontrollable affects our family, our well-being and our finances, the challenge is to regain control, so that once again you can take responsibility for your life. Timing is key, as illustrated so well in this quote:

> The greatest potential for control tends to exist at the point where action takes place. (Louis A. Allen)

While the healing of body and soul will take time, financial circumstances must be dealt with immediately. When critical illness strikes, it is often in an unlikely place that financial relief can exist: the family tax filing profile. In the case of the Hardy family, it turned out that this was a good place to start in coping with the fallout of Tom's accident.

FACTORS TO CONSIDER

The taxation system provides a series of provisions and benefits designed to address the needs of the critically ill and their families, whether the circumstances are temporary or permanent. These provisions are best discussed in light of their categories on a tax return:

- Income
- Deductions
- Non-refundable tax credits
- Refundable tax credits.

1. Income Provisions

Income continuation is of utmost importance to the critically ill and their families and a number of factors put into place in normal times can come to the rescue when tough times strike. However, because a number of different income supports can be received over a period of time and some of them are reduced by others, the reporting of the income and deductions for repayments of benefits can be confusing. In some instances, these circumstances can also lead to cash flow problems if taxpayers are unprepared for the repayments. There are half a dozen common income sources discussed in sections below.

Wage Loss Replacement

If the employee's company offered a group benefits plan, wage loss replacement benefits will be available. There are two ways these plans can be funded:

- **With Contributions by Both Employer and Employee.** in this case, the benefits are taxable but any premiums paid by the employee (all the way back to 1968) can be used to reduce benefits received in the first year the benefits start. The taxpayer must attach a letter from the employer which verifies the amount of the premiums paid over the years, and then only the net benefits are reported on the tax return on Line 104 Other Employment Income.
- **With Contributions Funded by the Employee Only.** In this case, the benefits received are not taxable at all. It is for this reason that employees often arrange to have any premiums paid by the employer taxed back to them as a benefit on the T4 slip. This is important planning that can make a significant difference when critical illness strikes.

Often, employers will continue to pay employees their salaries until disability payments begin, when amounts advanced must be repaid. In those cases, the employee may claim a deduction for any repayments, unless it can be shown that the amount was a bona fide loan. In this case, the employer may calculate an imputed interest charge as a taxable benefit.

Where wage loss replacement payments are received in a lump sum for a period of time in which eligibility was being established, the lump sum qualifies for special tax averaging, if the amount exceeds $3,000. This will provide the same tax treatment as if the amounts were received in the appropriate tax years. However, given recent tax reductions, the averaging may not be of benefit to the taxpayer, in which case CCRA allows the most advantageous treatment. The averaging is requested on *Form T1198*.

Often, wage loss replacement plans are reduced by CPP Disability benefits. As the wage loss replacement usually begins first and the CPP Disability benefits are received retroactively, the CPP benefits are generally used to repay the amounts advanced by the wage loss replacement plan. When the repayment is made, a tax deduction can be taken on Line 232 Other Deductions.

Worker's Compensation Benefits

Sometimes, employees will qualify for Worker's Compensation Benefits. These benefits must be reported as income on Line 144, but they are subtracted again on Line 250. The effect of this tax treatment is to increase net income for the purposes of calculating other social benefits, but to render the payments themselves as not taxable.

Again, because of the time period it can take to establish eligibility, employers will advance payments to the employee. This is verified by an "award letter" provided by the employer to the employee. This can cause a series of confusing tax filing results over a period of years:

- If the employer has included amounts advanced in the T4 Slip as employment income (Box 14), it is important to report the income on Line 144 Worker's Compensation Benefits instead of Line 101. Subtract the amount on the award letter from the Box 14 amount before reporting net income, net of the advance payments.
- If the advance is later repaid out of the Worker's Compensation Benefits, subtract these repayments made on Line 232 as Other Deductions.
- Should the Worker's Compensation claim be denied, but the employer waives the requirement to repay the advance, an adjustment to the tax return will have to be made to reflect the fact that the amounts received are actually wages.
- If the claim is denied and the employer requires repayment of the amounts advanced, the reimbursements are deductible on Line 229 Employment Expenses.

In each of these cases, all other provisions on the tax return must be revisited as a result of the adjustments to ensure that refundable and non-refundable tax credits are claimed by the right spouse in light of the changing taxable income picture.

Employment Insurance Sickness Benefits

When these amounts are received they are reported as income. These benefits are not subject to the Social Benefits Repayment on Line 235, which is required by those receiving regular EI benefits when income exceeds $48,750. However, it is possible that these benefits are reduced by other income sources received at the same time. For these reasons, most long term disability benefits do not begin until the EI sickness benefit period has expired.

Disability Benefits from the Canada Pension Plan

These payments, which usually result from a lengthy review procedure, are often paid retroactively in a lump sum, causing the income of the disabled person to spike. In these cases, CCRA will again perform an averaging calculation if the taxpayer remits *Form T1198* and the amounts are over $3,000. Once again, each tax return should be reviewed in these cases to ensure that transferable provisions are claimed on the right tax return and that taxes applied to those prior years' income levels are in fact lower than if the lump sum had all been taxed in the year the amounts were received.

It is also important to note that CPP Disability Benefits qualify as "earned income" for the purposes of building RRSP contribution room. They also form part of net income of dependants being claimed by supporting individuals (see later discussion).

Income Replacement from Registered Investments

Difficult times brought on by serious illness often require income replacement from savings. RRSP deposits should not be tapped if possible, as the withdrawal will result in a taxable income inclusion of both principal and earnings.

If RRSPs must be tapped, withdraw the amounts in the hands of the spouse with the lower net income in the year (assuming both spouses have RRSP deposits). However, remember that before any withdrawal is made out of a spousal RRSP, that there are special rules: the amounts withdrawn will be taxed in the hands of the contributor unless the deposits have been in the spousal plan for at least three years from the last contribution.

When withdrawals are made out of an RRSP, a withholding tax is required to be made by the financial institution. This should be taken into account in planning the withdrawal, in particular if there are specific allocations for the money. The withholding taxes are:

- 10% on the first $5,000
- 20% on amounts between $5,000 and $15,000
- 30% on amounts over $15,000.

Finally, remember that if you are making taxable withdrawals, timing is important. As we expect taxes to go down again due to inflation-adjustment brackets and personal amounts, it is usually best to defer the realization of income to January of the next tax year or split the withdrawal over two taxation years. This is especially true, if by doing so, the taxpayer stays in one of the lower tax brackets or on the right side of social benefit clawback zones. (See Introduction and Chapter 1.)

If the taxpayer is tapping into an RRIF, the same principles apply: try to defer the amounts into the next tax year or split them into two tax years. Remember that if you are over the age of 65, taxable RRIF withdrawals could cost you more if the withdrawals put you into a clawback zone for the Age Amount or Old Age Security.

Income Replacement from Non-Registered Investment Accounts

When savings in non-registered accounts are tapped, the factors to be weighed in making the decision regarding which investments to withdraw include current and future rates of return, current and future appreciation and tax efficiency:

- **Debt Obligations.** Withdrawing money sitting in bank accounts at zero rates of return or GIC/Canada Savings Bond investments at rates of return under 2% are obvious choices. However, remember that 100% of any interest generated is added to income in the year of withdrawal and taxed at higher rates than dividends or capital gains. Alternate uses of those funds include flips into an RRSP or LSIF which could generate new capital by way of tax savings. Be sure to weigh those options carefully.
- **Equity.** Because the appreciation in value of income producing assets accrues tax free until disposition, it may be best to leave those investments to grow quietly. It may be the wrong time to generate losses, if losses are a reflection of market conditions, rather than the potential of the company. This is particularly true if there are no offsetting capital gains in the current year or prior three years. Speak to your financial advisor for an informed opinion on whether to wait for market improvements and better returns.
  - However, there are a couple of other factors to consider if tax circumstances are different. For example, if the taxpayer realized capital gains taxed at a higher rate in a prior year and the outlook for any further gains on the asset is now bleak, generating a capital loss that results in a refund of previously paid taxes may be better cash flow management than waiting for the benefits of a loss claimed several years down the road, particularly after the ability to reclaim the taxes on previously reported gains has evaporated.
  - Also, those income-producing assets may be generating income in the form of dividends, which are subject to preferential tax treatment. That tax-efficient income source may well be the answer to solving short term cash flow needs, if the investment is large enough.
- **Shareholder's Loans.** Within a small business corporation, shareholder's loans may be taken out of the company to fund family needs. An imputed interest charge is calculated based on prescribed rates of interest and reported as a taxable benefit to the shareholder/employee. The amounts may not remain outstanding indefinitely, however; otherwise they are included as income. As a minimum, the loan must be repaid within one year from the end of the company's fiscal year, and such repayment may be the result of a declaration of dividends, salary or bonus paid to the shareholder/employee by the corporation. Where shareholders' loans are used to fund new investments, the imputed interest included in income as a taxable benefit may be deducted as a carrying charge.

- **Systematic Withdrawal Payments.** Taxpayers who hold mutual funds may wish to begin making a periodic withdrawal of a fixed amount in which capital and income is returned. This may provide a tax efficient way to top up the cash flow needs of the family, while the investment as a whole continues to earn returns.

All of the options above and others suggested by your financial advisor should be discussed in detail before taking action. This discussion should include an understanding of any fees payable on disposition and the tax cost, using a preliminary tax calculation or tax estimator.

2. Deductions

There are few tax deductions specific to those who are critically ill as most income tax relief in this area comes in the form of non-refundable credits. However, indirectly the deductions are influenced by the personal circumstances discussed in the following sections.

RRSP Deduction

The deduction for RRSP contributions is important in calculating the family unit's ultimate tax results, as it reduces net income (Line 236) of the return. By reducing net income of someone who became disabled during the year, one could increase:

- A Spousal Amount claimable for the disabled person
- A Medical Expense claim
- Transfers of Age Amounts, Pension Income Amounts, Disability Amounts and Tuition and Education Amounts from the disabled person to a supporting individual
- Refundable tax credits like the Child Tax Benefit, GST Credit, or provincial credits.

Or one could decrease:

- Clawbacks of Old Age Security or Employment Insurance benefits on Line 235
- Clawbacks of the Age Amount
- Clawbacks of the Child Tax Benefit or GST Credits.

Otherwise, reducing net income with an RRSP contribution could help a taxpayer to save other discretionary provisions for future use like:

- The application of capital or non-capital losses
- The use of Capital Cost Allowance deductions

- The use of charitable donations (which can be carried forward for five years).

Child Care Expenses

There are several provisions that apply to the sick and disabled under this deduction, claimed on Line 214 and by completing *Form T778*:

- **Child Care for Severely Disabled Children.** When a child qualifies for the purposes of making a Disability Amount claim, the maximum amount of child care expenses claimable on the return increases over the normal levels ($7,000 for children under 7 and $4,000 for children between the ages of 7 and 16) to **$10,000**, regardless of child's age.
- **Claims by Supporting Individuals.** Generally the claim for child care expenses must be claimed by the person with the lower net income. However, when that person is incapacitated and confined for a period of at least two weeks to a bed or wheelchair or as a patient in a hospital, an asylum or other similar institution, the higher income earner may make the claim for the child care expenses, but on a restricted basis, as outlined in Part C of *Form T778*. Also see Tip Sheet—Child Care Expenses, Figure 1-13 in Chapter 1.

Attendant Care Expenses

When the sick or disabled person with a severe and prolonged mental or physical impairment is ready to go back to work or school, but requires a paid attendant for assistance to do so, a special tax deduction on Line 215 may be claimed. The amounts paid must be to an unrelated person over the age of 18. The lesser of two amounts may be claimed by those who are not attending school: (a) the actual amount spent or (b) two-thirds of earned income.

Students must follow these restrictions if they are attending a designated educational institute, claiming the least of:

- The actual amount spent
- Two-thirds of income from other sources
- $15,000
- $375 times the number of weeks the person is in attendance at the school.

3. Non-Refundable Tax Credits

The non-refundable tax credits that are specific to the circumstances of the sick and disabled or their supporting individuals are often missed on the return. They are detailed in Figure 6-1.

Figure 6-1
Non-Refundable Credits for the Sick and Disabled

Provision:	2002	2001
Infirm dependant amount	$3,605	$3,500
Net income threshold	$5,115	$4,966
Caregiver amount	$3,605	$3,500
Net income threshold	$12,312	$11,953
Disability amount	$6,180	$6,000
Disabled child amount	$3,605	$3,500
Allowable child care and attendant care expenses	$2,112	$2,050
Medical expense tax credit—3% of net income ceiling	$1,728	$1,678
Refundable medical expense tax credit supplement	$535	$520
Minimum earnings threshold	$2,676	$2,598
Family net income threshold	$20,296	$19,705

The Spousal Amount

If the person who normally is the higher income earner becomes disabled, there is a "tax role reversal." Therefore, the other spouse may be claiming the disabled spouse for the first time for this provision, if net income of the disabled spouse is under approximately $7,000.

The Amount for Infirm Dependants Age 18 or Older

This amount can be claimed by a supporting individual caring for an adult dependant other than the spouse: adult children, grandchildren, parents, grandparents, brothers, sisters, aunts, uncles, nephews or nieces, including in-laws. These relatives must be living in Canada and the credit is reduced by their net income above the threshold amount. (See Figure 6-1.)

The Caregiver Amount

Since 1998, Canadian families have been able to claim an additional credit that allows for a higher net income earnings level (as shown in Figure 6-1) in calculating the claim for an adult who is disabled and being cared for in the home. Originally, the provision was meant for those who care for their parents or grandparents who are 65 years of age or older. However, this credit can now be claimed by those who care for the same list of relatives as described earlier under the amount for Infirm Dependants age 18 or older. Only one of the two credits is claimable for the same dependant, however.

The Disability Amount

This is possibly one of the most lucrative, yet most missed provisions on the tax return. It requires the signing of a form by a medical practitioner—*Form T2201 Disability Tax Credit Certificate*—and if the amount is not needed by the disabled person because that person is not taxable, the amount can be transferred to a supporting individual.

It is meant to support those with a severe and prolonged ailment that is expected to last for a continuous period of at least 12 months. This means that if a person was diagnosed with cancer in September and the condition of the disease became debilitating by the end of the year, the amount would be claimable for the whole year.

The condition must "markedly restrict" the patient. Examples are:

- Blindness at any time in the year
- Inability to feed or dress oneself (or situations in which this is possible but only after taking an inordinately long period of time to do so)
- Inability to perform basic functions, even with therapy or the use of devices and medication. This can include:
  - Perceiving, thinking, remembering or other cognitive functions
  - Speaking to be understood by a familiar person in a quiet setting
  - Hearing to understand a familiar person in a quiet setting
  - Walking
  - Controlling bowel and/or bladder functions.

In addition, those persons who receive therapy to support a vital function, like kidney dialysis for an average of at least 14 hours a week, will qualify to claim this credit.

Since 2000, an additional supplement has been added to this credit for those who support disabled children. However, if the child care expenses are claimed for the child, the supplement will be reduced.

The Disability Amount can be transferred to a supporting person. If that person is a spouse, use Schedule 2 of the federal return; otherwise a special line is allocated for transfers from other dependants: Line 318. If you have missed claiming this amount in any year (all the way back to 1985), the tax benefits can be recovered by filing *Form T1-ADJ* (See Bonus Chapter: Digging for Gold at the end of this book.)

There are some special rules in making this claim to take note of, however, particularly when deliberating the costs of hiring outside care for a severely disabled person:

- The Disability Amount and the Deduction for Attendant Care Expenses may both be claimed on the tax return, however, that deduction could limit the Disability Amount supplement claimed for minor children
- The taxpayer cannot claim both the costs of nursing home care or full-time attendant care as a medical expense, together with the Disability Amount. One or the other can be claimed but not both.
- Those who pay someone to come into the home to provide care for the sick may claim expenditures up to $10,000 ($20,000 in the year of death) and then still claim the Disability Amount.

Medical Expenses

This tax credit was discussed at length in Chapter 1. Please see the Tip Sheet at Figure 1-14 that lists all the individual types of medical expenses that can be claimed on the tax return. This provision is often missed and, if this happens, the prior-filed returns can be adjusted. (See Bonus Chapter: Digging for Gold for an example.) Costs for devices and equipment specific to the disabled include the following:

- 50% of air conditioner costs if required by a person with a severe and chronic ailment
- Artificial kidney machine
- Artificial limbs
- Braces, crutches, dentures
- Electronic bone-healing devices
- Electronic speech synthesizers
- Extremity pumps used to reduce swelling
- Iliostomy or colostomy pads, hernia trusses
- Iron lungs, oxygen tent, rocking beds, wheelchairs.

Note: The cost of funerals, cremation, cemetery, burial, etc. are not deductible.

4. Refundable Tax Credits

The federal government provides a refundable credit of 25% of medical expenses claimed of up to $535 in 2002 ($520 in 2001) for those who have very low earnings, but big medical costs. This claim—a sister to the medical expenses claimed on Line 330—is made on Line 452 and is often missed. If this happened to you, file an adjustment to your prior-filed returns.

To qualify, family net income must not exceed $20,296 in 2002 ($19,705 in 2001) but the family must have at least $2,676 of "earned income" from employment or self-employment in 2002 ($2,598 in 2001). So this provision is not meant for seniors whose primary income sources are pension or investment income. In addition, because the provision is based on family net income, RRSP and other deductions that reduce net income on Line 236 may help to create or increase this claim.

Reap Benefits at Year End and in Claiming Quarterly Instalments

Missing any of these provisions can make a large difference on the tax results, and on a stressed family's finances. In particular, we all think of the refund at the end of the year. We also should adjust quarterly instalment payments normally made by the individual who has recently become sick or disabled. Never overpay those quarterly instalments, particularly when the income picture changes dramatically from one year to the next. To reduce instalment payments from the billings CCRA automatically sends out, complete *Form T1033*. (See Bonus Section: Digging for Gold for an example.)

And remember that reaching back to recover missed provisions of the past can be very lucrative. For example, a blind person who has missed claiming the Disability Amount every year since 1985 (15 tax years) will have a very large refund sent back. In a true story, the amount in a similar case reaped over five figures with interest.

THE PLAN

To recap, Tom's income picture in 2001 and 2002 looks like this:

	2001	2002
Employment Income	$38,000	$0
Wage Loss Replacement benefits (net of premiums paid)	$2,812	$54,750
CPP disability benefits		$13,500 *
EI benefits	$7,106	$0
Interest income	$800	$800
Less: Repayment of Wage Loss Replacement befefits	$1,500	
Taxable Income	$47,218	$69,050

* $4,500 of CPP will be taxed as if it was received in 2001 using CCRA's special averaging provision.

1. **RRSP Strategies.** In 2001, Tom's reduced income level and increased medical expenses make an RRSP contribution impossible. He has RRSP contribution room based on his salary in 2000. Going into 2002, his RRSP room is increased by 18% of his $38,000 salary before the accident. In 2002, the $13,500 CPP disability pension is considered "earned income" for RRSP purposes. Unless medical costs in 2002 are high, Tom will once again contribute to his RRSP, at least to reduce his taxable income to $63,354 (the upper limit of the 22% federal tax bracket).

2. **LSIF to the Rescue.** To help cash flow in 2001, Tom has had to dip into his cash reserves. One measure he can take to increase cash flow is to transfer a portion of his RRSP funds into a LSIF. By transferring $10,000 of his RRSP funds to a LSIF in the first 90 days of 2002, he can claim a tax credit of $1,500 on his 2001 and on his 2002 returns.
3. **New Disability Credits.** Tom will qualify for the disability amount in both years. In addition, he will be able to claim the Caregiver Amount for grandma and transfer the unused part of her Disability claim, that she does not need, to his return.
4. **Savings with Emma's Return.** With Emma's income level at $30,000 each year, she will be in a better position to claim medical expenses, which will be reduced by 3% of her lower net income. When Emma files her return, she will claim the Employee and Partner GST rebate of $26.17 on the GST included in her professional fees. Emma will also request prior years returns be adjusted back to 1991 to claim the GST rebate (and add the rebate into income the next year).

THE RESULTS

Tax benefits savings relating to illness and disability in 2001 and 2002 are as outlined in Figure 6-2.

Figure 6-2
The Hardy Family's Financial Summary

Tom 2001:

Provision	Federal		Provincial	
	Claim	Tax Savings	Claim	Tax Savings
Caregiver Amount	$953	$152	$976	$60
Disability Amount	$6,000	$960	$6,000	$370
Disability Transfer	$2,531	$405	$2,426	$149
Totals		**$1,517**		**$579**
Total 2001 Tax Savings:	**$2,096**			

Note: With the LSF tax credit, Tom's return showed a small refund of just over $600 for 2001. With reduced withholding amounts on his wage loss replacement plan benefits and CPP disability, an instalment calculation should be done for tax year 2002 to ensure Tom will not be required to make quarterly instalment payments in the new year. However, instalment payments need not be made until Tom's return shows a balance in excess of $2,000 for the current year and either of the two preceding years.

Tom 2002:

Provision	Federal		Provincial	
	Claim	**Tax Savings**	**Claim**	**Tax Savings**
Caregiver Amount	$1,417	$227	$1,440	$87
Disability Amount	$6,180	$989	$6,180	$374
Disability Transfer	$3,092	$495	$2,934	$178
Totals		**$1,711**		**$639**
Total 2002 Tax Savings:	**$2,350**			

Emma 2001:

Provisions	Federal		Provincial	
	Claim	**Tax Savings**	**Claim**	**Tax Savings**
Medical Expenses	$14,511	$2,322	$14,511	$894
Total 2001 Tax Savings	**$3,216**			

Emma 2002:

Medical expenses for 2002 are unknown at this time.

Tax Secrets

For Dealing with Critical Illness

1. **Wage Loss Replacement Benefits.** The tax bite on these benefits, taxable if the employer participated in funding premiums, can be reduced in the year in which they begin to be received by offsetting the benefits with all undeducted premiums paid by the employee since 1968.
2. **Repayments of Advances on Wages.** Any taxable amounts later repaid to employers who extended advances, such as EI benefits repaid or Worker's Compensation benefits repaid, can be claimed either as Employment Expenses on Line 229 or Other Deductions on Line 232.
3. **Keep RRSP Contributions Intact if Possible.** RRSP withdrawals are taxable, so if possible, those deposits should not be tapped when critical illness strikes a younger family. If necessary, RRSP withdrawals should be made by the lower income earner. However if the amount comes out of a spousal plan, be sure at least three years from the last spousal contribution has passed before making the withdrawal. If not, the withdrawal is taxed in the hands of the contributor—generally the higher income earner. If that higher income earner is now the disabled person with the low income, however, this may be your intended result. Speak to your tax advisor before making such withdrawals.
4. **Plan withdrawals for "Emergency Money" in Non-Registered Accounts Carefully.** Be conscious of the tax consequences of generating withdrawals from non-registered accounts and do so in relation to other income levels of the year, whether capital losses are available to offset capital gains or to what extent prior year carryovers can assist in reducing the tax bill due to the withdrawal. Try to preserve as much capital as possible. Always discuss any withdrawal with your advisor.
5. **Use RRSP Deductions Wisely in Times of Change.** Even in times of personal challenge, an RRSP contribution can leverage other tax provisions: a variety of non-refundable tax credits based on net income, the reduction of clawbacks and the preservation of provisions that can be used in carryover years. It is therefore important to do RRSP planning even in the bleakest of economic times.
6. **Child Care Expense Claims Increase for Disabled Children.** Be sure to claim these expenses under the special provision for disabled minors—a maximum dollar limit of up to $10,000.
7. **Personal Injury Awards and their Earnings are Tax Exempt for Children.** When an injured child receives a personal injury award, the award is tax exempt (as is the case for recipients of all ages) and all earnings on the reinvested award are tax exempt until the child turns 21.

8. **Attendant Care Costs can be Claimed by Disabled Employees or Students.** The costs of hiring an unrelated adult attendant to help a disabled person get ready for work or school can be used to reduce net income on the return.
9. **Tax Role Reversals are Important when Circumstances Change.** When the higher income earner becomes the lower earner, many tax provisions are claimed in reverse: for example, the spousal amount (or amount for common-law partner), medical expenses, political contributions, etc. Be sure to review the entire family's tax filing profile in the year of change.
10. **The Caregiver Amount is Available for In-Home Caregivers.** Many people miss this credit of over $3,600 available for those who care for parents, grand-parents or other infirm adults with net incomes around the $12,000 mark. Available since 1998, this amount should be reclaimed by adjusting prior-filed returns. It is available only if care is provided in the home.
11. **Lucrative Disability Tax Credits are Often Missed.** A severe and prolonged ailment that begins in the taxation year, markedly restricting the patient's daily living activities and expected to last for a continuous period of at least 12 months, will likely qualify for the lucrative Disability Amount. Most people miss this in the stress of coping with severe illness, and therefore it is important to know that these missed provisions can be recovered all the way back to 1985, providing a medical practitioner completes *Form T2201* to verify the condition.
12. **Medical Expenses are Often Missed.** The claim for medical expenses is restricted to amounts above 3% of net income and so a better benefit generally results when the lower income earner makes the claim—provided that person is taxable. Devices, prescribed treatments and prescriptions are claimable, as are the costs of travelling to a location that is at least 80 kilometres away to receive medical treatments not available in your own community. The expenses are claimed for the best 12-month period ending in the tax year—24 months in the year of death—and so should be carefully planned for the best tax results.
13. **The Refundable Medical Expense Supplement can Assist with Medical Costs.** The federal government provides a refundable credit of up to $535 in 2002 for those who have very low earnings, but big medical costs. This claim is often missed and should be applied for retroactively if this happened to you.
14. **Always Adjust Quarterly Instalments when Circumstances Change.** Do not further stress your family by overpaying quarterly instalments to the government, if income is going to be much lower in the current year than in the last. In that case, Form *T1033* can be filed to estimate instalments based on this year's income reality, thereby retaining more for the family income at a difficult time.

CHAPTER 7

Parting Intelligently—And With a Tax Viewpoint

KEY PERSONAL TAX CONCEPTS:

- In today's complicated world there are many dimensions to co-habitation—resulting in new tax definitions for spouses and common-law partners
- Numerous important tax preferences are available when families join or separate
- In the year of separation, tax planning is required to minimize tax on income before and after separation
- The liquidation of assets at the time of separation or divorce can bring about a windfall that must be properly accounted for and invested
- RRSP contribution room and rollovers must be maximized to benefit from refundable and non-refundable tax credits
- Tax on support of the family should be limited
- Legal fees for a separation or divorce are not deductible—costs should be limited in favour of tax-deductible alternatives
- Single again? Revisit the tax consequences of income sources, investments, child care, etc.
- The Amount for an Eligible Dependant for one child can increase "tax free zones" for single parents

REAL LIFE

Marie and Jason had lived together in a married union for a dozen years. In that time they welcomed three lovely little girls into their lives, now aged 4, 6 and 8 and Jason was their full-time caregiver. Marie, a successful television reporter with an annual employment income of $135,000, also received dividends of $48,000 more from her small business corporation, stemming from her efforts as a freelance public speaker. She is the sole shareholder.

Marie pays Jason $600 a month as her administrative assistant, work he does out of a home office space. He has no other income. The home workspace, exclusively set aside for this work, is 250 square feet within their 3,000 square foot home and utility, insurance, mortgage interest, repair and property tax costs, without a claim for capital cost allowance, are $25,000 annually.

Marie has been conscientious about maximizing her RRSP contribution room and has invested half into a spousal plan every year.

Recently, Marie's dynamic career took a difficult turn when local news services downsized and her position there became uncertain. She decided to accept a position covering international war zones for a national network—a decision that caused an irreparable rift with Jason. The couple decided to separate, agreeing Jason would have sole custody of the children and Marie would have unlimited visitation rights.

The family's assets would be divided. Besides the RRSP savings, their non-registered investments include a house valued at $500,000 (Adjusted Cost Base with all improvements is $350,000), stocks and bonds valued at $150,000 (ACB of $160,000) which yielded $9,000 in investment income in 2001 and a second residence in Phoenix, Arizona, which they use as a rental property for most of the year. The family vacationed there at Christmas and during spring break. The ACB of that property is $150,000 U.S. and its Fair Market Value is $180,000 U.S. The net revenue earned from the property each year is $700 U.S. a month for ten months, before depreciation.

Marie and Jason wanted to minimize their legal costs, which were not tax deductible, split assets in a fair and equitable manner and continue investing in their children's bright futures.

THE CHALLENGE

This family had the right attitude going into a difficult period in their lives. They needed to set up the future, but understood resources would be limited for some time in the present in order to do so. They also understood that the tax system could provide some assistance in the process.

To begin, it was important to assess the resources required to meet basic needs of two households. The investment strategies for education, retirement and lifestyle then needed to be analyzed for all family members, with a view to maximizing tax provisions now available as a result of the new marital status.

How much more would they need to run separate households? What could the tax system provide? That was the challenge. A look at the tax consequences of their changes was a good place to begin deliberations.

FACTORS TO CONSIDER

In Canada we tax individuals rather than household units. This is so that each individual can take advantage of progressive tax rates. That is, lower earners pay little or no taxes; higher earners pay more.

As well, certain personal amounts provide a "tax free zone" to account for non-discretionary spending of the individual families. This includes a basic personal amount for each family member (but this is only valuable when each member earns taxable income). It also includes provisions for those who support spouses who do not work, children going to post-secondary school, the sick, the disabled and the elderly.

Depending on the family net income level, it is also possible to benefit from certain refundable tax credits that target the needs of children and compensate those who are forced to pay GST on non-discretionary items, despite very low income levels (the Canada Child Tax Benefit and Goods and Services Tax Credit, respectively).

With the exception of those special provisions, the sole earner must bear the tax cost of all earned income. That higher earner is also prohibited from reducing that load by transferring income or assets to the lower income earner, to take advantage of lower tax rates on that person's lower tax bracket. If such transfers take place, the income is "attributed back" to the higher income earner.

However, spouses and common-law partners can avoid those attribution rules in limited circumstances, as previously described in Chapter 4:

- When spousal RRSP contributions are made
- When income results from investment for which bona fide loans were drawn up between the spouses and interest is actually paid at least once a year during the year or within 30 days after the year end

- When taxable profits result from investments in a business
- When attributed income (second generation income) is reinvested
- Upon transfer of assets resulting from marriage breakdown.

So when a couple separates, each person will be taxed as an individual, income and assets will be separated and refundable and non-refundable tax credits will be allocated based on individual net income levels. Spousal RRSP contributions will no longer be allowed and income attribution becomes a non-issue. In fact, in some respects, it might be easier to accomplish some financial goals as non-arm's length individuals.

For one thing, it is easier to transfer income and property to an ex-spouse or ex-common-law partner. That's because under subsection 74.5(3) the attribution rules do not apply to any income or loss from property that relates to the period the individual is living separate and apart from their spouse because of marriage breakdown or the breakdown of a common-law partnership. More on that later.

In the comments above, two important terms were mentioned: spouse and common-law partner. Those terms have recently been changed for tax purposes.

When a union begins, a couple is considered for tax purposes to be in a conjugal relationship if they are members of the opposite sex and legally married, or in certain cases if they are in a common-law relationship. Effective the 1993 tax year, at least one of two conditions must exist to meet that common-law definition:

- Individuals living common-law must be of the opposite sex, living together as of December 31 of the tax year and have done so for a period of at least 12 months before this date either in the tax year or in any prior year or
- The individuals must be the natural or adoptive parents of a child who lives with the couple.

We have since built on that definition. In 2000, same sex partners who live together in a conjugal relationship could choose to be recognized as "common-law spouses" for tax purposes with transitional provisions to allow optional reporting in 1998, 1999 and 2000, under the same two conditions described above.

Starting in 2001 the term "spouses" would refer only to couples of the opposite sex who are legally married. All other common-law unions—same sex or opposite sex—would be identified with the term "common-law partners."

When a union ends, in general, a couple is considered to be separated if they cease co-habitation for a period of at least 90 days. Should the couple reconcile before year end, the spouse/common-law definition resumes, even if the separation exceeded the 90-day period. A couple need not be legally or formally separated for the tax provisions supporting divided families to begin.

Pre- and post-separation returns become an issue when separation occurs. Before separation, the household was required to observe and claim, as appropriate, the following tax provisions:

- The Spousal RRSP contribution provisions
- Child Care Expense provisions (usually claimed by the person with the lower net income)
- Moving expenses (claimable by either spouse as long as each had income in the new location)
- The Spouse or Common-law Partner Amount (to account for the support of a spouse with little or no income)
- Transferable Amounts, including the Age Amount, the Pension Income Amount, the Disability Amount and Tuition and Education Amounts, available if the spouse is not taxable
- Provisions claimable by either party include Medical Expenses, Charitable Donations, Political Contributions
- Labour-Sponsored Fund Tax Credits (when contributed to a spousal RRSP, either could claim the tax credits)
- Provisions based on net family income: Child Tax Benefits, Goods and Services Tax Credits, other provincial refundable tax credits.

In addition, family assets were pooled on a "per household basis." Provisions specific to family assets include the following:

- One tax-exempt principal residence was allowed per family unit
- Other assets were considered owned by the individual who earned the money to acquire the assets with subsequent gains or losses attributed to that person
- Transfers of those assets to the spouse during the other's lifetime generated a tax consequence
- Upon death of one spouse in the family, a tax free rollover of family assets to the surviving spouse is allowed.

Some of these provisions were discussed in detail in the context of use by a married couple in Chapter 1. When couples break up, however, the following new factors must be considered, relating to these provisions.

1. Unmatured RRSPs and RRIFs

Funds that have accumulated in RRSPs may be rolled over on a tax free basis to the ex-spouse when the parties are living apart and if the payments follow a written separation agreement, court order, decree or judgement. The transfer must be made directly between the RRSP plans of the two spouses and one spouse cannot be disqualified because of age (over age 69). The same rules for tax free transfer of funds apply to RRIF accumulations. *Form T2220* is used to authorize the transfers between the plans.

2. Spousal RRSPs

Accumulations can be withdrawn from spousal RRSPs upon marriage/partnership breakdown without generating the attribution rules when three years have not lapsed since the last spousal RRSP contribution.

3. Child Care Expense Provisions

When there is a marriage breakdown, child care expenses paid by each parent who subsequently looks after the children may be claimed under the rules extended to individuals. That is, there is no need for the parent with the lower net income to make the claim.

However, there is a specific tax twist to be aware of should you reconcile within the first 60 days of the next tax year. In that case, you are considered to be spouses/partners for the whole of the prior year (regardless of how long your separation was in the year before) and so the normal rules requiring deduction of child care by the lower earner, except in specific instances, will apply. See Chapter 1 for more details on making this claim.

4. Moving Expenses

The costs of a family move can only be claimed if the move was at least 40 kilometres closer to a new work or business location and the taxpayer had income at that new location. Therefore one spouse could pay the ex-spouse to move, but then the ex-spouse would claim the moving expenses, providing receipts were available. This would include the list of expenses itemized and discussed in Chapter 1.

5. The Spouse or Common-law Partner Amount

In the year of separation, the spousal amount is based on net income of the spouse before the separation. Therefore, to get the biggest benefit, one could plan:

- To separate early in the year (e.g. January 2)
- To reduce the spouse's net income with RRSP contributions.

After separation, there is no further claim for the spouse on the tax return under this provision. However, it may be possible to receive a tax deduction for spousal support payments or alimony and it may be possible to claim an "Amount for an Eligible Dependant" (formerly known as the Equivalent-to-Spouse Amount) elsewhere on the return.

6. Transferable Amounts

The Age Amount, the Pension Income Amount, the Disability Amount and Tuition and Education Amounts are no longer transferable between former spouses after separation.

7. Provisions Claimable by Either Party

Medical Expenses, Charitable Donations, Political Contributions are not transferable, but must be claimed on an individual basis.

8. Labour-Sponsored Fund Tax Credits

Those tax credits are earned and claimed individually. When contributed to a spousal RRSP before separation, either could claim the tax credits. Each newly separated spouse should look into this investment anew, if s/he has taxable income, as the credits can be used to fund life insurance policies, RRSP contributions or RESPs for the children if money is otherwise tight.

9. Refundable Tax Benefit Provisions based on Net Income

The Canada Child Tax Benefits, Goods and Services Tax Credits and other provincial refundable tax credits are all based on the individual's net income, not on combined net family income. This generally provides for much larger credits or the creation of first time credit receipts in the hands of the lower income spouse/partner.

However, there is another important provision that can bring significant money to a separated family immediately—CTBs can be paid retroactively for each month after separation based on the new net income of the separated family. The new net income should be disclosed to CCRA immediately after separation so that the benefits begin immediately. But if you miss doing so and if you notify CCRA before the eleventh month following separation, revised benefits will be received for each month after separation.

10. Other Family Assets

Tax treatment after separation of other assets belonging to the family is the following:

- **One Tax-exempt Principal Residence.** After separation, CCRA recognizes two family units and therefore it is possible for each to own one tax exempt residence. This provides for a more lucrative legacy for the children of the union.

- **Matrimonial Property.** Property brought into the marriage by one of the spouses will be considered owned by that person. Generally the property is then assigned to that person during the creation of the separation agreement. While this can vary with individual circumstances and in individual provinces, however, these general rules make it possible to obtain Adjusted Cost Base (ACB) information for the purposes of splitting the pool of assets.
- **Transfer of Property.** Property transferred upon relationship dissolution can be transferred at its ACB, (Undepreciated Capital Cost (UCC) in the case of depreciable property) so that there are no tax consequences at the time of transfer. This applies to property in settlement of marital property rights as well as any other voluntary transfers.

  That effectively transfers any accrued gains on the property from its original acquisition to the transferee.

  By special election, however, assets may be transferred at their Fair Market Value (FMV). This could result in significant tax savings if, for example, the transferor had unused capital losses to apply to the transferred property. The transferee would also receive a significant tax benefit in that future capital gains would be calculated based on the FMV at the time of transfer. Further, if the FMV of the property is less than its ACB, it may be advantageous to trigger the capital loss for application to other capital gains of the year, the previous three years or gains in the future.

  Also remember to take into account any capital gains election the individuals may have made in February 1994 and apply the elevated ACB to the deemed disposition brought on by the relationship breakdown.

  There are also changes in tax treatment of any property which was previously transferred to a spouse during the marriage/partnership and subject to the Attribution Rules (income earned on the property was attributed back to the transferor). The income attribution ends when there is a separation, providing that an election to this effect is made in the year of separation or after separation and providing that the couple continues to live apart. Therefore the new owner of the property after the relationship breakdown is responsible for all subsequent tax consequences on the earnings and capital appreciation (depreciation) of the property.

11. Ongoing Maintenance and Support

Finally, perhaps the most important tax provisions of all apply to the most contentious part of most separation agreements: the ongoing support of spouse and children. Here are factors to consider in striking a tax-efficient settlement:

Legal Fees

From a tax point of view, it is important to mention legal costs first in planning for relationship dissolution, for these reasons: legal fees to get the separation or divorce and establish rights to alimony and maintenance are **not** tax deductible. That means that if you are taxed in a 30% tax bracket, you'll have to earn $13,000 to pay a $10,000 legal bill. Think about that carefully. Wouldn't that money be better spent shoring up the children's RESP? Or by reaping tax rewards by topping up your or your former partner's RRSP? The best tax advice anyone can give a separating couple regarding the legal process, therefore, is the following: minimize non-deductible outlays.

Note that legal fees incurred to enforce payment of a previously established right to child support are deductible, however. This is allowed even if the payments are not taxable, as discussed below.

Spousal Support

Spousal support is taxable to the recipient and deductible to the payor, if certain conditions are met:

- The amounts paid are pursuant to a written separation agreement, judgement, order or decree
- The parties were separated and living apart when the payments were made
- The parties continued to live apart for the remainder of the year
- The payments were made to the former spouse or a third party for the maintenance of the spouse or children of the union
- The payments were made on a periodic basis (lump sum payments are not deductible).

Because of the taxable status of spousal support, tax planning is required for both recipients and payors to minimize tax erosion for the family as a whole.

Recipients of Taxable Spousal Support Payments

These taxpayers must set aside some money to pay for taxes at year end, and if amounts owed to CCRA are over $2,000 in the current year and either of the preceding two years, quarterly instalment payments will be necessary. This must be factored into cash flow planning.

In addition, taxable spousal support qualifies as earned income for RRSP purposes. Therefore, tax liabilities can be reduced by making RRSP contributions. That opens the possibility of making a Labour Sponsored Fund investment within the RRSP, which will create up to $1,500 in tax credits in some provinces (as discussed in Chapter 1, see Tip Sheet—LSIF).

Payors of Deductible Spousal Support Payments

Those who make spousal support or alimony payments may deduct these amounts on the tax return. The amounts so deducted also reduce RRSP contribution room.

It is important to identify amounts that are solely for spousal support in the agreement. Otherwise the amounts will be considered to be child support which is not taxable to the recipient or deductible to the payor.

Also, if payments are in arrears, all payments are considered to be non-deductible child support payments first. Only when all payments are current will deductible status be restored to spousal support. (See further details on child support below.)

Payors of support should review tax withholding at source by employers or quarterly tax instalment payments which can be reduced to account for these deductible payments.

Structuring Tax-Efficient Spousal Support

If the spouse has no other income, it would be wise to structure taxable spousal support payments according to the person's "tax free zone." This would normally be the Basic Personal Amount plus RRSP contributions and, if there are children, child care costs and the Amount for an Eligible Dependant.

For example, assume that a lower income spouse (no children involved) is negotiating for taxable spousal support payments for 2002. To arrive at a tax-efficient number, consider the following:

- The Basic Personal Amount is about $7,600
- The RRSP contribution will be $1,300 (that is 18% of earned income in the prior year, which was comprised of $7,400 in support equal to the Basic Personal Amount in 2001).

A taxable spousal maintenance amount of $8,900 (or $742 a month) could be paid before the recipient would be taxable. The $8,900 deduction allowed to the payor, on the other hand, would reap tax savings of almost $3,600, given a 40% marginal tax rate, money that could be reinvested in the payor's RRSP for future wealth accumulation.

And if the same general plan was followed each year, using the Basic Personal Amount as a base, an inflation-adjusted raise in payments, RRSP contributions and deductions would be built in for both parties.

Child Support

Child support payments negotiated after April 30, 1997, will not be taxable to the recipient or deductible to the payor.

Pre-May 1997 agreements will continue to be recognized—that is, payments for child support will continue to be deductible to the payor and taxable to the recipient, unless a joint election is filed with the CCRA to choose tax-exempt treatment under the new rules.

Payments from Non-Residents

Since 1985, based on an agreement in the Canada-U.S. Tax Treaty it is also important to note that Canada has agreed not to tax child support payments received from a U.S. resident. Similar treaties may exist with other countries and this should be explored with the CCRA, who can provide such information on an individual and current basis.

Amount for an Eligible Dependant (formerly Equivalent-to-Spouse Amount)

The recipient of the support payments will generally claim this credit, which mirrors the Spousal Amount available to married couples/common-law partners. (Note: Only one claim for the same dwelling and the same child per year).

However, because the amount is based on the net income of the child, this claim is generally more lucrative for single parents, who almost always benefit from the full claim of approximately $6,500 annually.

Also, it is important to note that if the couple reconciles before year end, it is still possible to make a claim for the Amount for Eligible Dependants, provided that the criteria for the claim is otherwise met (you must be separated and living apart from your spouse and supporting the dependant, who is under 19 in a home maintained by you). In addition, you must not have claimed an Amount for Spouse or Common-law Partner during the year.

THE PLAN

Jason and Marie decide to first review their current tax filing situation in order to understand their combined tax burdens as a married couple, including benefits received from refundable credits and non-refundable credits. A summary can be found in Figure 7-1.

Figure 7-1

Jason and Marie's Financial Summary—Before Separation

Before Separation	Jason	Marie
Total Income	$5,117.50	$217,780.00
Net Income	$5,047.94	$201,280.00
Taxable Income	$5,047.94	$201,280.00
Non-refundable credits	$1,197.05	$1,865.75
Taxes Payable	$139.11	$64,648.98
Marginal Tax Rate	0%	46.4%
GST	$0	
CTB	$0	

They must now explore the options under the new situation, taking into account the following:

1. Jason stops working for Marie, but she pays him taxable spousal support in the amount of $600 a month. Half of the family's non-registered investment portfolio—attributed entirely to Marie—is rolled over to Jason, by election at FMV*. This is reported as a taxable disposition on Marie's return. To minimize the tax liability, Marie chooses a date of separation in a period when the market has plunged. Her assets are therefore deemed disposed of at the low market values in effect as of that day. The Fair Market Value (FMV) of the assets on disposition becomes Jason's Adjusted Cost Base (ACB). He will pay taxes on later disposition based on this value (plus any improvements or additions made in the future).

* Long term use of losses and future tax liabilities should be contemplated carefully in choosing ACB or FMV.

The following shares will be transferred to Jason:

Number or shares	Stock Symbol	ACB	FMV	Gain (Loss)
500	Bell Canada Ent.	$6,750	$16,125	$9,375
500	Nortel Networks	$30,000	$5,875	($24,125)
500	Royal Bank	$15,500	$24,800	$9,300
1000	Lucent Tech.	$3,950	$6,600	$2,650
	Gov't of Canada Bonds	$23,800	$21,600	($2,200)
	Total	**$80,000**	**$75,000**	**($5,000)**

2. All RRSP accumulations are split equally and transferred on a tax free basis to Jason's and Marie's individual accounts.
3. Child support in the amount of $600 a month per child is paid—but is non-deductible and not taxable. Jason uses this money to fund basic needs of the children.
4. It is decided that the $500,000 family home should be sold, each moving into a smaller home. Marie will rent and invest her share of the equity; Jason will live in a 2,000 square foot home with a value of $200,000. He will invest the balance of the equity ($50,000) to provide additional income. The sale of a family home is a tax-exempt transaction. However, because the family has another property in Phoenix, they must consider which home should be considered that tax exempt principal residence. As that property has approximately the same value as Marie's small business corporation, she is considering giving the property to Jason in return for his agreement that she retains full rights, control and all inherent value in the SBC. The family needs to understand the tax consequences.
5. Marie will make third party payments directly to the children's dentist and doctor. She will recover costs through her medical plan at work. Jason's medical coverage will end, but his spousal support will be used to cover the costs of a separate plan for him, together with a small life insurance policy.
6. Child Tax Benefits received will fund the children's education, as will the benefits of the Amount for an Eligible Dependant (formerly Equivalent-to-Spouse Amount).
7. All pension rights—public and private—were split by agreement, as accrued up to the date of separation.

THE RESULTS

Before taking into account any of the options, the separation would have the effects as outlined in Figure 7-2, on Jason's and Marie's current tax situations, if all things remained equal.

Figure 7-2
Jason and Marie's Financial Summary—After Separation

After Separation	Jason	Marie
Total Income	$5,117.50	$217,780.00
Net Income	$5,047.94	$201,280.00
Taxable Income	$5,047.94	$201,280.00
Non-refundable Credits	$2,204.09	$1,565.74
Taxes Payable	$139.11	$64,921.68
Marginal Tax Rate Before Credits	0%	46.4%
GST	$741	
CTB	$7,161	

- Marie would pay $272.70 more taxes because she would lose the Spousal Amount
- Jason may claim the Amount for an Eligible Dependant for one of the girls—but this would have no tax effects at his income level
- Jason is eligible for $741 (more) GST
- Jason is eligible for $7,161 (more) CTB
- Total benefits of separation to this family, before accounting for actual financial consequences of property transfers and income support payments are **$7,629** or $636 a month (GSTC plus CTB less $272.70 more in taxes paid by Marie).

Now let's take a look at this family's tax consequences when spousal support and asset transfers are taken into account:

1. **Taxable Spousal Support.** The effects of the spousal support option are:
   - Jason's taxable income increases by $7,200 from this source, but this is cancelled out with his Basic Personal Amount and so he has no tax to pay here.
   - Marie's taxable income decreases by $7,200, reducing her tax bill by $3,132.64.
2. **Loss Application.** Marie will report an allowable capital loss of $2,500 (50% of $5,000 loss) as a result of the splitting of the non-registered portfolio. This will not affect the current year return but will fetch a refund of more than $1,000 when applied against prior year gains.

3. **Creation of Investment Income.** Marie's investment income will be cut in half by this transaction and Jason will have investment income to report for the first time. This will have income tax consequences and will reduce the Child Tax Benefit.
4. **No Tax Consequences: RRSP and Child Support.** There are no tax consequences regarding the payment of the child support or splitting of the RRSP funds. Third party payments for the children's benefit will have no tax consequences.
5. **New Amount for an Eligible Dependant (formerly Equivalent-to-Spouse Amount).** This tax provision for single parents reaps $6,500 in non-refundable tax credits for one of the children on Jason's return, increasing his "tax free zone." Jason can therefore earn about $6,500 more and still pay no taxes.
6. **Dealing with Family Residences.** By designating the family home as their principal residence, a gain of $150,000 is exempt from taxes. If the Phoenix home were to be designated, the $30,000 U.S. would be sheltered. Therefore it makes more sense to designate the family home in Canada as the tax exempt property.

   If the family home is consequently sold and designated as the couple's principal residence, there are no tax consequences. Marie's investment income will be increased because she will invest her portion of the proceeds. Jason will have $50,000 to invest as well, thus increasing his investment income and tax liability.

   If the Phoenix property is transferred to Jason at cost, there will be no immediate tax consequences. However, the rental income from the Phoenix property will now be reported by Jason and will have the following consequences.

   - The additional $10,780 rental income will add $1,480 to Jason's tax liability.
   - The rental income will also add to his RRSP contribution room.
   - The CTB will be reduced by about $400 by this income.

Jason also bears the full tax load of capital appreciation on a future sale of the property.

In summary, based on an estimated 5% return on investment income, Jason and Marie's income tax results after the separation are detailed in Figure 7-3.

Figure 7-3
Jason and Marie's Final Financial Summary

After Separation	Jason	Marie	Tax Savings
Total Income	$29,348	$211,250	
Net Income	$25,278	$190,550	
Taxable Income	$25,267	$190,550	
Non-refundable credits	$2,204	$1,566	
Taxes Payable	$1,947	$60,150	$2,691
Marginal Tax Rate*	48.1%	46.4%	
GST	$741		$741
CTB	$6,027		$6,027
		Total	**$9,459**

* Jason's marginal tax rate is high because he is in a CTB clawback zone.

Together Jason and Marie reap more than $17,000 in disposable income after the break-up (mainly as a result of investing the proceeds from the sale of their former home), but pay $9,459 less in taxes between them, when social benefit payments are taken into account. This will assist in the costs of running two households.

Further tax benefits can be obtained by creating Labour-Sponsored Fund Tax Credits, (up to $1,500 each in Ontario) if their financial plan can accommodate the risk and reward scenario this investment brings with it.

Clearly they are financially better off apart as a result of their planning decisions, even when bearing the costs of two households. This plan allows the family to carry on with little substantial change in their overall lifestyle in the short term and makes the trauma of their changes in tough times somewhat easier to deal with.

Tax Secrets

For Parting Your Ways Financially Sound

1. **In Contemplating Separation, Define Pre- and Post-tax Positions.** To fully understand the impact of separation on a family's after-tax financial position, it is important to review existing tax burdens to properly compare tax costs and cash flow after separation.
2. **The Progressive Nature of the Tax System can Work in a Separated Family's Favour.** Separation brings about income splitting, which can be advantageous under our progressive tax system. That is, the same income transferred to a lower income earning spouse/common-law partner can reap higher after-tax rewards.
3. **Provisions for Family Fairness and Equity can also Reap Tax Rewards.** Families at low income levels are supplemented in their living standards with certain "tax free zones"—non-refundable tax credits—and certain social benefit payments—refundable tax credits. These provisions can increase after-tax results by thousands of dollars annually for a separated family.
4. **The Tax Free Zone for Single Parents is Approximately $14,000.** A single parent can claim a Basic Personal Amount of approximately $7,600 and an Amount for Eligible Dependant for one child in the amount of approximately $6,500 in 2002; allowing for a tax free zone of around $14,000 or close to $1,200 a month. This should be taken into account in planning taxable spousal support payments. In fact, couples can create an "inflation-adjusted raise" for the recipient of the support payments by linking the payment amounts to the non-refundable tax credits available each year.
5. **Spousal Support is Taxable but Creates RRSP Contribution Room.** By contributing 18% of taxable spousal support received, lower income earners can top up their retirement savings and reduce net income for the purposes of calculating GST Credits and Child Tax Benefits.
6. **Multiply RRSP Tax Savings with an LSFTC.** If the RRSP contribution is invested in a Labour Sponsored Investment Fund, a further tax credit of up to $1,500 can be created (15% of the investment up to a maximum investment of $5,000 is available from both the provincial and federal governments in most provinces). This will only be of benefit to those who have federal/provincial taxes payable. The resulting tax credit can be reinvested in next year's RRSP contribution, or fund children's education savings or life insurance premiums for the single parent.

7. **Spousal Support Payments are Tax Deductible if Periodic.** This can save tax dollars—the more savings, the higher the payor's income—but the deduction will reduce RRSP contribution room. Those resulting tax savings can be used to fund RESP or other education savings for the children or the payor's own RRSP accumulations.
8. **Child Support Payments are Not Taxable or Deductible.** This is true if the separation agreement was negotiated after April 30, 1997, or old agreements were revised by mutual election to be treated as non-taxable/deductible. Otherwise, payments for agreements in effect prior to May 1, 1997, will still be taxable to the recipient and deductible to the payor.
9. **Income Attribution Ends After Separation.** Assets that were transferred to the spouse during the conjugal relationship were subject to income attribution except under very specific instances (i.e., when a spousal RRSP contribution is made, when a bona fide loan is drawn up or if the principal is invested to earn business profits). However, after separation, that income is properly taxed to the transferee, providing both parties make an election to agree to this.
10. **Capital Property of the Failed Relationship can be Transferred at FMV or ACB.** It is possible to divide the property of the failed union by transferring it at either its Adjusted Cost Base (in which case there are no immediate tax consequences) or at its Fair Market Value (in which case certain tax consequences can bring an immediate tax advantage). These options require careful review before agreements for separation and transfer of assets can be finalized.
11. **RRSP and RRIF Accumulations are Transferred on a Tax Free Basis.** By using *Form T2220*, registered assets can be split and transferred without tax consequence. Even the three year holding rules for spousal RRSP accumulations can be avoided upon relationship breakdown.
12. **Lower Income Earners can Now Claim Child Care Expenses.** When a couple is in a conjugal relationship for tax purposes, the child care expenses paid for care of children while parents work must be claimed by the person with the lower net income, except in very specific circumstances (see Chapter 1). After separation, each parent can claim their own child care expenses, until they begin co-habiting with another partner in the future.
13. **Time Separation to Maximize the Spouse or Common-law Partner Amount.** Because this approximately $6,500 amount is based on the spouse's/common-law partner's net income prior to separation, make the break in early January if possible, to win more tax savings.
14. **Calculate Canada Child Tax Benefits Receivable Before and After Separation.** Most couples will find that in cases where one spouse has little or no income, the CTB can provide significant monthly support on a

tax free basis, now that it is calculated based on that lower earner's net income only.

15. **Immediate Adjustments to CTB and GSTC are Possible.** The new net income should be disclosed to CCRA immediately after separation by filing *Form RC65* so that the benefits from the Canada Child Tax Benefit and Goods and Services Tax Credit can be based on that lower net income and therefore, begin immediately. If you do so before the eleventh month following separation, revised benefits will be received for each month after separation and, in the case of CTB and GST, credits will begin for the first quarter after the change in marital status. Note that, in the case of separation, you are not considered to be separated until you have been apart for 90 days so the CCRA will not process your request if you have not been separated at least 90 days at the time you notify them of the change.
16. **Payments from U.S. Residents for Child Support are Not Taxable.** Provisions within the U.S.-Canada Tax Treaty have provided a special tax break since 1985 for recipients of child support from U.S.-resident payors. Those receipts are not taxable. They must be reported as child support in Canadian funds for the purposes of increasing net income on the Canadian return (thereby reducing refundable tax credits and other provisions based on net income), but a deduction may be taken on Line 256.
17. **Minimize Non-deductible Expenditures on Legal Fees.** Always think of your separated family's legacy first. Legal fees to obtain a separation or divorce are not deductible. Spend your money shoring up RRSPs, RESPs or other non-registered investments for the benefit of the family, instead.
18. **Remember: There are Tax Consequences on Reconciliation.** When couples reconcile within 60 days of year end, child care expenses are deducted according to rules in effect for married/common-law unions for the whole year. However, the Amount for an Eligible Dependant (formerly Equivalent-to-Spouse Amount) may be claimed by one parent even if the couple reconciled before year end, if all other criteria for making the claim were met.

CHAPTER 8

Creating Tax-Driven Prosperity

KEY PERSONAL TAX CONCEPTS:

- The Canadian tax system is full of tax preferences people can take advantage of to drive new capital creation and long term wealth
- Employees can plan to reduce tax withholding, negotiate for tax free and taxable benefits, tax exempt death benefits, stock options, and low interest employment loans
- Pre-retirees can plan to maximize savings accumulations by maximizing RRSP contributions every year, splitting income with spouse, and sheltering non-registered assets
- Small business owners can use start-up losses to offset prior taxes paid and accumulate equity on a tax free, tax deferred and possibly tax-exempt basis
- The tax consequences of death can be minimized and the role of life insurance should be considered in planning intergenerational wealth opportunities
- Canadian taxpayers will turn over approximately 22% to almost 50% of their taxable income and capital gains over their lifetimes ... tax efficiency can result in significant savings over time

It doesn't take tough times to realize that the provisions of the Canadian tax system are complicated and large in size and scope. In fact, the mere filing of a tax return every year brings on tough times (albeit temporarily) for many!

But it is especially during times of great change that financial assets and the tax consequences of their liquidation, transfer or changing values must be carefully addressed. Tough times can, in fact, be the prelude to prosperity and the time to launch new personal and professional adventures.

As mentioned in the Introduction, tough times are also the right times to review tax filing profiles, long and short term financial priorities and to look to the combined dynamics of change in tax law, personal circumstances and market conditions to make informed decisions (or at least educated guesses) about your future.

While tax preparation is an activity based in history (the reconciliation of last year's tax obligations), tax planning aims to arrange a taxpayer's affairs within the framework of the law to minimize future tax obligations of the whole family unit. This is done by using all known tax provisions of the past, present and foreseeable future to eliminate, reduce or defer taxes.

For our foreseeable future in Canada, despite economic uncertainty, taxpayers know that recent federal tax reductions will prevail over the next several years and bring savings from tax rate reductions, the indexing of income brackets subject to those rates and new refundable and non-refundable tax credits and their clawback levels.

In that context, be on the lookout for the following top tax filing errors in your affairs. Discuss these mistakes of the past and your options for wise tax management in the future with your financial advisors.

15 TOP TAX FILING ERRORS

Error #1: Overpaid Tax Withholding or Tax Installment Payments

The government returns over $16 billion in tax refunds to Canadians annually ... which means we willingly give an interest-free loan to the government with every pay cheque (in the case of employees) or every quarterly instalment payment (in the case of seniors, investors, small business owners and others).

Employees, tell CCRA to let your employer take into account the legitimate tax deductions you'll claim on your return—carrying charges, employment expenses, charitable donations, RRSP contributions, etc.—so that periodic tax withholdings can be reduced throughout the year. You can request this by filing *Form T1213* with CCRA, who will then forward a letter of authority to reduce tax withholdings to your employer.

If you are paying tax by instalment, recalculate the estimated taxable income for the year. If you know it has dropped, request a reduction in your instalment payments by filing *Form T1033*. When income levels fall, many people don't have to make their December 15 instalment payment—which is a great surprise at holiday time.

Error #2: Missed Capital Loss Carryovers

Investors have many reasons they want to forget about their non-registered market losses, but it's just not smart to forget about them on your tax return. Although those capital losses can only be used to offset capital gains of the year, they can be carried back to offset gains in the previous three years or carried forward indefinitely into the future for the same purpose. And, in the year of death, if unused, capital loss balances can offset other income of the year or the immediately preceding year.

So, if you haven't previously reported losses—for whatever reason—go back and adjust your tax returns to include all capital losses since 1985, the last year in which we can request adjustments. Capital loss balances can be carried forward from 1972, however, as that was the first year of capital gains taxation in Canada.

Error # 3: Underused RRSP Room

Now is not a good time to slack off on RRSP contributions ... the overwhelming majority of Canadians have not maximized their RRSP contributions. In an era of progressively reducing tax burdens (largely due to indexing and tax bracket/rate adjustments), an RRSP contribution made this year will be worth marginally more than one made next year (all things being equal).

So the worst mistake you could have made from a tax point of view last year was to miss your RRSP top-up—it can be the worst mistake you make this year too. Prepare a preliminary tax calculation early in the year and then top-it up.

Remember you can switch assets from non-registered funds to make the RRSP contribution to maximize your tax savings, if you can't come up with the cash; but beware of "superficial loss rules" that could render losses on such flips non-deductible.

Error #4: Generating Actual Losses in RRSPS

For many Canadians, their RRSP is their only savings. In times of market turmoil, so many people feel compelled to take action, but to do so within an RRSP may not be wise, particularly if losses are crystallized.

In general, there is no good tax reason for realizing losses in an RRSP. They will give no immediate tax benefits (although projecting forward, total RRSP accumulations will be reduced by the losses generated, and therefore taxes on the accumulations as a whole will be less). In addition, if market conditions improve, those unrealized losses may once again turn into gains over time.

It is much more important to deal with diminished values in RRSPs by investing as much new money as possible as soon as possible (provided the taxpayer is eligible, of course). This will allow the taxpayer to average back into the market, reap tax savings and make up for lost values with new performance.

Remember, too, that your RRSP savings can multiply your wealth creation opportunities: you can switch assets into a Labour-Sponsored Investment Fund to create tax credits (federally and in most provinces) of up to $1,500 or you can withdraw your accumulated funds tax free under the Lifelong Learning Plan or Home Buyer's Plan if you need cash to continue your education or buy a new home.

Error # 5: Failure to Take Advantage of Tax Loss Selling Opportunities

Taxpayers who had capital losses in the current or any of the prior three years should discuss the benefits of selling losers within their non-registered accounts to offset taxable capital gains in current or prior years.

If capital gains arose in 1999 or 2000, when capital gains inclusion rates were higher and tax brackets, rates and surtaxes were higher, a loss carryback can reap rich rewards. Tax year 1998 drops off with losses carried back from 2001.

Taxpayers can use the tax refund to average back into the market. However, if they want to buy back into the same equities, they must wait the requisite 30 days after the disposition to avoid the superficial loss rules.

Error #6: Failure to Leverage Equity

One of the key ways Canadians accumulate equity is through home ownership. While any kind of leveraging using this equity should be carefully discussed with financial advisors, it is a fact that by using that asset to borrow money for investment purposes you may be able to increase your wealth significantly over time, while deducting the interest on the loan. At today's low interest rates that may be an affordable and viable option.

However, this plan is not right for everyone. Its use will depend on availability of equity, other debt loads, ability to repay the loan and current age. Never contemplate a large mortgage on your home if you are retired or in danger of losing your job. Always seek unbiased, professional opinions before taking the loan.

Error #7: Failure to Split Income with Family Members

Always contribute to a spousal RRSP. You can't reverse a decision to accumulate all the retirement funds in one person's name later. Income splitting provides important tax benefits that can save you thousands of dollars.

You can also help low income earners shore up their own non-registered investment accounts by providing inter-spousal or intergenerational loans at prescribed rates of interest, which were very low at the time of writing (3%). As long as the interest is actually paid to the lender within the first 30 days of the end of the year, resulting investment income is taxed to the borrower. This is a good (and currently inexpensive) way to build up equity in the name of the lower earner.

Higher earners can also finance the start up of the lower earner's business, with the resulting profits being properly taxed to the lower earner. Family members can be hired in the business for further income splitting and RRSP accumulation opportunities. Think about the wealth creation possibilities of the family unit as a whole, then think big tax savings!

Error # 8: Failure to Realize Values in Assets

Market downturns present a good opportunity to crystallize values in capital assets, held outside registered plans, for the purposes of deemed dispositions, including transfers to other family members, into registered accounts and so on.

It may be a good time, for example, for small business corporation owners to plan an estate freeze, maximizing the use of their lifetime capital gains deduction and ensuring future growth of the company accrues in the hands of other family members. Remember every Canadian may use one $500,000 capital gains deduction in their lifetime based on an accumulation of gains from the disposition of qualifying small business corporation shares or qualifying farms. This presents important family income splitting opportunities.

Cottage and vacation property transfers should also be contemplated when asset values are low. However, losses generated on personal use properties are not recognized for tax purposes.

Always bear in mind that the transferor's proceeds of disposition becomes the transferee's adjusted cost base. If the proceeds of disposition are low upon transfer, the capital appreciation in the future is transferred to the transferee. That may be desirable in some, but not all cases.

In addition, while most transfers take place at Fair Market Value, in the case of a transfer to spouse the proceeds of disposition and adjusted cost base are deemed to be cost, unless an election is made to use fair market value. This allows for a tax free rollover of the property at the time of transfer. The same rules may be applied when farm land or depreciable property is transferred to a farmer's child or grandchildren during the farmer's lifetime. Careful planning should take place to ensure the best tax consequences now and in the future.

Error #9: Failure to Think Out of the Tax Box

Bad times are usually temporary. So, if your income picture has changed dramatically in the wrong direction, think "out of the tax box." That is, your normal tax filing profile will be different and that means you may qualify for the first time for tax provisions otherwise unavailable to you.

For example, Child Tax Benefits, GST Credits, child care expenses (if your spouse is now the higher income earner), medical expenses, loss carryovers, etc., all may be available to you for the first time. Or you may be able to avoid the clawback of your Old Age Security or Age Credit and reduce your quarterly tax instalment payments if your investment income has dropped off.

It is therefore important to speak to your tax advisor immediately upon the significant change to your family structure, job or business or investment performance. By sharing the changes in your life with those professionals and discovering how those changes will impact your tax filing profile and obligations this year, you can make informed decisions about your future.

You may be surprised, in short, to find that the tax system can offer you ways to get over temporary spells of bad luck with targeted tax breaks for you and your family.

Error #10: Overpayment of Taxes on Death of a Taxpayer

The death of a taxpayer has many tax consequences and in that time of high stress, many people miss out on lucrative tax provisions. For this reason it is important to plan ahead for this inevitable event and leave instructions with executors through a valid will, which should be updated at least once a year during tax filing time.

Remember that the death of a taxpayer triggers a deemed disposition of assets which in general are rolled over to the surviving spouse at cost, resulting in a tax free rollover. However, because it is possible to elect to use Fair Market Value on some or all of the assets on transfer, tax preferences can be used to their fullest advantage.

For example, the final mandatory tax return (reporting income from January 1 to date of death) should report taxable assets in such a manner as to use up the deceased's capital loss carry forward balances. If possible, increase the Adjusted Cost Base of assets for the survivors to minimize their taxes on dispositions in the future.

If a capital gains election was made to pre-report accrued gains held on February 22, 1994 (this provision allowed taxpayers to use up their $100,000 capital gains deduction which was eliminated as of that date), remember to include those increased values as the Adjusted Cost Base on the deemed disposition of elected assets on the final return. Look for *Form T664* from 1994 and keep it with the will to ensure that legal representatives do not overlook this important election.

As well, other special provisions allow the claiming of medical expenses in the best 24-month period ending in the final year (normally this is the best 12-month period ending in a tax year) and the claiming of donations up to 100% of net income (normally this is 75% of net income). Many who care for a terminally ill patient fail to make claims for the Caregiver Amount, the Disability Amount and Medical Expenses, all of which can be claimed by adjusting prior-filed returns. However, if they can be claimed immediately their lucrative benefits can help with expensive drug costs or non-deductible funeral expenses.

Also a final RRSP contribution can be made, to reduce income on the deceased's final return, if that deposit is made within 60 days of year end and if the deceased had the required RRSP contribution room. It should be made to a spousal RRSP.

If the deceased, who may normally have been the higher income earner, passes away early in the year, the net income up to the date of death will be very low. This may allow the surviving spouse to claim the amount for spouse or common-law partner, or transfer the Age Amount, Pension Income Amount, Disability Amount or Tuition/Education Amounts to that survivor's return.

Finally, because death will trigger the payment of tax exempt life insurance policy proceeds, many survivors are overwhelmed by the receipt of such large sums of money and stressed by the decisions that have to be made to properly invest it. It is most important not to make quick or uninformed decisions with long term consequences. In fact, for most survivors, it is important to get through the first year after the trauma of loss before major lifestyle changes should be decided upon. Therefore, it is important for family members and executors to know and trust financial advisors before the inevitable occurs.

Error #11: Unnecessary Asset Liquidation to Pay Taxes on Death

When taxes result on the final return due to the deemed disposition of assets, it is possible to make an election under subsection 159(5) to pay taxes owing in instalments over a ten year period. This election applies to certain liabilities including income inclusion resulting from the recapture of capital cost allowance on depreciable properties, capital gains (net of losses), rights or things filed on an optional return.

Security for payment must be provided if the election to pay by instalment is made and the first payment must be made at the time the final return is filed. The remaining payments must be made within one year on that anniversary date.

Form T2075 Election by a Deceased Taxpayer's Legal Representative to Defer Payment of Income Tax must be filed and interest will be charged at the prescribed rate on the taxes deferred.

This provision will help the executor avoid the hasty sale of assets to pay tax liabilities on deemed disposition at death and enable the actual sale when market conditions are more advantageous. In addition, at that time, the actual cash will be available to pay the taxes.

These options and the use of life insurance to offset taxable liabilities on death should be discussed with financial advisors early in one's lifetime, to ensure affordable insurability and avoid unintended consequences for the family legacy due to premature and unexpected death.

Error #12: Failure to File Tax Returns as a Family

Because of the numerous transferable tax provisions available to family members (as illustrated in Chapter 1), it is best to file the annual tax returns of the family together, starting with the lower income earner and moving on in order to the highest. In this way, refundable and non-refundable tax credits can be maximized, savings and investment plans for the future can be discussed in the context of the family's combined tax load, income splitting opportunities can be contemplated and estate planning can be reviewed.

Particularly if the family is actively involved in a family business, it is important to discuss diversification of time and money and to arrange to minimize tax withholding at source for all members of the family who work as employees. Each should regularly contribute through a payroll plan to an RRSP and family donations, medical expenses, child care, moving and Labour-Sponsored Investment Fund acquisitions should be taken into account when determining the amount of withholding taxes.

All tax savings from tax preferences used by the family should be identified and treated as "capital bonuses" to be invested. Also, inter-family loans (if formally set up with interest payable and actually paid at the prescribed rate within 30 days of year end) may provide income splitting opportunities to share wealth and minimize the effect of taxation.

Finally, remember that those who attend post-secondary school in the family now qualify for lucrative education tax credits ($400 a month for full-time students and $120 a month for part-time students) as well as a $3,000 exemption on scholarship income. Because of these lucrative new provisions, taxes will be reduced for many families. It is important not to overpay quarterly instalments or tax withholding at source in those instances.

Error #13: Overpayment of Taxes on Job Termination

When job termination results in long term reduction of income and the immediate and unexpected receipt of cash windfalls, the combination of the two can spell "mistake!"

It is important to ensure, as illustrated in Chapter 2, that receipt of severance is carefully planned from a tax viewpoint, and that clawbacks on Employment Insurance benefits received after job loss are avoided.

When negotiating for the next position, be tax wise: look for a good cash remuneration package, but the availability of stock options, tax free benefits (like athletic club memberships), taxable benefits (like use of a company car), death benefits (up to $10,000 is tax exempt on death of the employee) and the ability to tap into group insurance or access to low or no-interest loans all can significantly improve lifestyle now and in the future. It is therefore important to visit with a tax advisor before signing up for the next career move.

Relocation can also bring lucrative moving expense claims (see Figure 1-12 in Chapter 1). The stress of changes in career can also bring on other unintended stressors: illness or separation for example. All of those circumstances require tax knowledge to maximize cash flow in difficult times.

Error #14: Failure to Generate Investment Losses

When saddled with the reality of insolvency, tax consequences should be reported immediately to provide some relief. Losses in non-registered holdings, including losses on shares of insolvent public companies due to guarantee fulfillment, defaults of money loaned to others, and other uncollectible debt, result in deemed dispositions at a value of nil. Capital losses may be claimed against other gains of the year, carried back three years and claimed against capital gains in those years, or carried forward for use against capital gains in the future.

When investments in a small business corporation are reduced to nil, a Business Investment Loss (BIL) results. In general, one-half of that loss can be used to reduce all other income of the year. If unapplied loss balances remain, they can be carried back three years and forward seven years. Unapplied balances remaining after this period turn into a normal capital loss with the usual consequences.

BILs can also be reduced or eliminated by prior capital gains deduction claims. Also, if the person who incurred the BIL or other capital or non-capital losses previously had a debt forgiven, loss balances claimable may be reduced.

It is important to receive professional tax assistance in all of these instances to maximize tax preferences in the current year and in carryover periods.

Error # 15: Not Claiming Tax Deductible Carrying Charges

Many errors are made in claiming carrying charges. The most common is the failure to write off the costs of the safety deposit box. But it is in the claiming of interest cost for investment purposes that people can really go wrong.

Remember that interest paid on loans taken to invest in registered plans—RRSPs, RESPs for example—is not deductible.

Nor is money borrowed to transfer equities to minor children. While they are legitimately able to avoid the attribution rules and report resulting capital gains on their returns, interest costs on an investment loan taken out by Mom or Dad for these purposes will not be deductible.

Also, when the value of an asset diminishes or the asset is worthless, the CCRA will still allow the taxpayer to continue to write off the interest charges on loans taken for that asset acquisition, as the asset's original value is deemed to continue for income-producing purposes.

It is also necessary for assets acquired to show potential for income—rents, royalties, dividends, interest, business profits—for interest costs to be deductible. If the asset is not income-producing (i.e., only capital appreciation is expected), interest will not be deductible.

In tough times, it may also be wise to capitalize the costs of interest on business assets, thereby saving bigger tax deductions for the future when income may be higher. All of these provisions should be discussed in detail with your tax advisor.

CONCLUSION: CONQUERING THE FEAR OF FLYING

When great change occurs, we feel out of control and suffer from fear. Fear is caused by uncertainty and uncertainty is caused by a lack of knowledge. Will the market go up or further down; will my workplace be safe from bombs or poisoning; will my air travel end successfully on the ground at my destination of choice?

These important questions have had dramatic personal and economic effects. Many people have been crippled in their decision-making in the aftermath of shocking life events. But it is important to gain control again, to start making our own decisions again.

In the aftermath of the September 11, 2001, terrorist attacks, for example, many people chose not to fly, which may have been the right decision at the time. It was based on fear caused by uncertainty. But, in contemplating the effects of those fear-based decisions, while sitting on a plane, I had to wonder: who was terrorized—the people in the air going about their normal business or those who chose to stay in fear on the ground at home?

To turn that to a financial perspective, many people have feared—legitimately—that perhaps they have not saved enough or that their diminished assets will not provide them with the retirement lifestyle they had envisioned.

Fortunately, the greatest antidote to fear is knowledge and then knowledge-based action. The greatest power that people have is the power to choose—their actions, their relationships and their possessions. When we choose to act (or not to act), we immediately put ourselves on a path—and the road to success is full of forks. Whichever fork in the road we choose, we face potential risk and obstacles.

This is where a relationship with experienced professionals in the financial services can really pay off. They will be able to give you perspective. Many people, for example, don't realize that market fluctuations are not their greatest accumulation risk. Rather, sitting out of the marketplace can have greater consequences over the long term. Others don't know that their biggest lifetime expense is not their mortgage, food, clothing, shelter or current market losses—it is the taxes they pay day in and day out over a productive lifetime of 40 years and more.

So, the good news is that increased knowledge, with the help of your trusted financial advisors can help you offset current financial or personal setbacks and put you back into the driver's seat on your personal road to success. And when it comes to your biggest lifetime expense—the taxes you will pay—remember that the income tax system allows you to exercise your personal power to arrange your affairs within the framework of the law so as to pay the least amount of taxes possible throughout your lifetime.

For all of those reasons ... you may not need to fear flying again. Whether in the air or on the ground, decisions made as a result of knowledge will help you take control of your destiny and decide on the right course of action.

We hope you have found ways to save tax dollars contemplating the "Tax Secrets" in this book, so that you and your family can achieve peace of mind when it comes to your tax planning affairs, and *use tax savings as a driver to new prosperity*.

In the meantime, be safe and pay only the correct amount of tax ... not one cent more.

Evelyn Jacks

BONUS CHAPTER

Digging for Gold: How to Recover Errors and Omissions on Prior-Filed Returns

KEY PERSONAL TAX CONCEPTS:

- **Many Canadians overpay their federal and provincial income taxes every year, by missing out on tax deductions and credits or by mistakenly over- or under-reporting their income**
- **Failing to file a tax return is unnecessarily costly on several fronts:**
  - If money is owed, the taxpayer will be subject to late filing penalties and interest costs
  - If taxes were over-paid, the taxpayer misses out on the investment returns this money could otherwise be earning
  - RRSP room is not created until a return is filed, therefore private retirement savings are underfunded and taxes are overpaid in the year the RRSP deduction is missed
  - If the taxpayer's income level is low enough, refundable tax credits, like the Child Tax Benefit, will be lost which effects monthly income levels.
- **Errors and omissions on income tax returns happen most often when there is a significant change in an individual's personal or financial affairs:**
  - Births and deaths
  - Marriages and divorces
  - Hiring or job termination

- The starting or selling of a business
- The acquisition or sale of assets
- Moving from one city to another
- Illness and disability
- Retirement
- Post-secondary education
- Bankruptcy, immigration or emigration.

- **Canadian governments allow "voluntary compliance." That is, gross negligence and tax evasion penalties may be avoided when taxpayers voluntarily comply by filing tax returns to report income, or claim deductions, or credits**
- **The federal government's "Fairness Provisions," as outlined in their *Information Circular 92-3*, allow taxpayers to request refunds of overpaid taxes beyond the normal three year Statute of Limitations**
- **Taxpayers may request refunds on overpaid taxes all the way back to tax year 1985 for most federal tax provisions**
- **Provincial tax provisions can be corrected and refunds of resulting overpaid taxes can be obtained only for the normal three year period: the current year and the two prior years**
- **CCRA is bound by the three year Statute of Limitations in reassessing taxpayer's returns—except if fraud is expected, in which case older returns may be reassessed**
- **Taxpayers must keep their tax records for a six-year-period following the last day of the tax year in which the Notice of Assessment was received. Taxpayers who wish to dispose of records sooner must request permission to do so—which can lead to an audit**
- **Never destroy any tax records without doing a prior-year review to collect refunds due to missed tax provisions**

REAL LIFE

On the following pages you will find 16 of the most common tax errors made on the federal return and how to reclaim your overpaid taxes—all the way back to tax year 1985 if applicable—by using *Form T1 ADJ*.

The adjustments are presented in the same order as the lines on the income tax return:

- Income
- Deductions
- Non-refundable tax credits
- Refundable tax credits
- Provisions that reduce federal taxes
- Instalment payment reduction requests.

A brief true-to-life scenario brings the error or omission to life, using some basic details.

Hopefully, you will identify a few of these items in your own personal affairs and then use these guidelines—and the sample adjustment requests—to recover tax refunds you didn't know you were entitled to. The chart on the next page will provide you with a listing of the errors or omissions and the category under which they fall. Look at the ones that match your situation, but come back and review them all to make sure you don't miss out on any savings.

When requesting an adjustment, send all receipts, even if you would not normally send them in when filing a tax return.

Remember: It's tax wise to commit to investing all tax savings windfalls to create additional wealth for your family unit.

TAX SECRETS

Important tax tips surrounding the error or omission and the reason for the adjustment request are outlined, together with other areas of the tax return that may be affected by the changes.

TAX SAVINGS RESULTS

The fiscal result of the adjustment is computed to quantify the new capital created by making the adjustment.

The table on the following page lists the categories under which the Request for Adjustment falls and a brief description of the error or omission and the page on which it can be found.

Adjustment # 1 To:	**Other Employment Income (Line 104) and GST Rebate (Line 457)**
Error or Omission:	**Missed GST Rebate on Union Dues**
Tax Years in Question:	**1991 to 2000**

KEY PERSONAL TAX CONCEPTS:

- **Professionals, like nurses, often pay association dues directly to their associations. Others, like commission sales reps, often claim tax-deductible employment expenses for out-of-pocket costs incurred in their employment pursuit.**
- **A recovery of the GST paid on these costs is possible via the tax return.**

REAL LIFE

Sarah is a nurse who paid annual professional dues of $450 to her association. GST of $31.50 was added to this for a total of $481.50 in each year since 1991. While she claimed the dues as a deduction on Line 212, she was unaware this amount qualified for a GST Rebate.

TAX SECRETS

- Employees who make a claim for tax deductible union or professional dues on Line 212, or for employment expenses on Line 229 qualify for a refund of any GST paid on these expenses (Line 457) by filing *Form GST 370.*
- The year the rebate is received, it must be reported as income on Line 104.
- The amounts can be recovered for each year in which the GST becomes payable: 1991 forward; and in the case of the HST: 1997 forward.

TAX SAVINGS RESULTS

This tax adjustment has the following financial impact for Sarah:

- Net Refund of $31.50 for each year adjusted
- Note the GST Rebate is requested for each individual tax year on which the Union Dues were claimed.
- The rebate refund received is reported on Line 104 in the year received.

Sarah's Request for Adjustment for 2000 is shown on the following page.

Canada Customs and Revenue Agency / Agence des douanes et du revenu du Canada

T1 ADJUSTMENT REQUEST

- Use this form to request an adjustment (a reassessment) to an individual income tax return.
- See the back of this form for information on how to complete it.
- Send the completed form to the Enquiries & Adjustments Division of your tax centre. You can find the address on the back of this form.

Date of action:

A Identification

For filing ☐ DO NOT USE THIS AREA

PSN

Social insurance number: 1 0 0 0 0 0 0 2 5

Adjustment request for the 2000 tax year (complete a separate form for each year)

Full name: (please print your given name first, surname last) Sarah

Address: (please print)
☒ same as on the return
☐ or:

CORLOC # ☐ Ack. ☐ St. Code

Assessor | Date | Rev. | Date

B Authorization - complete this area if a person or firm is preparing this request for you; otherwise, go to Area C.

Name and address of person or firm preparing this request: (please print)

Letter of authorization (or Form T1013, *Consent Form*) for the year under review:
☐ was submitted previously
☐ is attached

C Adjustment details

Using your copy of your tax return and your *Notice of Assessment or Reassessment*, list below the details of your requested change.
If you have received an assessment or reassessment notice with an amount that is different from the amount on the return, use the amount stated on the notice.
See the back of this form for information about required documentation and for examples of how to complete this area.

Line number from return or schedule	Name of line from return or schedule	Previous amount	+ −	Amount of change	Revised amount
457	Employee and partner GST rebate	–	+	31.50	31.50
	(prepare one adjustment for each year Union dues were claimed)				

Other details or explanations (attach an extra sheet if required)

1. Add 1999 GST rebate to income (per prior T1ADJ)
2. Claim GST rebate on GST included in union dues. Form GST 370 attached

D Certification

I certify that the information given on this form and on any documents attached is, to the best of my knowledge, correct and complete.

2001 12 02
Date

Client's/Representative's signature

(Home) ( )
(Business) ( )
Telephone

You can get more copies of this form from any Canada Customs and Revenue Agency office.
(Ce formulaire existe en français.)

T1-ADJ E (01)

Canada

Adjustment # 2 To: Other Employment Income (Line 104)

Error or Omission: Missed Premium Deduction on Wage Loss Replacement Benefits Received

Tax Years in Question: 2000

KEY PERSONAL TAX CONCEPTS:

- **It is common for employers and employees to fund wage loss replacement plans through a payroll deduction plan.**
- **Most taxpayers, who must later draw benefits, are unaware of their tax rights and overpay tax on this income source.**
- **If the employee covered all the costs personally (or the premiums the employer paid through the year on his/her behalf are included in his income as a taxable benefit), the benefits would not be taxable upon receipt.**

REAL LIFE

Tom suffered from a permanent disability this year: his chronic asthma made it impossible for him to continue to work. He started to receive wage loss replacement benefits during the year and these were shown as other income on a T4A slip received. While he reported the amounts as income, he missed reducing the benefits by premiums he had paid since he started working in 1975. The premiums amounted to $150 each year.

Taxpayer Details Before Adjustments	Year: 2000	Year:	Year:	Year:	Year:
Marital Status	Married				
Taxpayer's Total Income	$40,000				
Net Income	$39,550				
Taxable Income	$39,550				
Marginal Tax Rate	31%				
Residency	MB				
Family Net Income	$48,550				

TAX SECRETS

- When both employer and employee participate in funding a wage loss replacement plan, benefits received from the plan are taxable on Line 104.
- Such benefits may be reduced by premiums paid by the employee.
- Simply attach a letter from the payroll department which itemizes premiums paid since 1968. The amounts can be claimed all in one tax year.

TAX SAVINGS RESULTS

This tax adjustment has the following financial impact for Tom:

- Additional refund of $1,236.60
- Increased CTB of $75 for their youngest child who is still living at home.
- Reduced earned income for RRSP purposes. RRSP contribution room is reduced by $540.

Tom's Request for Adjustment is shown on the following page.

Canada Customs and Revenue Agency / Agence des douanes et du revenu du Canada

T1 ADJUSTMENT REQUEST

- Use this form to request an adjustment (a reassessment) to an individual income tax return.
- See the back of this form for information on how to complete it.
- Send the completed form to the Enquiries & Adjustments Division of your tax centre. You can find the address on the back of this form.

Date of action:

For filing ☐ DO NOT USE THIS AREA

PSN

CORLOC # ☐ Ack. ☐ St. Code

Assessor | Date | Rev. | Date

A Identification

Social insurance number: 1 0 0 0 0 0 0 3 3

Adjustment request for the 2000 **tax year** **(complete a separate form for each year)**

Full name: (please print your given name first, surname last)

Tom

Address: (please print)

☒ same as on the return

☐ or:

B Authorization - complete this area if a person or firm is preparing this request for you; otherwise, go to Area C.

Name and address of person or firm preparing this request: (please print)

Letter of authorization (or Form T1013, *Consent Form*) for the year under review:

☐ was submitted previously

☐ is attached

C Adjustment details

Using your copy of your tax return and your *Notice of Assessment or Reassessment*, list below the details of your requested change.
If you have received an assessment or reassessment notice with an amount that is different from the amount on the return, use the amount stated on the notice.
See the back of this form for information about required documentation and for examples of how to complete this area.

Line number from return or schedule	Name of line from return or schedule	Previous amount	+ −	Amount of change	Revised amount
104	Other employment income	15,000.00	−	3,000.00	12,000.00

Other details or explanations (attach an extra sheet if required)

Adjust income from wage loss replacement plan to deduct
$3,000 for premiums I paid for this plan and have not previously deducted

D Certification

I certify that the information given on this form and on any documents attached is, to the best of my knowledge, correct and complete.

2001 12 02
Date

Client's/Representative's signature

(Home) (   )
(Business) (   )
Telephone

T1-ADJ E (01)

You can get more copies of this form from any Canada Customs and Revenue Agency office.
(Ce formulaire existe en français.)

Canada

Adjustment # 3 To: Taxable Capital Gains (Line 127)
Error or Omission: Missed Claiming Brokerage Fees
Tax Years in Question: 2000

KEY PERSONAL TAX CONCEPTS

- **Certain costs of buying or selling assets are deductible when taxable dispositions arise.**
- **These costs reduce capital gains or increase capital losses of the year.**

REAL LIFE

Jason, a self employed plumber earning a net income from his proprietorship of $64,000 annually, reported capital gains in June 2000 but failed to claim his brokerage fees. In addition, he sold a revenue property in October 2000. He incurred appraisal costs and real estate commissions. Finally, he sold some mutual fund units during the year and failed to take into account all the reinvested earnings he had previously reported from his T3 and T5 slips.

Taxpayer Details Before Adjustments	Year: 2000	Year:	Year:	Year:	Year:
Marital Status	Single				
Taxpayer's Total Income	$86,583				
Net Income	$81,583				
Taxable Income	$81,583				
Marginal Tax Rate	47.9%				
Residency	ON				
Family Net Income	$81,583				

TAX SECRETS

- Costs associated with acquiring a capital asset form part of the cost base. This includes brokerage fees on acquiring shares, legal fees when acquiring real estate, sales commissions on purchase of mutual funds, etc.
- Costs of improving assets such as upgrades to real property increase the cost base of the asset.

- Capital gains reported each year on mutual funds increase the cost base of the mutual fund units.
- Costs of disposing of capital assets, such as brokerage fees for shares, "back end loads" for mutual funds, and real estate commissions, legal fees and property appraisals when selling real estate are deductible in calculating the gain when disposing of the asset.

TAX SAVINGS RESULTS

This tax adjustment has the following financial impact for Jason:

- Refund of $3,083.

Jason's Request for Adjustment for 2000 is shown on the following page.

Canada Customs and Revenue Agency / Agence des douanes et du revenu du Canada

T1 ADJUSTMENT REQUEST

- Use this form to request an adjustment (a reassessment) to an individual income tax return.
- See the back of this form for information on how to complete it.
- Send the completed form to the Enquiries & Adjustments Division of your tax centre. You can find the address on the back of this form.

Date of action:

For filing ☐ DO NOT USE THIS AREA

PSN

CORLOC # ☐ Ack. ☐ St. Code

Assessor | Date | Rev. | Date

A Identification

Social insurance number: 1 0 0 0 0 0 0 8 2

Adjustment request for the 2000 tax year (complete a separate form for each year)

Full name: (please print your given name first, surname last)

Jason

Address: (please print)

☒ same as on the return

☐ or:

B Authorization - complete this area if a person or firm is preparing this request for you; otherwise, go to Area C.

Name and address of person or firm preparing this request: (please print)

Letter of authorization (or Form T1013, *Consent Form*) for the year under review:

☐ was submitted previously

☐ is attached

C Adjustment details

Using your copy of your tax return and your *Notice of Assessment or Reassessment*, list below the details of your requested change.
If you have received an assessment or reassessment notice with an amount that is different from the amount on the return, use the amount stated on the notice.
See the back of this form for information about required documentation and for examples of how to complete this area.

Line number from return or schedule	Name of line from return or schedule	Previous amount	+ –	Amount of change	Revised amount
127	Taxable capital gains	22,853.33	–	6,462.50	16,120.83

Other details or explanations (attach an extra sheet if required)

Please make the following corrections to capital gains reported (revised Schedule 3 attached)

1 Add $750 brokerage fees on sale of shares

2 Adjust cost base of mutual funds to $9,000 to adjust for previously reported income

3 Add real estate commission ($7,500) and appraisal fee ($450) on sale of real property

D Certification

I certify that the information given on this form and on any documents attached is, to the best of my knowledge, correct and complete.

2001 12 02
Date

Client's/Representative's signature

(Home) ( )
(Business) ( )
Telephone

You can get more copies of this form from any Canada Customs and Revenue Agency office.
(Ce formulaire existe en français.)

T1-ADJ E (01)

Canada

Adjustment # 4 To: RRSP Deduction (Line 204)
Error or Omission: Lost RRSP Receipt
Tax Years in Question: 2000

KEY PERSONAL TAX CONCEPTS

- **Taxpayers often find lost slips—T4s, T5s, charitable donations, RRSP contribution records, medical expenses, etc., after their tax returns have been filed.**
- **Never file another tax return in this case. Simply request an adjustment to the return.**
- **When the Notice of Reassessment arrives, study it carefully to be sure all provisions of the return affected by the omission are addressed.**

REAL LIFE

The taxpayer, Marion, a single mother of two pre-schoolers and a manager of a dry cleaning retail outlet, found a receipt for an RRSP contribution made during the tax year 2000 (December 31), in the amount of $4,000. This was in addition to monthly contributions of $1,200 during the year and another contribution of $2,000 on March 1st of 2001. Contribution room for the tax year 2000 was $8,500. She also claimed child care costs of $4,000 during the year.

Taxpayer Details Before Adjustments	Year: 2000	Year:	Year:	Year:	Year:
Taxpayer's Total Income	$47,000				
Net Income	$39,800				
Taxable Income	$39,800				
Marginal Tax Rate	41.5%				
Residency	AB				
Family Net Income	$39,800				

TAX SECRETS

- Net income is reduced by additional deductions such as RRSP deductions, union dues, moving expenses, employment expenses, etc. This reduction in net income will affect non-refundable credits, refundable credits and possibly transfers of credits to supporting persons.

TAX SAVINGS RESULTS

This tax adjustment has the following financial impact for Marion's family:

- Income tax refund of $1,460.00
- Increased Child Tax Benefit of $200.00
- GST Credit of $189.05 (without the additional $4,000 deduction, Marion did not quality for the GST credit).

Marion's Request for Adjustment for 2000 is shown on the following page.

Canada Customs and Revenue Agency / Agence des douanes et du revenu du Canada

T1 ADJUSTMENT REQUEST

- Use this form to request an adjustment (a reassessment) to an individual income tax return.
- See the back of this form for information on how to complete it.
- Send the completed form to the Enquiries & Adjustments Division of your tax centre. You can find the address on the back of this form.

Date of action:

A Identification

For filing ☐ DO NOT USE THIS AREA

PSN

Social insurance number: 1 0 0 0 0 0 1 0 8

Adjustment request for the 2000 **tax year** **(complete a separate form for each year)**

Full name: (please print your given name first, surname last)

Marion

Address: (please print)

☒ same as on the return
☐ or:

CORLOC # – ☐ Ack. ☐ St. Code

Assessor	Date	Rev.	Date

B Authorization - complete this area if a person or firm is preparing this request for you; otherwise, go to Area C.

Name and address of person or firm preparing this request: (please print)

Letter of authorization (or Form T1013, *Consent Form*) for the year under review:

☐ was submitted previously
☐ is attached

C Adjustment details

Using your copy of your tax return and your *Notice of Assessment or Reassessment*, list below the details of your requested change.
If you have received an assessment or reassessment notice with an amount that is different from the amount on the return, use the amount stated on the notice.
See the back of this form for information about required documentation and for examples of how to complete this area.

Line number from return or schedule	Name of line from return or schedule	Previous amount	+ –	Amount of change	Revised amount
208	RRSP contributions	\$3,200.00	+	\$4,000.00	\$7,200.00

Other details or explanations (attach an extra sheet if required)

Please include a deduction for the \$4,000 RRSP contribution per attached receipt.

D Certification

I certify that the information given on this form and on any documents attached is, to the best of my knowledge, correct and complete.

2001 12 02 — Date

Client's/Representative's signature

(Home) ( )
(Business) ( )
Telephone

T1-ADJ E (01)

You can get more copies of this form from any Canada Customs and Revenue Agency office.
(Ce formulaire existe en français.)

Canada

Adjustment # 5 To: Child Care Expenses (Line 214)
Error or Omission: Claimed by High Income Earner
Tax Years in Question: 2000

KEY PERSONAL TAX CONCEPTS

- **Child care expenses are a deduction that is claimable by working parents with qualifying earned income sources for children under the age of 17 or, under certain conditions, for disabled children.**
- **The claim must generally be made by the spouse with the lower earned income. However, there are some instances when the spouse with the higher income can make the claim.**

REAL LIFE

Jack and Jennifer have been married for three years and were delighted to welcome baby Jackson Allan into the world in January 2000. Julie, who returned to college as a full-time student in September of that year, left the baby in the care of a sitter at a cost of $120 each week for 13 weeks. As she had no income that year, she did not claim babysitting expenses at all, following the normal rules for the child care claim. However, she recently became aware that Jack, who earned $35,000 net income from his courier business, could have made the claim.

TAX SECRETS

- Child care expenses are a lucrative deduction that reduces net income on the return. This means that certain refundable tax credits, like the Child Tax Benefit, or non-refundable amounts, like the spousal amount or medical expenses, could be increased as a result of making this claim.
- While child care usually is claimed by the spouse with the lower net income, in the following cases the higher earning spouse can make the claim:
  - The other supporting person was a full- or part-time student
  - The other supporting person was incapable of caring for the children because of mental or physical infirmity
  - The other supporting person was confined to a prison or similar institution for at least two weeks

  - You have separated from the other supporting person due to a breakdown in your relationship for a period of at least 90 days but have reconciled within the first 60 days after the taxation year
- Child care expenses claimed will reduce the Child Tax Benefit supplement for children under 7 and may reduce a claim for a disabled dependant who is under 18. Care should be taken not to claim more child care expenses than are needed to reduce taxes to zero.

TAX SAVINGS RESULTS

This tax adjustment has the following financial impact for Jack and Jennifer:

- Income tax savings of $583.44
- Increased GSTC of $78
- Decreased CTB of $182 (due to clawback of supplement for children under 7 when child care expenses are claimed).

  Jack's Request for Adjustment for 2000 is shown on the following page.

Canada Customs and Revenue Agency — Agence des douanes et du revenu du Canada

T1 ADJUSTMENT REQUEST

- Use this form to request an adjustment (a reassessment) to an individual income tax return.
- See the back of this form for information on how to complete it.
- Send the completed form to the Enquiries & Adjustments Division of your tax centre. You can find the address on the back of this form.

Date of action:

For filing ☐ DO NOT USE THIS AREA

PSN

CORLOC # ☐ Ack. ☐ St. Code

Assessor | Date | Rev. | Date

A Identification

Social insurance number: 1 0 0 0 0 0 1 1 6

Adjustment request for the *2000* tax year (complete a separate form for each year)

Full name: (please print your given name first, surname last)
Jack

Address: (please print)
☒ same as on the return
☐ or:

B Authorization - complete this area if a person or firm is preparing this request for you; otherwise, go to Area C.

Name and address of person or firm preparing this request: (please print)

Letter of authorization (or Form T1013, *Consent Form*) for the year under review:
☐ was submitted previously
☐ is attached

C Adjustment details

Using your copy of your tax return and your *Notice of Assessment or Reassessment*, list below the details of your requested change.
If you have received an assessment or reassessment notice with an amount that is different from the amount on the return, use the amount stated on the notice.
See the back of this form for information about required documentation and for examples of how to complete this area.

Line number from return or schedule	Name of line from return or schedule	Previous amount	+ –	Amount of change	Revised amount
214	Child care expenses	–	+	1,560.00	1,560.00

Other details or explanations (attach an extra sheet if required)

Please include child care expenses of $1,560 incurred while my wife was in full-time attendance at college.

Completed Form T778 and receipts are attached.

D Certification

I certify that the information given on this form and on any documents attached is, to the best of my knowledge, correct and complete.

Date: *2001 12 02*

Client's/Representative's signature

Telephone: (Home) ( ) (Business) ( )

T1-ADJ E (01)

You can get more copies of this form from any Canada Customs and Revenue Agency office.
(Ce formulaire existe en français.)

Canada

Adjustment # 6 To: Moving Expenses (Line 219)
Error or Omission: Missed Real Estate Commissions
Tax Years in Question: 2000

KEY PERSONAL TAX CONCEPTS

- **Moving expenses can be claimed by taxpayers who incur expenses in moving their residence to work, start a business or, in some cases, to go to school in a location that is at least 40 kilometres closer to the new work or school location.**
- **These expenses are deductible against income at the new location; when there is none, the deduction can be carried forward for use next year.**
- **The amounts claimable can be sizable and are generally audited before CCRA sends your tax refund back, so receipts are necessary.**

REAL LIFE

When Jim, an employed executive earning $125,000 annually, moved his family to Moncton from Toronto, he claimed the cost of the movers, air, hotel and meals for a 15 day period before they were able to move into their home—all eligible expenses. However, he did not realize he could claim the real estate commissions he paid on his Toronto home sale: in the amount of $15,000.

Taxpayer Details Before Adjustments	Year: 2000	Year:	Year:	Year:	Year:
Marital Status	Married				
Taxpayer's Total Income	$125,000				
Net Income	$105,500				
Taxable Income	$105,500				
Marginal Tax Rate	48.8%				
Residency	NB				
Family Net Income					

TAX SECRETS

Eligible moving expenses, claimed on *Form T1-M* include the following:

- Cost of selling your former residence, including real estate commissions, penalties for paying off a mortgage, legal fees, advertising costs
- Costs of keeping a vacant old residence up for sale (to a maximum of $5,000) while you attempt to sell it, including mortgage interest, property taxes, insurance premiums, heat and power
- Expenses of purchasing the new home, including transfer taxes and legal fees (as long as the old home was owned)
- Temporary living expenses (meals and lodging) for up to 15 days
- Removal and storage costs
- Transportation costs
- Costs of meals on route
- Cost of cancelling an unexpired lease
- Cost of revising legal documents to show the new address, replacing drivers' licenses and auto permits, cost of utility connections and disconnections.

TAX SAVINGS RESULTS

This tax adjustment has the following financial impact for Jim's family:

- Income tax refund of $7,130.98
- CTB of $504.00 (before the Adjustment, the family did not qualify for any CTB).

Jim's Request for Adjustment for 2000 is shown on the following page.

Canada Customs and Revenue Agency / Agence des douanes et du revenu du Canada

T1 ADJUSTMENT REQUEST

- Use this form to request an adjustment (a reassessment) to an individual income tax return.
- See the back of this form for information on how to complete it.
- Send the completed form to the Enquiries & Adjustments Division of your tax centre. You can find the address on the back of this form.

Date of action:

For filing ☐ DO NOT USE THIS AREA

PSN

CORLOC # ☐ Ack. ☐ St. Code

Assessor | Date | Rev. | Date

A Identification

Social insurance number: 1 0 0 0 0 0 1 2 4

Adjustment request for the 2000 tax year (complete a separate form for each year)

Full name: (please print your given name first, surname last)

Jim

Address: (please print)

☒ same as on the return
☐ or:

B Authorization - complete this area if a person or firm is preparing this request for you; otherwise, go to Area C.

Name and address of person or firm preparing this request: (please print)

Letter of authorization (or Form T1013, *Consent Form*) for the year under review:

☐ was submitted previously
☐ is attached

C Adjustment details

Using your copy of your tax return and your *Notice of Assessment or Reassessment*, list below the details of your requested change.
If you have received an assessment or reassessment notice with an amount that is different from the amount on the return, use the amount stated on the notice.
See the back of this form for information about required documentation and for examples of how to complete this area.

Line number from return or schedule	Name of line from return or schedule	Previous amount	+ / –	Amount of change	Revised amount
219	Moving expenses	6,000.00	+	15,000.00	21,000.00

Other details or explanations (attach an extra sheet if required)

Please adjust my claim for moving expenses to include $15,000 real estate commission on sale of my old residence.

A copy of the real estate sales contract is attached

D Certification

I certify that the information given on this form and on any documents attached is, to the best of my knowledge, correct and complete.

2001 12 02
Date

Client's/Representative's signature

(Home) ( )
(Business) ( )
Telephone

T1-ADJ E (01)

You can get more copies of this form from any Canada Customs and Revenue Agency office.
(Ce formulaire existe en français.)

Canada

Adjustment # 7 To: **Carrying Charges (Line 221)**
Error or Omission: **Missed Safety Deposit Box Fees**
Tax Years in Question: **1985 to 2000**

KEY PERSONAL TAX CONCEPTS

- **One of the most commonly missed deductions on the tax return is the safety deposit box fees.**
- **Taxpayers, who often make errors in claiming carrying charges, are pleasantly surprised by the tax refunds they can recover with this simple and common expenditure.**

REAL LIFE

Vivienne, a radio announcer, whose income was $105,000 this year, had never claimed a deduction for her safety deposit box charges. Upon contacting her bank for a printout of what she had paid, she discovered it was $75 a year for the period 1985 to 2000, a total of $1,125. Her earnings level were around the $100,000 mark throughout that period.

TAX SECRETS

- Multiple year adjustments for the missed safety deposit box requires the careful completion of *Form T1 ADJ* to ensure that the adjustment is made for each year in which the expenditure occurred. The letter from the financial institution verifying the payments must be attached.
- Other carrying charges often missed include:
  - Investment counsel fees and investment management fees
  - Tax return preparation fees for those with significant investment or business income
  - Taxable benefits on employee loans when loans are used for investment purposes
  - Interest costs on loans to purchase investments when the value of the asset has diminished or disappeared.

NOTE: When interest costs relating to the acquisition of qualifying investments are related to loans or lines of credit with mixed use (i.e., some investment component and some personal uses), the interested costs claimed on the return must be prorated appropriately to reflect only the costs pertaining to the investments.

TAX SAVINGS RESULTS

This tax adjustment has the following financial impact for Vivienne:

- A refund of about $35 per year adjusted for a total of over $500.

Vivienne's Request for Adjustment for 2000 is shown on the following page.

Canada Customs and Revenue Agency / Agence des douanes et du revenu du Canada

T1 ADJUSTMENT REQUEST

- Use this form to request an adjustment (a reassessment) to an individual income tax return.
- See the back of this form for information on how to complete it.
- Send the completed form to the Enquiries & Adjustments Division of your tax centre. You can find the address on the back of this form.

Date of action:

For filing ☐ DO NOT USE THIS AREA

PSN | | | | | – | | | – | | – | | | | | | |

CORLOC # | | – | | | | | | | | ☐ Ack. ☐ St. Code

Assessor | Date | Rev. | Date

A Identification

Social insurance number: 1 0 0 0 0 0 1 3 2

Adjustment request for the *2000* **tax year** **(complete a separate form for each year)**

Full name: (please print your given name first, surname last)

Vivienne

Address: (please print)

☒ same as on the return

☐ or:

B Authorization - complete this area if a person or firm is preparing this request for you; otherwise, go to Area C.

Name and address of person or firm preparing this request: (please print)

Letter of authorization (or Form T1013, *Consent Form*) for the year under review:

☐ was submitted previously

☐ is attached

C Adjustment details

Using your copy of your tax return and your *Notice of Assessment or Reassessment*, list below the details of your requested change.
If you have received an assessment or reassessment notice with an amount that is different from the amount on the return, use the amount stated on the notice.
See the back of this form for information about required documentation and for examples of how to complete this area.

Line number from return or schedule	Name of line from return or schedule	Previous amount	+ –	Amount of change	Revised amount
221	*Carrying charges and interest*	*1,234.00*	+	*75.00*	*1,309.00*

Other details or explanations (attach an extra sheet if required)

Please include a claim for safety deposit box rental ($75.00) as documented in the attached letter from my bank

D Certification

I certify that the information given on this form and on any documents attached is, to the best of my knowledge, correct and complete.

2001 12 02
Date

Client's/Representative's signature

(Home) ( )
(Business) ( )
Telephone

T1-ADJ E (01)

You can get more copies of this form from any Canada Customs and Revenue Agency office.
(Ce formulaire existe en français.)

Canada

Adjustment # 8 To: Non-capital Losses of Other Years (Line 252)

Error or Omission: Business Loss Remained Unused

Tax Years in Question: 2000

KEY PERSONAL TAX CONCEPTS

- **Proprietors who incur net business losses may reduce all other income of the year in which the loss occurs, provided the expenses claimed were reasonable, supported by receipts and there is a reasonable expectation of profit from the enterprise.**
- **Most taxpayers are unaware that excess losses can be carried back up to three years or forward up to seven years to offset other income.**

REAL LIFE

Straight out of school, Jack began building his proprietorship three years ago and things are finally beginning to pay off. In 1998, his fledgling business lost $10,000 (of borrowed money). In its second year it showed a profit of $7,000 and in 2000, it showed a net profit of $45,000. When Jack filed his return, he had no idea that his losses in 1998 could be applied to his income in 2000.

Taxpayer Details Before Adjustments	Year: 2000	Year:	Year:	Year:	Year:
Marital Status	Single				
Taxpayer's Total Income	$45,000				
Net Income	$37,800				
Taxable Income	$37,800				
Marginal Tax Rate	41%				
Residency	MB				
Family Net Income	$37,800				

TAX SECRETS

- Non-capital losses are created when the calculation of taxable income results in a negative amount. Generally this is caused by a self-employment loss although other deductions may result in a non-capital loss as well. These losses can be used to reduce taxable income in any of the prior three tax years or in any of the following seven taxation years.

- In a year when a non-capital loss occurs, use of other discretionary provisions that can be carried forward—like RRSP deductions, medical expenses, charitable donations and Capital Cost Allowance (CCA) deductions—should be reviewed to ensure that the taxpayer will not lose the benefit of non-refundable credits.
- Where business operations result in a loss before claiming CCA, but the taxpayer has other sources of income, generally CCA or RRSP deductions should only be claimed to the extent that they reduce taxable income to the level of the non-refundable credits.
- If business operations result in a loss before claiming CCA, and the losses exceed income from other sources, consider using a CCA deduction to increase the loss to be carried to another year to reduce taxes.

TAX SAVINGS RESULTS

This tax adjustment has the following financial impact:

- Income tax refund of $3,470.

Jack's Request for Adjustment for 2000 is shown on the following page.

Canada Customs and Revenue Agency / Agence des douanes et du revenu du Canada

T1 ADJUSTMENT REQUEST

- Use this form to request an adjustment (a reassessment) to an individual income tax return.
- See the back of this form for information on how to complete it.
- Send the completed form to the Enquiries & Adjustments Division of your tax centre. You can find the address on the back of this form.

Date of action:

For filing ☐ DO NOT USE THIS AREA

PSN

CORLOC # ☐ Ack. ☐ St. Code

Assessor | Date | Rev. | Date

A Identification

Social insurance number: 1 0 0 0 0 0 1 5 7

Adjustment request for the *2000* **tax year** **(complete a separate form for each year)**

Full name: (please print your given name first, surname last) *Jack*

Address: (please print)

☒ same as on the return

☐ or:

B Authorization - complete this area if a person or firm is preparing this request for you; otherwise, go to Area C.

Name and address of person or firm preparing this request: (please print)

Letter of authorization (or Form T1013, *Consent Form*) for the year under review:

☐ was submitted previously

☐ is attached

C Adjustment details

Using your copy of your tax return and your *Notice of Assessment or Reassessment*, list below the details of your requested change.
If you have received an assessment or reassessment notice with an amount that is different from the amount on the return, use the amount stated on the notice.
See the back of this form for information about required documentation and for examples of how to complete this area.

Line number from return or schedule	Name of line from return or schedule	Previous amount	+ −	Amount of change	Revised amount
252	Non-capital losses of other years	−	+	10,000.00	10,000.00

Other details or explanations (attach an extra sheet if required)

Please apply my undeducted business loss from 1998 to my 2000 return.

D Certification

I certify that the information given on this form and on any documents attached is, to the best of my knowledge, correct and complete.

2001 12 02
Date

Client's/Representative's signature

(Home) ( )
(Business) ( )
Telephone

T1-ADJ E (01)

You can get more copies of this form from any Canada Customs and Revenue Agency office.
(Ce formulaire existe en français.)

Canada

Adjustment # 9 To: Capital Losses of Other Years (Line 253)
Error or Omission: Prior Year Losses Not Recorded
Tax Years in Question: 1985 to 2000

KEY PERSONAL TAX CONCEPTS

- **Capital losses incurred on asset dispositions can be used to reduce other capital gains of the year for most asset classes (except personal use properties like personal residences).**
- **When there are no capital gains in the year, capital losses benefits are not lost, provided the taxpayer has had capital gains in the past, or may have capital gains in the future.**

REAL LIFE

Douglas has been dabbling in the stock market for years. In good years, he dutifully reported his capital gains each year but had no idea that he should be reporting his losses. In 1997, he reported a $18,000 gain. 1998 was another good year—he reported a $15,000 gain. However, in 1999 Douglas got caught up in the Bre-X debacle and lost $50,000. After Bre-X, Douglas stayed out of the market in 2000.

TAX SECRETS

- Beginning in 1972, increases in the value of capital property are taxable when the property is disposed of. Over the years, the inclusion rate has been changed several times. The rate is shown in the table following. After May 23, 1985, capital losses could only be claimed against capital gains.
- Where capital losses exceed capital gains in a year, the excess loss may be applied against capital gains in any of the previous three years. Losses not applied to the current or prior years may be carried forward indefinitely to be applied against future capital gains.
- When applying capital losses to other years, the losses must be adjusted for any difference in the inclusion rate for the year the loss was incurred to the inclusion rate in which the loss is applied. The table following shows how a $1,000 allowable capital loss from another year would be applied to 2001.

Year	Capital Gains Inclusion Rate	Sample Allowable Capital Loss	Carryover Conversion Rate	Loss Applied to 2001
1972–1987 and Oct. 18, 2000 to date	50% (1/2)	$1,000	(1/2)/(1/2) = 1	$1,000
2000–use inclusion rate per Schedule 3	66.67%(2/3)	$1,000	(1/2)/(2/3) = 3/4	$750
1990–Feb. 27, 2000	75%(3/4)	$1,000	(1/2)/(3/4) = 2/3	$667

TAX SAVINGS RESULTS

This tax adjustment has the following financial impact:

- 1999: no effect—capital losses are only deductible against capital gains
- 1998: carry back of $13,500 capital loss from 1999 results in refund of $6,325
- 1997: carry back of $11,250 capital loss from 1999 results in a refund of $5,037
- Future years: unused capital losses ($12,750) may be applied against capital gains in any future year.

Douglas' Request for Adjustment for 1999 is shown on the following page.

Canada Customs and Revenue Agency / Agence des douanes et du revenu du Canada

T1 ADJUSTMENT REQUEST

- Use this form to request an adjustment (a reassessment) to an individual income tax return.
- See the back of this form for information on how to complete it.
- Send the completed form to the Enquiries & Adjustments Division of your tax centre. You can find the address on the back of this form.

Date of action:

For filing ☐ DO NOT USE THIS AREA

PSN

CORLOC # ☐ Ack. ☐ St. Code

Assessor | Date | Rev. | Date

A Identification

Social insurance number: 1 0 0 0 0 0 1 6 5

Adjustment request for the 1999 tax year (complete a separate form for each year)

Full name: (please print your given name first, surname last)
Douglas

Address: (please print)
☒ same as on the return
☐ or:

B Authorization - complete this area if a person or firm is preparing this request for you; otherwise, go to Area C.

Name and address of person or firm preparing this request: (please print)

Letter of authorization (or Form T1013, *Consent Form*) for the year under review:
☐ was submitted previously
☐ is attached

C Adjustment details

Using your copy of your tax return and your *Notice of Assessment or Reassessment*, list below the details of your requested change.
If you have received an assessment or reassessment notice with an amount that is different from the amount on the return, use the amount stated on the notice.
See the back of this form for information about required documentation and for examples of how to complete this area.

Line number from return or schedule	Name of line from return or schedule	Previous amount	+ −	Amount of change	Revised amount

Other details or explanations (attach an extra sheet if required)

Please adjust my return to include capital losses of $37,500 ($50,000 actual loss) per attached Schedule 3. Apply these losses to 1998 and 1997 per attached Form T1A.

D Certification

I certify that the information given on this form and on any documents attached is, to the best of my knowledge, correct and complete.

2001 12 02
Date

Client's/Representative's signature

(Home) ( )
(Business) ( )
Telephone

You can get more copies of this form from any Canada Customs and Revenue Agency office.
(Ce formulaire existe en français.)

T1-ADJ E (01)

Canada

Adjustment # 10 To: Amount for an Eligible Dependant
Error or Omission: File When Marital Status Changes
Tax Years in Question: 2000

KEY PERSONAL TAX CONCEPTS

- **The amount for Eligible Dependants (called the Equivalent-to-Spouse Amount before 2001) is a non-refundable tax credit available to single parents who support a child under 19. The claim is based on the child's net income.**
- **This claim can affect other provisions on the return including the Good and Services Tax Credit (GSTC), the Amount for Infirm Dependants Age 18 and Over and the Caregiver Amount.**

REAL LIFE

Karen and Andy decided in 2000 that their relationship was over. Andy moved out on July 7, leaving Karen to look after Andy Jr. Both Karen and Andy were working all year. When filing her return, Karen made no claim for Andy Jr., unaware of her eligibility for the Amount for Eligible Dependants.

Taxpayer Details Before Adjustments	Year: 2000	Year:	Year:	Year:	Year:
Marital Status	Separated				
Taxpayer's Total Income	$24,000				
Net Income	$20,000				
Taxable Income	$20,000				
Marginal Tax Rate	$25.4%				
Residency	BC				
Family Net Income	$20,000				

TAX SECRETS

- The amount for an eligible dependant can be claimed by singles (or those who are divorced, separated from and not supporting their spouses, widows (widowers) supporting a minor, or an adult relative who is infirm.

- The dependant must be related by blood, marriage or adoption and living with you in a home you maintain.
- Those who separated from, but reconciled with, their spouse during the same year may still claim this amount, provided no Spousal Amount is also claimed by the family.

TAX SAVINGS RESULTS

This tax adjustment has the following financial impact:

- Tax refund of $1,584.06 as a result of an Equivalent to Spouse amount
- Increase in GST Credit of $98.

Karen's Request for Adjustment for 2000 is shown on the following page.

Canada Customs and Revenue Agency / Agence des douanes et du revenu du Canada

T1 ADJUSTMENT REQUEST

- Use this form to request an adjustment (a reassessment) to an individual income tax return.
- See the back of this form for information on how to complete it.
- Send the completed form to the Enquiries & Adjustments Division of your tax centre. You can find the address on the back of this form.

Date of action:
For filing ☐ DO NOT USE THIS AREA
PSN
CORLOC # ☐ Ack. ☐ St. Code
Assessor | Date | Rev. | Date

A Identification

Social insurance number: 1 0 0 0 0 0 1 8 1

Adjustment request for the *2000* tax year (complete a separate form for each year)

Full name: (please print your given name first, surname last)
Karen

Address: (please print)
☒ same as on the return
☐ or:

B Authorization - complete this area if a person or firm is preparing this request for you; otherwise, go to Area C.

Name and address of person or firm preparing this request: (please print)

Letter of authorization (or Form T1013, *Consent Form*) for the year under review:
☐ was submitted previously
☐ is attached

C Adjustment details

Using your copy of your tax return and your *Notice of Assessment or Reassessment*, list below the details of your requested change. If you have received an assessment or reassessment notice with an amount that is different from the amount on the return, use the amount stated on the notice.
See the back of this form for information about required documentation and for examples of how to complete this area.

Line number from return or schedule	Name of line from return or schedule	Previous amount	+ −	Amount of change	Revised amount
305	*Equivalent-to-spouse amount*	–	+	*6,140.00*	*6,140.00*

Other details or explanations (attach an extra sheet if required)

Please include a claim for the equivalent-to-spouse amount for my son Andy Jr. who has lived with me all year. Attached is a completed Schedule 5.

D Certification

I certify that the information given on this form and on any documents attached is, to the best of my knowledge, correct and complete.

2001 12 02
Date

Client's/Representative's signature

(Home) (   )
(Business) (   )
Telephone

T1-ADJ E (01)

You can get more copies of this form from any Canada Customs and Revenue Agency office.
(Ce formulaire existe en français.)

Canada

Adjustment # 11 To: Caregiver Amount (Line 315)
Error or Omission: Missed Claiming for Infirm Parent
Tax Years in Question: 1999, 2000

KEY PERSONAL TAX CONCEPTS

- **Taxpayers who care for infirm adult relatives in their home may qualify to claim the Caregiver Amount.**
- **This claim is generally more lucrative than the Amount for Infirm Dependent Adults on Line 306 because it is based on a higher net income of the dependant.**

REAL LIFE

After his Dad died in 1998, Paul's ailing Mother came to live with Paul and his wife Georgina. Paul's Mother was 66 at the time and her only income was her Old Age and Canada Pensions, which totalled $12,079 in 2000. Paul and Georgina were unaware that any claim could be made for his Mother.

Taxpayer Details Before Adjustments (Paul)	Year: 2000	Year: 1999	Year: 1998	Year:	Year:
Marital Status	Married	Married	Married		
Taxpayer's Total Income	$45,000	$43,600	$41,000		
Net Income	$41,000	$39,600	$37,000		
Taxable Income	$41,000	$39,600	$37,000		
Marginal Tax Rate	36.5%	38%	38%		
Residency	AB	AB	AB		
Family Net Income	$44,500	$42,850	$40,100		

TAX SECRETS

- The Caregiver Amount may be claimed by individuals who, at any time in the year, provided care in their own home for an infirm dependant.
- This amount may be claimed for a parent or grandparent who is over 65 or for an infirm dependant such as your child or grandchild, your brother, sister, niece, nephew, aunt or uncle who is over 18.
- If more than one person qualifies to make this claim, the claim must be shared between them.
- If anyone, including you, claims the Caregiver Amount, no one may claim the Amount for Infirm Dependants for the same person.

- You may claim the Amount for an Eligible Dependant for this same person, but your claim for the Caregiver Amount must be reduced by your Amount for an Eligible Dependant claim.
- If anyone else makes a claim for the Amount for an Eligible Dependant for the same person, you cannot claim the Caregiver Amount.

TAX SAVINGS RESULTS

This tax adjustment has the following financial impact:

- For 2000, an additional refund of $482
- For 1999, an additional refund of $576
- For 1998, an additional refund of $582.
- Total $1,640

Paul's Request for Adjustment for 2000 is shown on the following page.

Canada Customs and Revenue Agency / Agence des douanes et du revenu du Canada

T1 ADJUSTMENT REQUEST

- Use this form to request an adjustment (a reassessment) to an individual income tax return.
- See the back of this form for information on how to complete it.
- Send the completed form to the Enquiries & Adjustments Division of your tax centre. You can find the address on the back of this form.

Date of action:

A Identification

For filing ☐ DO NOT USE THIS AREA

PSN

Social insurance number: 1 0 0 0 0 0 1 9 9

Adjustment request for the 2000 tax year (complete a separate form for each year)

Full name: (please print your given name first, surname last)
Paul

Address: (please print)
☒ same as on the return
☐ or:

CORLOC # – ☐ Ack. ☐ St. Code

Assessor | Date | Rev. | Date

B Authorization - complete this area if a person or firm is preparing this request for you; otherwise, go to Area C.

Name and address of person or firm preparing this request: (please print)

Letter of authorization (or Form T1013, *Consent Form*) for the year under review:
☐ was submitted previously
☐ is attached

C Adjustment details

Using your copy of your tax return and your *Notice of Assessment or Reassessment*, list below the details of your requested change.
If you have received an assessment or reassessment notice with an amount that is different from the amount on the return, use the amount stated on the notice.
See the back of this form for information about required documentation and for examples of how to complete this area.

Line number from return or schedule	Name of line from return or schedule	Previous amount	+ –	Amount of change	Revised amount
315	Caregiver amount	–	+	1,968.00	1,968.00

Other details or explanations (attach an extra sheet if required)

Please include a claim for the Caregiver Amount for my mother who has lived with us since 1998.
Attached is a completed Schedule 5.

D Certification

I certify that the information given on this form and on any documents attached is, to the best of my knowledge, correct and complete.

2001 12 02
Date

Client's/Representative's signature

(Home) ( )
(Business) ( )
Telephone

T1-ADJ E (01)

You can get more copies of this form from any Canada Customs and Revenue Agency office.
(Ce formulaire existe en français.)

Canadä

Adjustment # 12 To: Disability Amount (Line 316/318)
Error or Omission: Missed Claim for Sick Husband
Tax Years in Question: 1996 to 2000

KEY PERSONAL TAX CONCEPTS

- **The Disability Amount is claimed by a taxpayer with a severe and prolonged disability that restricts the individual's activities of daily life for a continuous period of at least 12 months, beginning in the tax year. It can also be claimed by that person's supporting individual.**
- ***Form T2201 Disability Tax Credit Certificate* must be completed by the individual's doctor and submitted to CCRA in the first year the claim is made.**
- **The credit has recently been enhanced significantly for minor children.**

REAL LIFE

In 1995, Ray was diagnosed with lung cancer and was unable to continue working. Soon after, his wife Yvonne had to return to work to cover household expenses as Ray's only income was a small disability pension of $330 per month. Ray's health deteriorated until he passed away early in 2001. Yvonne only found out about the disability amount when she had a professional file Ray's final return.

Taxpayer Details Before Adjustments (Yvonne)	Year: 2000	Year: 1999	Year: 1998	Year: 1997	Year: 1996
Marital Status	Married	Married	Married	Married	Married
Taxpayer's Total Income	$24,000	$23,200	$22,600	$21,900	$21,200
Net Income	$23,760	$22,970	$22,374	$21,681	$20,988
Taxable Income	$23,760	$22,970	$22,374	$21,681	$20,988
Marginal Tax Rate	23.4%	24.2%	25.0%	25.7%	27.0%
Residency	ON	ON	ON	ON	ON
Family Net Income	$27,812	$26,904	$26,193	$25,389	$24,948

TAX SECRETS

- Qualifying conditions for this amount include:
  - Severe mental or physical impairment that restricts the taxpayer's basic activities all or most of the time
  - The impairment has lasted or is expected to last at least 12 months
  - *Form T2201* must be certified by a medical doctor.
- Those receiving life-sustaining therapy such as kidney dialysis for an average of at least 14 hours per week now qualify.
- When making this claim you cannot also claim medical expenses for full-time attendant care or care in a nursing home. If you have such costs, you may claim them on Line 215 as well as claiming the Disability Amount.
- Beginning in 2000, an additional supplement of $3,500 may be claimed if the taxpayer is under 18. This supplement is reduced by any claim for child care or attendant care expenses in excess of $2,050 (for 2001).
- If the taxpayer does not require the Disability Amount, it can be transferred to a supporting individual.

TAX SAVINGS RESULTS

This tax adjustment has the following financial impact:

- Additional tax refunds totalling $7,452 from the following years:
  - 1995: none as Ray's income was too high
  - 1996: $1,702
  - 1997: $1,477
  - 1998: $1,426
  - 1999: $1,417
  - 2000: $1,430

Yvonne's Request for Adjustment for 1996 is shown on the following page.

Canada Customs and Revenue Agency / Agence des douanes et du revenu du Canada

T1 ADJUSTMENT REQUEST

- Use this form to request an adjustment (a reassessment) to an individual income tax return.
- See the back of this form for information on how to complete it.
- Send the completed form to the Enquiries & Adjustments Division of your tax centre. You can find the address on the back of this form.

A Identification

Social insurance number: 1 0 0 0 0 0 2 0 7

Adjustment request for the *1996* tax year (complete a separate form for each year)

Full name: (please print your given name first, surname last) *Yvonne*

Address: (please print)

☒ same as on the return
☐ or:

Date of action:
For filing ☐ DO NOT USE THIS AREA
PSN
CORLOC # ☐ Ack. ☐ St. Code
Assessor | Date | Rev. | Date

B Authorization - complete this area if a person or firm is preparing this request for you; otherwise, go to Area C.

Name and address of person or firm preparing this request: (please print)

Letter of authorization (or Form T1013, *Consent Form*) for the year under review:
☐ was submitted previously
☐ is attached

C Adjustment details

Using your copy of your tax return and your *Notice of Assessment or Reassessment*, list below the details of your requested change.
If you have received an assessment or reassessment notice with an amount that is different from the amount on the return, use the amount stated on the notice.
See the back of this form for information about required documentation and for examples of how to complete this area.

Line number from return or schedule	Name of line from return or schedule	Previous amount	+ –	Amount of change	Revised amount
326	*Amounts transferred from spouse*	1,000.00	+	4,233.00	5,233.00

Other details or explanations (attach an extra sheet if required)

Please amend my claim for amounts transferred from spouse to include a disability amount. Attached is a revised Schedule 2 and a certified Form T2201.

D Certification

I certify that the information given on this form and on any documents attached is, to the best of my knowledge, correct and complete.

2001 12 02
Date

Client's/Representative's signature

(Home) ( )
(Business) ( )
Telephone

T1-ADJ E (01)

You can get more copies of this form from any Canada Customs and Revenue Agency office.
(Ce formulaire existe en français.)

Canada

Adjustment # 13 To: Tuition and Education Credits
Error or Omission: Missed Transfer to Parents
Tax Years in Question: 2000

KEY PERSONAL TAX CONCEPTS

- **Tuition and Education Credits have been doubled for 2001.**
- **They must be claimed by students first, but if the student is not taxable, up to $5,000 can be transferred to supporting parents, grandparents or spouses.**
- **Full-time students who receive scholarships or bursaries and qualify for the Tuition and Education Amount are eligible for an exemption of $3,000 of their scholarship income**

REAL LIFE

When Troy graduated high school in June 2000, he was excited about attending college in the fall. During the summer, he earned $3,600 from his summer job. During the fall, he worked part-time and earned another $3,200. He also earned a bursary for $4,500 to aid in his tuition, books, fees and other expenses. After claiming his tuition of $3,000, Troy still had taxable income. He was unaware, however, that he could reduce his bursary with a $3,000 exemption.

Taxpayer Details Before Adjustments	Year: 2000	Year: 1999	Year: 1998	Year: 1997	Year: 1996
Marital Status	Single				
Taxpayer's Total Income	$11,300				
Net Income	$11,300				
Taxable Income	$11,300				
Marginal Tax Rate	17%				
Residency	ON				
Family Net Income	$11,300				

TAX SECRETS

- Tuition fees must be relating to studies at a post-secondary institution and must exceed $100 to be claimable.
- Costs relating to books (except if part of a correspondence school), student activity fees, board and lodging, transportation, parking and entrance fees to professional organizations will not qualify.
- The education amount is $400 a month for full-time students and $120 a month for part-time students.
- The first $3,000 of scholarship income is exempt for students who qualify for the Education Amount.
- File tax returns for all teenagers to report income from part-time work efforts (babysitting, lawn care, retail work, etc.) to create RRSP contribution room. Then make an RRSP contribution for that child later when s/he goes to university. This will reduce his or her net income so Tuition and Education Amounts can be transferred to the parents.

TAX SAVINGS RESULTS

This tax adjustment has the following financial impact:

- For Troy, a tax refund of $17 versus taxes payable of $108 under the first attempt
- After claiming the scholarship exemption, Troy has an unused Tuition and Education Amount of $2,341 which may be transferred to his father
- This transfer will save his father $568.

Troy's Request for Adjustment for 2000 is shown on the following page. Troy's father will also have to request an adjustment to claim the Tuition/ Education Amount transfer.

Canada Customs and Revenue Agency / Agence des douanes et du revenu du Canada

T1 ADJUSTMENT REQUEST

- Use this form to request an adjustment (a reassessment) to an individual income tax return.
- See the back of this form for information on how to complete it.
- Send the completed form to the Enquiries & Adjustments Division of your tax centre. You can find the address on the back of this form.

Date of action:

For filing ☐ DO NOT USE THIS AREA

PSN

CORLOC # ☐ Ack. ☐ St. Code

Assessor | Date | Rev. | Date

A Identification

Social insurance number: 1 0 0 0 0 0 2 1 3

Adjustment request for the 2000 tax year (complete a separate form for each year)

Full name: (please print your given name first, surname last)

Troy

Address: (please print)

☒ same as on the return

☐ or:

B Authorization - complete this area if a person or firm is preparing this request for you; otherwise, go to Area C.

Name and address of person or firm preparing this request: (please print)

Letter of authorization (or Form T1013, *Consent Form*) for the year under review:

☐ was submitted previously

☐ is attached

C Adjustment details

Using your copy of your tax return and your *Notice of Assessment or Reassessment*, list below the details of your requested change. If you have received an assessment or reassessment notice with an amount that is different from the amount on the return, use the amount stated on the notice.

See the back of this form for information about required documentation and for examples of how to complete this area.

Line number from return or schedule	Name of line from return or schedule	Previous amount	+ −	Amount of change	Revised amount
130	Other income	4,500.00	−	3,000.00	1,500.00
323	Tuition and education amount	3,240.00	−	2,341.10	898.90
327	Tuition and education amounts transferred	−	+	2,341.00	2,341.00

Other details or explanations (attach an extra sheet if required)

Scholarship income of $4,500 was reported in full. It is eligible for the $3,000 exemption. Based on this exemption I would like to transfer $2,341.00 of my unused credit to my father.

D Certification

I certify that the information given on this form and on any documents attached is, to the best of my knowledge, correct and complete.

2001 12 01
Date

Client's/Representative's signature

(Home) ( )
(Business) ( )
Telephone

T1-ADJ E (01)

You can get more copies of this form from any Canada Customs and Revenue Agency office.
(Ce formulaire existe en français.)

Canada

Adjustment # 14 To: Medical Expenses (Line 330)
Error or Omission: Missed Multiple Expenses
Tax Years in Question: 1990 to 2000

KEY PERSONAL TAX CONCEPTS

- **Medical expenses are claimed generally by the lower taxable spouse because total expenses must be reduced by 3% of net income.**
- **The expenses can be claimed for the best 12 month period ending in the tax year or the best 24 month period in the year a taxpayer dies.**
- **Most taxpayers miss claiming common expenditures every year.**
- **When claiming medical expenses for a dependant other than your spouse or common-law partner, you must reduce your medical expenses by 425% of the dependant's income over the Basic Personal Amount.**

REAL LIFE

Martha is a single Mom with three children in high school. She also cares for her Mom, who lives with her, while her Dad has been in a nursing home since 1990. When preparing her return for 2000, Martha did not make any claim for her ailing father's nursing home care which amounted to $12,000. In addition, she made no claim for the taxable benefit for $660 Blue Cross premiums shown on her T4 slip.

Taxpayer Details Before Adjustments	Year: 2000	Year:	Year:	Year:	Year:
Marital Status	Widowed				
Taxpayer's Total Income	$48,000				
Net Income	$48,000				
Taxable Income	$48,000				
Marginal Tax Rate	34.6%				
Residency	ON				
Family Net Income	$48,000				

TAX SECRETS

Common medical expenses missed by Canadians include costs for:

Medical Practitioners

- Dentist
- Medical Doctor
- Medical Practitioner
- Optometrist
- Pharmacist
- Psychologist
- Speech-language Pathologist
- Osteopath
- Chiropractor
- Naturopath
- Therapeutist (or Therapist)
- Physiotherapist
- Chiropodist (or Podiatrist)
- Christian Science Practitioner
- Psychoanalyst who is a member of the Canadian Institute of Psychoanalysis or a member of the Quebec Association of Jungian Psychoanalysts
- Psychologist
- Speech-language Pathologist or Audiologist
- Occupational Therapist who is a member of the Canadian Association of Occupational Therapists
- Acupuncturist
- Dietician
- Dental Hygienist
- Nurse including a Practical Nurse whose full-time occupation is nursing as well as a Christian Science Nurse
- Audiologist (after Feb 18, 1997)

Treatments

- medical and dental services
- attendant care
- nursing home care
- ambulance fees
- transportation
- travel expenses
- eyeglasses
- guide dogs
- transplant costs
- alterations to the home for disabled persons
- lip reading or sign language training
- sign language services
- moving expenses for a disabled person to a more suitable dwelling
- caregiver training
- therapy for a disabled patient
- tutoring services for a patient with a learning disability or mental impairment
- lab tests
- private health plan premiums
- prescribed drugs

Devices

- artificial limb
- iron lung
- rocking bed for poliomyelitis victims
- wheelchair
- crutches
- spinal brace
- brace for a limb
- ileostomy or a colostomy pad
- truss for a hernia
- laryngeal speaking aid
- aid to hearing
- artificial kidney machine
- van for wheelchair

Source: CCRA's Interpretation Bulletin 519R and the Income Tax Act.

TAX SAVINGS RESULTS

This tax adjustment has the following financial impact:

- In 2000, an income tax refund of $2,142
- Note: Martha's claim is reduced by 425% of her Father's income over the Basic Personal Amount
- Additionally, a similar amount was available for each year starting in 1990 when Martha began paying her father's nursing home costs
- The total of these refunds will exceed $23,000!

Martha's Request for Adjustment for 2000 is shown on the following page.

Canada Customs and Revenue Agency / Agence des douanes et du revenu du Canada

T1 ADJUSTMENT REQUEST

- Use this form to request an adjustment (a reassessment) to an individual income tax return.
- See the back of this form for information on how to complete it.
- Send the completed form to the Enquiries & Adjustments Division of your tax centre. You can find the address on the back of this form.

Date of action:

For filing ☐ DO NOT USE THIS AREA

PSN

CORLOC # ☐ Ack. ☐ St. Code

Assessor | Date | Rev. | Date

A Identification

Social insurance number: 1 0 0 0 0 0 2 3 3

Adjustment request for the 2000 **tax year** **(complete a separate form for each year)**

Full name: (please print your given name first, surname last)
Martha

Address: (please print)
☒ same as on the return
☐ or:

B Authorization - complete this area if a person or firm is preparing this request for you; otherwise, go to Area C.

Name and address of person or firm preparing this request: (please print)

Letter of authorization (or Form T1013, *Consent Form*) for the year under review:
☐ was submitted previously
☐ is attached

C Adjustment details

Using your copy of your tax return and your *Notice of Assessment or Reassessment*, list below the details of your requested change.
If you have received an assessment or reassessment notice with an amount that is different from the amount on the return, use the amount stated on the notice.
See the back of this form for information about required documentation and for examples of how to complete this area.

Line number from return or schedule	Name of line from return or schedule	Previous amount	+ / –	Amount of change	Revised amount
330	Medical expenses	–	+	12,660.00	12,660.00
331	Medical expenses adjustment	–	+	3,076.00	3,076.00
332	Allowable medical expenses	–	+	8,144.00	8.144.00

Other details or explanations (attach an extra sheet if required)

Please add the following medical expenses:

1 Blue Cross premiums paid by my employer and included as a taxable benefit.

2 Nursing home fees paid for my father's care

D Certification

I certify that the information given on this form and on any documents attached is, to the best of my knowledge, correct and complete.

2001 12 02
Date

Client's/Representative's signature

(Home) ( )
(Business) ( )
Telephone

You can get more copies of this form from any Canada Customs and Revenue Agency office.
(Ce formulaire existe en français.)

T1-ADJ E (01)

Canada

Adjustment # 15 To: Charitable Donations
Error or Omission: Carry Forward Unused Donations
Tax Years in Question: 1999, 2000

KEY PERSONAL TAX CONCEPTS

- **Charitable donations can be claimed by either spouse. Because a better tax benefit is available when donations exceed $200 in the year, it is often best for spouses to claim all donations on one spouse's return.**
- **Donations can be saved for up to five years to maximize the tax benefits.**

REAL LIFE

Sol and Lisa are a wealthy couple living in Vancouver. Saul owns a small proprietorship which normally shows a profit of $75,000 to $100,000 each year. The couple donates $5,000 to charity each year. Since Lisa has no income of her own, Sol claims this on his tax return. Unfortunately, the business suffered a setback in 2000 which resulted in a $10,000 net loss. As a result, Sol's total income for the year was only $15,000. As Sol's non-refundable credits exceed his taxable income, his claim for the donation credit was wasted. He wanted to adjust his tax return to carry forward the charitable donation for a better claim in future years.

Taxpayer Details Before Adjustments	Year: 2000	Year:	Year:	Year:	Year:
Marital Status	Married				
Taxpayer's Total Income	$15,000				
Net Income	$15,000				
Taxable Income	$15,000				
Marginal Tax Rate	0%				
Residency	BC				
Family Net Income	$15,000				

TAX SECRETS

- Donations made by yourself or your spouse (or common-law partner) to registered charities in Canada as well as certain "qualified donees" are eligible for this credit. Some common qualified donees are:
  - Registered Canadian amateur sports associations
  - Canada or a province
  - Charities outside Canada to which the Government of Canada has made a donation in the prior 12 months
  - The United Nations and its agencies.
- Donations to U.S. charities will also qualify to the limit of 75% of U.S. source income.
- Qualified gifts include:
  - Cash
  - Capital property such as publicly traded shares, mutual fund units
  - Cultural property
  - Life insurance policies
  - Ecological gifts
  - Personal use property.

TAX SAVINGS RESULTS

This tax adjustment has the following financial impact:

- In 2000, there is no impact as the donation credit was wasted
- In 2001, if the business income returns to normal, adding this amount to the 2001 donations will result in a decreased liability of about $2,300. Sol's Request for Adjustment for 2000 is shown on the following page.

Canada Customs and Revenue Agency / Agence des douanes et du revenu du Canada

T1 ADJUSTMENT REQUEST

- Use this form to request an adjustment (a reassessment) to an individual income tax return.
- See the back of this form for information on how to complete it.
- Send the completed form to the Enquiries & Adjustments Division of your tax centre. You can find the address on the back of this form.

Date of action:

A Identification

For filing ☐ DO NOT USE THIS AREA

PSN

Social insurance number: 1 0 0 0 0 0 2 4 9

Adjustment request for the 2000 tax year (complete a separate form for each year)

Full name: (please print your given name first, surname last)
Sol

Address: (please print)
☒ same as on the return
☐ or:

CORLOC # – ☐ Ack. ☐ St. Code

Assessor | Date | Rev. | Date

B Authorization - complete this area if a person or firm is preparing this request for you; otherwise, go to Area C.

Name and address of person or firm preparing this request: (please print)

Letter of authorization (or Form T1013, *Consent Form*) for the year under review:
☐ was submitted previously
☐ is attached

C Adjustment details

Using your copy of your tax return and your *Notice of Assessment or Reassessment*, list below the details of your requested change.
If you have received an assessment or reassessment notice with an amount that is different from the amount on the return, use the amount stated on the notice.
See the back of this form for information about required documentation and for examples of how to complete this area.

Line number from return or schedule	Name of line from return or schedule	Previous amount	+ –	Amount of change	Revised amount
340	Allowable donations	5,000.00	–	5,000.00	0

Other details or explanations (attach an extra sheet if required)

Please remove my claim for donations made in 2000. This amount should be carried forward to 2001.

D Certification

I certify that the information given on this form and on any documents attached is, to the best of my knowledge, correct and complete.

2001 12 01
Date

Client's/Representative's signature

(Home) ( )
(Business) ( )
Telephone

T1-ADJ E (01)

You can get more copies of this form from any Canada Customs and Revenue Agency office.
(Ce formulaire existe en français.)

Canada

Adjustment # 16 To: Instalment Payments
Error or Omission: Request Reduction
Tax Years in Question: 2002

KEY PERSONAL TAX CONCEPTS

- **If your return for the current year and your return for either of the previous two years shows an underpayment of taxes of $2,000 or more, you will be required to make quarterly instalment payments.**
- **If you are required to make instalments, the CCRA will calculate the amount, based on your prior year income, and send you an Instalment Reminder notice specifying the amount they have calculated.**
- **If your income in the current year varies significantly from the last, the instalment calculation will not accurately predict your tax liability for the year. If your income increases and you pay the requested instalments, you will not be penalized for underpaying your instalments. If your income decreases, it is in your best interest to adjust your instalments so as not to overpay your taxes by making instalments that are too large.**

REAL LIFE

In 2000, Jim and Wilma sold their small business. The result was a significantly larger income than in prior years. In 2001, their income from their new business is, as with many start-up businesses, nearly zero. Jim's Instalment Reminder notice indicates that Jim should be paying over $10,000 each quarter. Jim figures that if he pays these instalments, he will have overpaid his taxes by thousands of dollars. He prepares *Form T1033* (following) to recalculate his instalment requirements.

TAX SECRETS

There are three methods available to determine your instalment payments:

1. CCRA's Billing Option—pay the amount shown on the CCRA Instalment Requirement Notices.
2. Prior Year Option—complete *Form T1033* using the figures from your prior year income tax return.

3. Current Year Option—complete *Form T1033* estimating your income for the current year.

The best method to conserve your capital is to calculate the amount under all three options and select the one which results in the lowest payment. However, be warned that if you use option 2 or 3 and you underpay your instalments, you will be liable for instalment interest on the shortfall.

TAX SAVINGS RESULTS

- After filing the form shown, Jim may reduce his instalment payments to $2,405, saving him $7,600 each quarter which can be used as capital in building their new business.
- Wilma should file her own copy of the form based on her projected income for 2001.

Canada Customs and Revenue Agency / Agence des douanes et du revenu du Canada

WORKSHEET FOR CALCULATING 2001 INSTALMENT PAYMENTS

Please read the instructions on the back of this worksheet before you complete this form.

Social insurance number: 1 0 0 0 0 0 2 5 6

Calculating net tax owing by instalments

Note: The line references are from the General income tax return.

Net federal tax (line 420)	6,477	A		
Old Age Security (OAS) repayment (from line 422)	–	B		
Provincial or territorial tax (line 428)	2,586	C		
First Nations tax (line 432)	–	D		
Total payable (add lines A, B, C, and D)	9,063	►	9,063	1
Total income tax deducted (line 437)* (If you are a resident of Quebec, use line 439.)	–	E		
Refundable abatement (line 440 plus line 441)	–	F		
Refundable medical expense supplement (line 452)	–	G		
Refund of investment tax credit (line 454)	–	H		
Part XII.2 trust tax credit (line 456)	–	I		
Provincial or territorial tax credits (line 479)	–	J		
Total credits (add lines E, F, G, H, I and J)	–	►	0	2
Net tax owing by instalments (line 1 minus line 2)			9,063	3

*If you are calculating your **2000** net tax owing (prior year option), include in the amount on line E the total amount withheld from your OAS pension benefits during **2000.** If you are estimating your **2001** net tax owing (current year option), do the calculation for "line E" on the back of this worksheet.

Canada Pension Plan (CPP) contributions payable by instalments

If you reported self-employment income on lines 135 to 143 of your return or business or professional income from a partnership on line 122 of your return, complete Schedule 8, *Canada Pension Plan Contributions on Self-Employment and Other Earnings*, included with your individual tax package. If you are using the prior year option, report the amount you calculated on line 10 of Schedule 8 on line 4 below. If you are estimating your 2001 CPP contributions payable (current year option), use the following figures to complete Schedule 8:

- $3,500 on line 6
- $34,800 on line 7
- 8.6% on line 8

CPP contributions payable by instalments 559 4

Total amount payable by instalments

Add lines 3 and 4 .... 9,622 5

Instalment amount due:

If you have to make instalment payments every three months, divide the amount on line 5 by 4 and send it by each due date. 2,405 6

If your main source of income is self-employment income from farming or fishing, calculate 2/3 of the amount on line 5 and send it in one instalment payment by December 31 .... ______ 7

Note

If the amount on line 6 or 7 is more than the amount on your instalment reminders, and you pay only the amount on each of your reminders by the due date, you will not have to pay instalment interest or penalties.

T1033-WS E (00) (Ce formulaire existe en français.) Canada

Appendix

Canada Customs and Revenue Agency / Agence des douanes et du revenu du Canada

T1 GENERAL 2001

Income Tax and Benefit Return

Identification

7

Attach your personal label here. Correct any wrong information.
If you are not attaching a label, print your name and address below.

First name and initial

Last name

Mailing address: Apt. No. – Street No. Street name

P.O. Box, R.R.

City | Prov./Terr. | Postal code

Information about you

Enter your social insurance number (SIN) if it is not on the label, or if you are not attaching a label:

Enter your date of birth: Year Month Day

Your language of correspondence: / Votre langue de correspondance : English ☐ Français ☐

Check the box that applies to your marital status on December 31, 2001: (see the "Marital status" section in the guide for details)

1 ☐ Married 2 ☐ Living common law 3 ☐ Widowed
4 ☐ Divorced 5 ☐ Separated 6 ☐ Single

Information about your spouse or common-law partner (if you checked box 1 or 2 above)

Enter his or her SIN if it is not on the label, or if you are not attaching a label:

Enter his or her first name:

Enter his or her net income for 2001 to claim certain credits: (see the guide for details)

Check this box if he or she was self-employed in 2001: 1 ☐

If this return is for a deceased person, enter the date of death: Year Month Day

Do not use this area

Information about your residence

Enter your province or territory of residence on **December 31, 2001**:

Enter the province or territory where you **currently** reside if it is not the same as that shown above for your mailing address:

If you were self-employed in 2001, enter the province or territory of self-employment:

If you became or ceased to be a resident of Canada **in 2001**, give the date of:

entry Month Day or departure Month Day

Elections Canada (Canadian citizens only; see the guide for details)

Do you authorize the Canada Customs and Revenue Agency to provide your name, address, and date of birth to Elections Canada for the **National Register of Electors**? .... Yes ☐ 1 No ☐ 2

Your authorization is needed each year. This information will be used for electoral purposes only.

Goods and services tax / Harmonized sales tax (GST/HST) credit application

Are you applying for the GST/HST credit? (see the guide for details)........ Yes ☐ 1 No ☐ 2

If *yes*, we will now get the number of children for purposes of this credit from the Canada Child Tax Benefit information we have on file.

Your guide contains valuable information to help you complete your return.

When you come to a line on the return that applies to you, look up the line number in the guide for more information.

Do not use this area	172					171				

2

Please answer the following question

Did you own or hold foreign property at any time in 2001 with a total cost of more than CAN$100,000? (read the "Foreign income" section in the guide for details) .... 266 Yes ☐ 1 No ☐ 2

If *yes*, complete Form T1135.

If you had certain dealings with a non-resident trust or corporation in 2001, see the "Foreign income" section in the guide.

As a Canadian resident, you have to report your income from all sources both inside and outside Canada.

Total income

Employment income (box 14 on all T4 slips)			101
Commissions included on line 101 (box 42 on all T4 slips)	102		
Other employment income			104 +
Old Age Security pension (box 18 on the T4A(OAS) slip)			113 +
CPP or QPP benefits (box 20 on the T4A(P) slip)			114 +
Disability benefits included on line 114 (box 16 on the T4A(P) slip)	152		
Other pensions or superannuation			115 +
Employment Insurance benefits (box 14 on the T4E slip)			119 +
Taxable amount of dividends from taxable Canadian corporations (see the guide)			120 +
Interest and other investment income (complete Schedule 4)			121 +
Net partnership income: limited or non-active partners only (complete Schedule 4)			122 +
Rental income	Gross 160		Net 126 +
Taxable capital gains (complete Schedule 3)			127 +
Support payments received	Total 156		Taxable amount 128 +
RRSP income (from all T4RSP slips)			129 +
Other income	Specify:		130 +
Self-employment income (see lines 135 to 143 in the guide)			
Business income	Gross 162		Net 135 +
Professional income	Gross 164		Net 137 +
Commission income	Gross 166		Net 139 +
Farming income	Gross 168		Net 141 +
Fishing income	Gross 170		Net 143 +
Workers' compensation benefits (box 10 on the T5007 slip)	144		
Social assistance payments	145 +		
Net federal supplements (box 21 on the T4A(OAS) slip)	146 +		
Add lines 144, 145, and 146	=	▶	147 +
Add lines 101, 104 to 143, and 147 This is your **total income.**			150 =

3

Attach here all of the schedules, information slips, forms, receipts, and other documents that you need to attach to your return.

Net income

Enter your **total income** from line 150		150
Pension adjustment (box 52 on all T4 slips and box 34 on all T4A slips) 206		
Registered pension plan deduction (box 20 on all T4 slips and box 32 on all T4A slips)	207	
RRSP deduction (see Schedule 7; attach receipts)	208 +	
Saskatchewan Pension Plan deduction (maximum $600)	209 +	
Annual union, professional, or like dues (box 44 on all T4 slips, or from receipts)	212 +	
Child care expenses (complete Form T778)	214 +	
Attendant care expenses	215 +	
Business investment loss Gross 228 Allowable deduction	217 +	
Moving expenses	219 +	
Support payments made Total 230 Allowable deduction	220 +	
Carrying charges and interest expenses (complete Schedule 4)	221 +	
Deduction for CPP or QPP contributions on self-employment and other earnings (complete Schedule 8)	222 +	•
Exploration and development expenses (complete Schedule 4)	224 +	
Other employment expenses	229 +	
Clergy residence deduction (complete Form T1223)	231 +	
Other deductions Specify:	232 +	
Add lines 207 to 224, 229, 231, and 232.	233 =	► –
Line 150 minus line 233 (if negative, enter "0"). This is your **net income before adjustments.**		234 =
Social benefits repayment (if you reported income on line 113, 119, or 146, see line 235 in the guide)		235 – •
Line 234 minus line 235 (if negative, enter "0"). If you have a spouse or common-law partner, see line 236 in the guide. This is your **net income.**		236 =

Taxable income

Employee home relocation loan deduction (box 37 on all T4 slips)	248	
Stock option and shares deductions	249 +	
Other payments deduction (if you reported income on line 147, see line 250 in the guide)	250 +	
Limited partnership losses of other years	251 +	
Non-capital losses of other years	252 +	
Net capital losses of other years	253 +	
Capital gains deduction	254 +	
Northern residents deductions (complete Form T2222)	255 +	
Additional deductions Specify:	256 +	
Add lines 248 to 256.	257 =	► –
Line 236 minus line 257 (if negative, enter "0") This is your **taxable income.**		260 =

Use your taxable income to calculate your federal tax on Schedule 1.

Starting this year you will also use Schedule 1 to claim your federal non-refundable tax credits.

Refund or Balance owing

4

Net federal tax: Complete Schedule 1 and enter the amount from line 19 of that schedule	420	
CPP contributions payable on self-employment and other earnings (from Schedule 8)	421 +	
Social benefits repayment (enter the amount from line 235)	422 +	
Provincial or territorial tax (complete Form 428)	428 +	
Add lines 420 to 428 This is your **total payable.**	435 =	•

Total income tax deducted (from all information slips)	437	•
Refundable Quebec abatement	440 +	•
CPP overpayment (enter your excess contributions)	448 +	•
Employment Insurance overpayment (enter your excess contributions)	450 +	•
Refundable medical expense supplement (see the guide)	452 +	•
Refund of investment tax credit (complete Form T2038(IND))	454 +	•
Part XII.2 trust tax credit (box 38 on all T3 slips)	456 +	•
Employee and partner GST/HST rebate (complete Form GST370)	457 +	•
Tax paid by instalments	476 +	•
Provincial or territorial credits (complete Form 479 if it applies)	479 +	•
Add lines 437 to 479 These are your **total credits.**	482 =	▶ –

Line 435 minus line 482 =

If the result is negative, you have a **refund**.
If the result is positive, you have a **balance owing**.
Enter the amount below on whichever line applies.

We do not charge or refund a difference of less than $2.

Refund 484 •

Balance owing 485 •

Amount enclosed 486 •

Attach to page 1, a **cheque** or **money order** payable to the Receiver General. Your payment is due no later than April 30, 2002.

Direct deposit – Start or change (see line 484 in the guide)

You do not have to complete this area every year. Do not complete it this year if your direct deposit information for your refund has not changed.

Refund and GST/HST credit – To start direct deposit or to change account information only, attach a "void" cheque or complete lines 460, 461, and 462.

Note: To deposit your **CCTB** payments (including certain related provincial or territorial payments) into the **same** account, also check box 463.

Branch number	Institution number	Account number	CCTB
460 ____ (5 digits)	461 ____ (3 digits)	462 ____ (maximum 12 digits)	463 ☐

I certify that the information given on this return and in any documents attached is correct, complete, and fully discloses all my income.

Sign here ______________________

It is a serious offence to make a false return.

Telephone ( ) Date

490 **For professional tax preparers only.**

Name:
Address:

Telephone: ( )

Do not use this area 487 ☐ 488 ☐ •

Privacy Act Personal Information Bank number CCRA/P-PU-005

T1-2001 **Federal Tax** **Schedule 1**

Use this schedule to claim your federal non-refundable tax credits and to calculate your net federal tax. Be sure to attach a copy of this schedule to your return.

Enter your **taxable income** from line 260 of your return ______ 1

Use the amount on line 1 to determine which **ONE** of the following columns you have to complete.

If the amount on line 1 is:	$30,754 or less		more than $30,754, but not more than $61,509		more than $61,509 but not more than $100,000		more than $100,000	
Enter the amount from line 1 above		2		2		2		2
Base amount	– 0 00	3	– 30,754 00	3	– 61,509 00	3	– 100,000 00	3
Line 2 minus line 3 (this amount cannot be negative)	=	4	=	4	=	4	=	4
Rate	× 16%	5	× 22%	5	× 26%	5	× 29%	5
Multiply the amount on line 4 by the rate on line 5	=	6	=	6	=	6	=	6
Tax on base amount	+ 0 00	7	+ 4,921 00	7	+ 11,687 00	7	+ 21,694 00	7
Add lines 6 and 7	=	8	=	8	=	8	=	8

Federal non-refundable tax credits (Read the guide for details about these credits.)

		Line	
Basic personal amount	**claim $7,412**	300	
Age amount (if you were born in 1936 or earlier)		301	+
Spouse or common-law partner amount:			
Base amount	6,923 00		
Minus: His or her net income (from page 1 of your return)	–		
Result: (if negative, enter "0") (maximum $6,293)	= ►	303	+
Amount for an eligible dependant	(maximum $6,293)	305	+
Amount for infirm dependants age 18 or older		306	+
CPP or QPP contributions:			
through employment from box 16 and box 17 on all T4 slips	(maximum $1,496.40)	308	+ •
on self-employment and other earnings (from Schedule 8)		310	+ •
Employment Insurance premiums from box 18 on all T4 slips	(maximum $877.50)	312	+ •
Pension income amount	(maximum $1,000)	314	+
Caregiver amount		315	+
Disability amount		316	+
Disability amount transferred from a dependant		318	+
Interest paid on your student loans		319	+
Tuition and education amounts (complete Schedule 11)		323	+
Tuition and education amounts transferred from a child		324	+
Amounts transferred from your spouse or common-law partner (complete Schedule 2)		326	+
Medical expenses (attach receipts)	330		
Minus: $1,678, or 3% of line 236, whichever is **less**	–		
Subtotal	=		
Minus: Medical expenses adjustment	331 –		
Allowable portion of medical expenses (if negative, enter "0")	= ►	332	+
Add lines 300, 301, 303 to 326, and 332.		335	=
Multiply the amount on line 335 by 16% =		338	
Donations and gifts (complete Schedule 9)		349	+
Total federal non-refundable tax credits: Add lines 338 and 349.		350	=

continue on the back

Enter the amount from line 8 on the other side				9
Federal tax on split income (from line 4 of Form T1206)			424 +	• 10
			Add lines 9 and 10 =	11
Enter your total federal non-refundable tax credits from line 350 on the other side	350			
Federal dividend tax credit (13.3333% of the amount on line 120 of your return)	425 +	•		
Overseas employment tax credit (complete Form T626)	426 +			
Minimum tax carry-over	427 +	•		
Add lines 350, 425, 426, and 427	=	►	–	12
Basic federal tax: Line 11 minus line 12 (if negative, enter "0")			429 =	13
Federal foreign tax credit: Complete the federal foreign tax credit calculation below and enter the amount from line (i) or line (ii), whichever is **less**			–	14
Federal tax: Line 13 minus line 14 (if negative, enter "0")			406 =	15
Total federal political contributions (attach receipts) 409				
Federal political contribution tax credit (see the guide)	410	•		
Investment tax credit (complete Form T2038(IND))	412 +	•		
Labour-sponsored funds tax credit — Net cost 413 — Allowable credit	414 +	•		
Add lines 410, 412, and 414.	416 =	►	–	16
Line 15 minus line 16 (if negative, enter "0") (if you have an amount on line 424 above, see Form T1206)			417 =	17
Additional tax on RESP accumulated income payments (complete Form T1172)			418 +	18
Net federal tax: Add lines 17 and 18 Enter this amount on line 420 of your return.			420 =	19

Federal foreign tax credit: (see lines 431 and 433 in the guide)

Make a separate calculation for each foreign country.

Non-business-income tax paid to a foreign country 431 ________ •(i)

Net foreign non-business income * 433 ________ / Net income ** ________ X Basic federal tax *** ________ = ________ (ii)

* Reduce this amount by any income from that foreign country for which you claimed a capital gains deduction, and by any income from that country that was, under a tax treaty, either exempt from tax in that country or deductible as exempt income in Canada (included on line 256). Also reduce this amount by the lesser of lines E and F on Form T626.

** Line 236 plus the amount on line 3 of Form T1206, minus the total of the amounts on lines 248, 249, 250, 253, 254, and minus any foreign income deductible as exempt income under a tax treaty or any income deductible as net employment income from a prescribed international organization (included on line 256). If the result is less than the amount on line 433, enter your **Basic federal tax***** on line (ii).

*** Line 429 plus the amount on lines 425 and 426, and minus any refundable Quebec abatement (line 440) and any federal refundable First Nations abatement (line 441 on the return for residents of Yukon).

Index

About the Author

Evelyn Jacks has established a nation-wide reputation as a leading writer, speaker and entrepreneur in the tax preparation and financial services industries, as well as a community leader promoting the partnership of educators and businesses for economic prosperity.

Evelyn is the best-selling author of almost 30 books on the subject of personal taxation, tax planning and business practices. She has been a regular tax columnist for numerous papers and magazines, including *The National Post, Advisor's Edge, CARPNews, Reader's Digest, The Globe and Mail, The Canadian Consumer, The Canadian MoneySaver, Chatelaine* and numerous other newspapers and industry publications across the country. She has developed and published regular monthly newsletters for both income tax and business management matters.

A popular and respected featured commentator on radio and television programs across the nation, Evelyn is sought after regularly to comment on tax policy, as well as federal or provincial budgets and tax proposals. Recently she served an appointment by the Premier of Manitoba as a Commissioner for the Lower Tax Commission.

Evelyn is President of Evelyn Jacks Productions, Inc., a national firm specializing in producing speeches, seminars, workshops and training sessions for industry and government. Her numerous speaking engagements for financial institutions, mutual fund companies, independent financial services, associations and government departments cover topics such as tax-related issues, pre-retirement planning, business development, marketing, communications, family finance and entrepreneurship.

Throughout her business-building activities, Evelyn has specialized in developing relationships with a variety of professional associations and industries. She is also an award-winning entrepreneur several times over, including the recipient of the prestigious Canadian Woman Entrepreneur of the Year Award.

Evelyn lives with her family in Winnipeg.